Wise Teacher, Wise Student

Wise Teacher, Wise Student

Tibetan Approaches to a Healthy Relationship

Alexander Berzin

Snow Lion Publications
ITHACA, NEW YORK

Snow Lion Publications
P.O. Box 6483
Ithaca, New York 14851 U.S.A.
Telephone: 607-273-8519
www.snowlionpub.com

ISBN 978-1-55939-347-8

Printed in the USA on acid-free recycled paper.

*The Library of Congress cataloged the previous edition
of this book as follows:*

Berzin, Alexander.
Relating to a spiritual teacher : building a healthy relationship
/ by Alexander Berzin.
p. cm.
Includes bibliographical references.
ISBN 1-55939-139-1
1. Teacher-student relationships—Religious aspects—Buddhism.
2. Spiritual life—Buddhism. 3. Buddhism—China—Tibet—
Doctrines. I. Title.
BQ7756 .B47 2000
294.3'61—dc21
00-008944

Designed and typeset by Gopa & Ted2, Inc.

⁓Table of Contents

～Preface

Initial Contacts between Western Seekers
and Tibetan Spiritual Teachers

SINCE THE MIGRATION of the Kalmyk Mongols to the Volga region of European Russia in the early seventeenth century, the Tibetan form of Buddhism has been present in the West. Over the centuries, contact increased as Germans settled along the lower stretches of the Volga and czars recruited Kalmyk horsemen into the imperial army. Slowly, the Kalmyks' beliefs and Buddhist practices attracted the attention of Western spiritual seekers.

Language barriers and a lack of translated materials naturally led to an initial romanticization. For example, the nineteenth-century Russian mystic Madame Blavatsky, the founder of theosophy, popularized the image of mysterious spiritual adepts sending secret teachings telepathically from Himalayan caves to especially receptive persons in the West. This image fired the imagination of many sincere seekers and led to further inflation of Tibetan masters and the types of relationship possible with them. Tibet has long stood high at the pinnacle of the "mysterious East."

Fittingly, the first contact with Tibetan Buddhism in the United States came with another migration of Kalmyk Mongols. Displaced in Germany after the Second World War, a group of them settled in New Jersey in the early 1950s. In 1955, Geshey Wangyal, a great Kalmyk teacher, moved to America as their spiritual leader. Bursting the bubble of fantasy, he introduced many Americans, including me, to the more realistic face of Tibetan Buddhism.

With the exile in India in 1959 of His Holiness the Fourteenth Dalai Lama and about a hundred thousand of his followers, more opportunities opened for Westerners to meet authentic Tibetan Buddhist teachers. The earliest crew of foreign seekers consisted mostly of young spiritual adventurers who traveled to India and Nepal in the late 1960s, sparked by romantic ideals. I too was part of that wave, though I came as a more sober Fulbright scholar rather than as a hippie on a magical mystery tour. With few competent translators and scarcely any reliable books available, much remained incomprehensible. Relatively easy access, however, to the older generation of masters, including the Dalai Lama, his tutors, and the heads of the four Tibetan traditions, more than made up for this limitation.

Deeply moved by our initial impressions, many of us began to build relationships with these spiritual teachers and started to learn and to practice Tibetan Buddhism. With no precedent available from our Western backgrounds, most of us modeled our relationships with these teachers after those between Tibetan disciples and their spiritual mentors. Some even adopted Tibetan dress. The promise of an alternative, Shangri-la culture spurred on our interest.

Most young Westerners of the sixties generation had little or no respect for their elders at home. Unable to understand the hardships our parents had faced with the Depression and the Second World War, we found the older generation materialistic and emotionally stiff. We sought openness and unconditional love. Our clumsy attempts at free love with each other had failed to remove our underlying tension and alienation. On the other hand, the natural warmth and acceptance we felt from the Tibetan masters was undeniable, even if the spiritual practices behind their attainments remained incomprehensible. The authenticity of these teachers' realizations spoke loudly to us. Here, at last, were persons worthy of respect—something we had desperately sought, though perhaps only unconsciously. With joy and enthusiasm, we freely prostrated at these masters' feet.

The Establishment of Dharma Centers and the Start of Confusion

The phenomenon of Western Dharma centers began in the mid-1970s as a natural outgrowth of enthusiasm and of several additional factors. The Chinese Cultural Revolution was raging in Tibet and the destruction of the monasteries that had begun in 1959 was nearly complete. The Tibetan refugees in India felt insecure. Many of them had witnessed firsthand India's border war with China in 1962 and its wars with Pakistan in 1965 and 1971. Unable to support the millions of Bangladeshi refugees they had initially accepted, the Indian authorities had sent them back. There was fear that they might easily do the same with the Tibetans.

At the same time, the Tibetan refugees in Nepal watched with apprehension as the Chinese built a road with military capacity between Lhasa and Kathmandu. Two decades earlier, the Chinese had done the same between Western China and Lhasa. As tension grew, Sikkim became an Indian state in 1975, throwing the Tibetans settled there into great uncertainty. Feeling threatened from all sides, Bhutan soon took measures to foster cultural unity and national pride. Tibetan refugees living there began to feel unwelcome. Throughout the Himalayan regions, Tibetans looked for safer havens in case of emergency. The wish for a secure home is universal.

Several older Tibetan teachers had moved to the West at the end of the fifties and the beginning of the sixties. They had kept a low teaching profile, primarily associated with universities. A few younger high-ranking Tibetan monks had also come to the West in the late sixties and early seventies, mostly to receive a modern education. Responding to the growing thirst for spiritual guidance, they began to teach Buddhism in the West by the mid-seventies, with some of them using nontraditional, adaptive methods. They soon invited their own teachers from India and Nepal to tour the West and to inspire their students.

Initially, the great Tibetan masters they invited mostly imparted tantric empowerments (initiations), performed with elaborate rituals. *Tantra* is an advanced form of meditation entailing visualization of multiheaded, multiarmed Buddha-figures (deities). Receiving empowerment is the entranceway to this practice. The primary motivation of the Tibetan masters in performing these rituals was to plant seeds of positive potential (merit) in the minds of those attending, so that these people would reap beneficial results in future lives. After all, the average Tibetan would attend such ceremonies with the aim of receiving these seeds. Most Westerners who went, however, had little if any thought of improving future lives. The majority came out of curiosity, or to fulfill their fantasies of the mystical East, or to find a miracle cure for their problems. With hardly any translation or explanation of the proceedings available, people's imaginations soared. The exotic splendor of the rituals enchanted many, and Tibetan Buddhism soon became the latest fad.

In response to the enthusiastic interest among Westerners and to the mounting insecurity felt in India and in the surrounding countries, many Tibetan teachers from both the older and younger generations thought to establish a base in the West. Nearly everyone who came West founded his or her own center for study and meditation, usually referred to as a Dharma center (*Dharma* means Buddha's teachings). No such phenomenon had existed before in the history of Buddhism. Previously, teachers who traveled to lands that were new to Buddhism had established only monasteries, not meditation and study facilities for laypeople.

Some of the more dynamic teachers attracted groups in several cities and countries. To meet the growing demand, a few of them invited other instructors—known as *gesheys* or *lamas*—from the Tibetan communities in the Himalayan countries to live and to teach at their various centers. Also coming from insecure backgrounds, many members of this second wave of teachers similarly wished to create stable situations for themselves in the West.

Most of these junior teachers would have remained unnoticed in Tibet or among their fellow compatriots in exile. Circumstances, however, thrust them in the West into positions of spiritual authority normally reserved for those of much higher attainment and then left them to manage on their own. The abbots and heads of the four Tibetan Buddhist traditions do not serve as supervisors for those under their care. Their primarily role is to preside over ceremonies and, if they are monastics, to ordain monks and nuns. Thus, isolated from their teachers and peers, and lacking any checks or balances, many junior teachers in their loneliness adopted modes of behavior familiar from precommunist Tibet. They assumed the roles of benevolent lords of spiritual fiefdoms, expecting to be supported and served with loyal devotion.

The Western students who returned from India and Nepal played the other side of these teachers' fantasies by mimicking the behavior they had seen Tibetan disciples show toward the highest masters there. Those without personal experience of Asia learned this mode of conduct by watching how their Tibetan teachers treated their own masters on tour in the West. Traditional teachings on so-called guru-devotion and the advanced practice of seeing the teacher as a Buddha, when only superficially explained and poorly understood, led to further confusion.

Further Forces Leading to Misunderstanding

Several additional forces played a role in shaping the relationships that grew between Western students and Tibetan teachers. Most Tibetan teachers came to the West with little, if any, previous information about the basic beliefs of Western culture and took for granted that Westerners share most, if not all, Tibetan assumptions, such as the existence of rebirth without a beginning. Moreover, most of these teachers were unaware of the wide diversity of cultures and customs that they would find. To most Tibetans, all Westerners are *Injis*—the Tibetan term for the English—and share the same cultural background. The average Tibetan's picture of the diversity of Western countries is about as jumbled and vague as is that of most Westerners concerning the rich palette of Asian societies.

The few adventurous Westerners these teachers might have met in India or Nepal were certainly not representative of what they would find in the West. Nor did their experience with Indian or Nepalese culture prepare them for the encounter. They had to face not only teaching laypeople rather than exclusively monks, but also addressing a mixed audience of men and women rather than exclusively men. Moreover, Western women were assertive and demanded equal treatment with the men. For many Tibetan teachers, the cultural gap was more than they could handle. The widely held impression in India, gained from movies, that all Western women are open and eager for sex did not help matters.

In addition, many Tibetan teachers were the only persons from their land to live in a particular city or country. Alternatively, they were there with merely a lone attendant or translator with whom they could speak their mother tongue. When faced with the language barrier in India or Nepal, most Tibetans had learned the local vernacular. The ability to communicate was essential for shopping and for all other practical aspects of life. In the West, however, these teachers led a privileged existence, with students readily available to serve their daily needs. Consequently, many Tibetan teachers did not learn the language of the country they were in and thus they became rather isolated. They had little or no contact with the real lives of their students. Many retreated into an inner world and spent most of their time either reading or meditating.

Further, with the end of the Cultural Revolution and the Chinese relaxation of the Tibetan-Nepalese border, large numbers of Tibetans flooded to India in the 1980s. Deprived for more than two decades of the possibility of becoming monks and nuns, these "new arrivals" flocked to the monasteries and nunneries. The gesheys and lamas teaching in the West had already borne the burden of expectation for raising the funds to build the temples for the reestablished monastic institutions. Now they received unrelenting pressure to finance the housing and feeding of the newly ordained monks and nuns.

The Rise of Unhealthy Relationships

The dynamic of these forces led in many cases to less than optimal relationships between Western spiritual seekers and Tibetan teachers. Westerners, for the most part, speak their minds openly, whereas Tibetans tend to verbalize less or to speak circuitously. For example, if offered a second helping of dessert, Westerners straightforwardly accept if they want more. Tibetans, on the other hand, typically refuse three times before acceding. Immediately saying yes indicates greed and attachment. Because of cultural differences such as these and the universal policy of teachers not sharing their personal problems with their students, the lack of communication steadily worsened. Members of the Dharma centers had little idea of the emotional and financial pressures their Tibetan teachers were facing.

Sexual, financial, and power abuses soon began to occur. Traditional Tibet also had its share of religious corruption. No society is immune. However, abuse did not happen to the extent that Chinese communist propaganda would lead us to believe. On the other hand, not everyone who was a teacher was a saint, despite what starry-eyed Westerners might fantasize. The challenging circumstances of living in the West merely brought out the worst in some of the teachers who were already prone to scurrilous behavior.

As senior Western practitioners also began teaching Tibetan Buddhism in the early eighties in the West, a lack of proper supervision sometimes led to instances of similar abuse among them. The older generation of truly inspiring masters was slowly but steadily passing away. Power struggles over succession and Dharma-protector issues among respected spiritual leaders within the Tibetan community added fuel to the growing confusion. Dharma-protectors are powerful, invisible beings enlisted by great masters to safeguard Buddha's teachings from destructive forces. Most Western seekers have little understanding of protectors or of the sociopolitical issues underlying the disputes about them.

By the late 1980s and early nineties, the situation became critical. Scandals surfaced and received public outcry. Disillusionment followed in many circles. Some Westerners left their teachers in disgust and gave up Buddhist practice, while others went into states of denial and became defensive. Dharma groups polarized over succession and protector issues and by the mid-1990s several began making public protests against others. The image of Tibetan Buddhism and its spiritual leaders became tarnished. Cynical circles freely used pejorative labels such as "authoritarian," "patriarchal," and "sexist."

As the millennium drew to an end, many Westerners called for a purely Western Buddhism, free of irrelevant religious and cultural trappings of the East. Differentiating the essence from the trappings, however, is never a simple task. People sometimes discard important factors in haste, without deeply examining the possible consequences. The zealous attitude of such people reminded others of Victorian scholars and missionaries self-righteously proclaiming "Lamaism" a degenerate form of Buddhism. Consequently, furious debate flared up between "traditionalists" and "modernists" within the Western Buddhist community. Topics of debate included the language to use for performing rituals in the West and the place of belief in rebirth in following the Buddhist path.

Now, as the twenty-first century dawns, many of the problems persist and fallout from them remains unresolved. Public protest, abuse, and heated debate still occur. As with recurrent scenes of violence and injustice on television, the recurring misconduct has led some Dharma practitioners to become indifferent. No longer believing in anyone, many find their spiritual practice has weakened and become ineffective. Resolution of the problems and a healing of wounds are desperately needed so that sincere seekers may get on with the work of spiritual development. The student-teacher relationship as understood and developed in the West needs reexamination and perhaps revision.

The Approach Suggested for Revising the
Student-Teacher Relationship

The first place to look for guidelines is within the Buddhist teachings themselves, as did Tsongkapa, the founder of the Gelug tradition of Tibetan Buddhism, who substantiated all his reforms with textual evidence. By indicating the valid sources from which he derived his innovations and the valid lines of reasoning that led to his insights, he dispelled any suspicion that he was making up "false Dharma"— teachings contradictory to the intention of Buddha's words. Even when Tsongkapa received a pure vision of Manjushri, the embodiment of the Buddhas' wisdom, he obtained advice primarily about which classic texts to reexamine in order to gain a correct understanding.

In the present book, I have attempted to follow Tsongkapa's lead. Since all four Tibetan Buddhist schools derive from India, where none of them existed as such, they have equally valid claims as authentic traditions. Therefore, in the search for guidelines, I have drawn upon textual material from each of the four schools and from some of their Indian sources.

Clarification of misunderstood points in Buddha's teachings can bring only benefit to sincere practitioners trying to follow the Buddhist path. Clarification, however, requires great care. To disparage points found personally distasteful—perhaps because of misinterpretation— and to invent new teachings more personally pleasing, but which contradict Buddha's deepest intentions, clearly violate the basic vows taken by most Buddhists. Tsongkapa's example commands respect. Those who take safe direction (refuge) in the Dharma need to trust that Buddha's teachings themselves provide the principles for solving problems concerning the Dharma.

Various schools of Western psychology provide useful analytical tools for understanding some of the problems that may be causing unhealthy relationships with spiritual teachers. Although I have used these tools to identify several syndromes, I have correlated them with the Buddhist analysis and shown how traditional Buddhist methods may address the problems. In this way, I have attempted to highlight the broad applicability of the Buddhist teachings, rather than to adulterate the teachings with Western psychology.

Any approach at restructuring the student-teacher relationship needs to avoid two extremes. The first is justifying the deification of the teacher to the point that it encourages a cult-mentality and white-washes abuse. The second is justifying the demonization of the teacher to the point that paranoia and distrust prevent the benefits to be gained from a healthy disciple-mentor relationship. In trying to prevent the first extreme, we need great care not to fall to the second.

The Present Book

The purpose of this book is to suggest several guidelines for consideration. I have written it based on textual research and on personal experience of Buddhist disciple-mentor relationships for thirty years, twenty-nine of which were spent living primarily with the Tibetan exile community in Dharamsala, India. Especially significant have been the nine years of disciple/apprenticeship I spent with Tsenzhab Serkong Rinpochey, the late Master Debate Partner and Assistant Tutor of His Holiness the Dalai Lama, during which I trained and served as his interpreter, English secretary, and foreign tour manager. I also have drawn on nineteen years of experience teaching Buddhism in Dharma centers and universities in seventy countries. Unless specifically stated, the opinions and interpretations I have given are merely my own. I do not claim to speak with any authority. I merely hope that the textual information and personal insights given here may stimulate further thought and discussion.

The intended audience for this book includes both people already practicing Buddhism and potential students who wish to avoid the problems that others have previously encountered. Practitioners who have been abused by their teachers or who have been disenchanted or confused by their behavior may find it particularly helpful. In addition, those who are fervently devoted to their teachers may find useful points for helping to stabilize their emotions in the relationships. Although the book discusses student-teacher relations specifically in Tibetan Buddhism, those involved with other Buddhist traditions or with any spiritual path that involves relating to a teacher may also find it relevant.

Since this book does not specifically address scholars, I have cited Sanskrit and Tibetan sources in the traditional Buddhist manner, by title and author's name alone, rather than with footnotes. I have used the English translation of all text titles and, for ease of reading, have used a simplified phonetic transliteration system for Sanskrit and

Tibetan names. The standard transcription of these names, as well as the Tibetan, and Sanskrit when available, for the titles of cited texts are included in the bibliography. The bibliography also comprises a detailed list of primary sources consulted, together with available English translations and secondary sources. I also have employed the simplified transliteration system for the Sanskrit and Tibetan technical terms used in the text, and have provided the standard transcription of the Tibetan terms in parentheses. For selected technical terms in English, I also have given in parentheses the Tibetan transliterations and transcriptions and, where indicated, the Sanskrit equivalents, occasionally with the more common English translations.

I am totally indebted to my spiritual mentors, especially to His Holiness the Dalai Lama, the late Tsenzhab Serkong Rinpochey and his fifteen-year-old reincarnation, and the late Geshey Ngawang Dhargyey, whose unending inspiration has enabled this work. This book was also made possible by a grant from the Kapor Family Foundation, administered by the Nama Rupa Foundation, for which I am extremely grateful. I deeply thank my assistant, Peter Green, and my editor at Snow Lion, Christine Cox, whose contributions have been invaluable. I also thank Caitlin Collins, Thubten Chodron, Dr. Catherine Ducommun-Nagy, Alnis Grants, Aldemar Hegewald, Dr. Martin Kalff, Israel and Alis Lifshitz, Dr. Rainer and Renata Noack, Sönam Tenzin, Alan Turner, Roberto Volpon, Sylvia Wetzel, and numerous other Dharma friends for their helpful suggestions and advice with this project. May this book be of some benefit.

Alexander Berzin
Berlin, Germany

PART I

Spiritual Seekers and Spiritual Teachers

~1
Cultural Considerations

CULTURES PLAY a large role in shaping the form of the personal inter-actions of their members. Just as the child-parent relation differs from one society and time to another, so does the relationship between spiritual seeker and spiritual teacher. It is only natural, then, that the relationship will differ according to whether the parties are both Tibetan, or both Western, or one of each. Trouble occurs when one or both sides think that they need to mimic an alien culture or expect the other to adopt foreign ways. For example, Western students may think that they need to act like Tibetans, or that Tibetan teachers should behave more like Westerners. Alternatively, Tibetan teachers may expect that Western students will act as Tibetan disciples would. When each side understands and respects the other's cultural background, however, flexibility and adjustment become possible. This often eliminates some of the problems. To understand a few of the differences, let us profile the average spiritual seeker from each of these cultures.

The Typical Spiritual Seeker in Traditional Tibet

Traditionally, most Tibetan spiritual seekers, as well as their teachers, were celibate monks or nuns with limited knowledge of family life, gained primarily from their childhood. Most had limited knowledge also of secular matters. Nearly everyone entered monasteries or nunneries as illiterate children. Premodern Tibet never developed a public education system and, in fact, had hardly any secular education at all. The major exceptions were in the capital, Lhasa, which had a government school to train civil servants and a medical and astrological college. Admission was normally limited to children of the nobility.

Further, monastic education covered only subjects directly related to spiritual matters. Even in monasteries that also taught medicine and astrology, these topics were strongly interlaced with Buddhist theory and ritual.

Few opportunities existed for spiritual study for laypeople. Nearly the only possibility was to study with a *ngagpa* (*sngags-pa*), a married tantric yogi devoted to meditation and to performing rituals in people's homes. Ngagpas, however, normally taught only children from their own families and a few local youths who would live with them. While staying for several months in a patron's home in a distant region, they might also instruct the adolescents in the house and several other teenagers from prominent families in the area. The number of ngagpas in Tibet, however, hardly compared with the number of monastics. Lay spiritual seekers were the exception and not the rule.

Some ngagpas were also *tulkus* (*sprul-sku*, reincarnate lamas) and were usually the lay throneholders of one or more monastic institutions, responsible for giving empowerments and for leading major rituals. Discovered as children to be the reincarnations of previous tantric masters, tulkus stand at the peak of Tibetan society. Monasteries and nunneries normally did not admit lay students. Nevertheless, if ngagpa tulkus were associated with monastic institutions, they often received much of their education there. Similarly, their younger family members and later their children might also take classes in the monasteries or nunneries. Thus, lay spiritual seekers such as these often had close contact with monks and nuns.

Joining a Tibetan Monastery or Nunnery in Traditional Tibet

Traditionally, Tibetans joined monasteries or nunneries at a young age. The prerequisite was to be healthy and old enough to chase away a crow. This ability indicated that the children had enough self-assuredness to live away from home. Most who joined were about seven or eight years old, although tulkus were sometimes as young as four.

The decision to enter a monastery or nunnery always came through mutual agreement between parents and child. The initiative could come from either side. Becoming a monk or a nun was not only prestigious in Tibet, it was a commonplace occurrence. Over one-sixth of the population were monastics. Moreover, because sending some of the family's children to monastic institutions helped to prevent the overfragmentation of inherited property, almost every household sub-scribed to the custom.

Although child monks and nuns shaved their heads and wore robes, they normally did not take novice vows before early or middle adoles-cence or full vows until age twenty-one. Unlike their Christian coun-terparts, they normally maintained contact with their families. If they lived in local monasteries or nunneries during adolescence, they fre-quently spent summer holidays at home helping with the fields or the herds.

One could argue that children hardly qualified as sincere spiritual seekers. Many, of course, wished to join monasteries or nunneries to enjoy the camaraderie of living with other children their age. Others, who yearned for knowledge, were keen to go to monastic institu-tions since studying Buddhism was the route to receiving an educa-tion. Spiritual interest often manifested first in playfully imitating the older monastics meditating and performing rituals. Sincere spiritual interest came mostly with education and maturity. Many monks and nuns, however, never actually developed that interest, but remained in monastic institutions for a secure way of life.

The young monks and nuns traditionally lived in the homes of their teachers. If they entered great monasteries or nunneries outside their native regions, the students and teachers from one area lived in the same compounds, forming subunits within the larger institutions. They had their own temples for communal prayers and, like most mountain people, bonded strongly with each other through regional loyalty and common dialects.

During both their childhood and teenage years, the young monks and nuns performed household chores and joined the adult attendants in serving their teachers. They received strict discipline from both their teachers and the monastic authorities. Scolding and beatings were nor-mal fare, even for tulkus. Nevertheless, children also received a certain amount of physical affection from the older members of the household, who served as substitute parents. The teachers fulfilled the parental functions of being the authority figures and role models.

Joining a Monastery or Nunnery Nowadays in Exile

The Tibetan refugee community has reestablished many of its major monasteries and nunneries in India and Nepal. The new institutions maintain most of the traditional customs, although those in South India require communal agricultural work of most of their able-bodied members. Joining a monastery or nunnery is less widespread than it was before. Mostly poor families and new arrivals send a few of their children to become monks or nuns, primarily because of financial pressure. Often, novice candidates receive at least some secular education before entering monastic institutions, and many wait until adolescence. Tulkus, however, still join at a tender age. Since the early 1980s, modern schooling forms a part of the monastic education, but only at the major institutions.

The households of tulkus and senior teachers in exile still have young disciples living in them. Many monks and nuns, however, now live either in dormitories with communal kitchens or with a few others in small houses. The larger monasteries and nunneries still have regional divisions. Although the reestablished institutions lack many of the modern conveniences of the West, they have far more than their original institutions did in traditional Tibet. Consequently, maintaining a household requires far less menial work than before. Thus, serving the teacher plays a less dominant role in the disciple-mentor relationship than it did previously. Some service, however, is still standard fare.

As in traditional Tibet, child monks and nuns do not receive special treatment. On the other hand, child tulkus have always had, and continue to have, better food and clothing than everyone else. Their person and everything around them are kept scrupulously clean. Waited on by special attendants, they have almost no contact with ordinary child monastics, who are considered too rough and filthy for them to play with.

Strict discipline has traditionally prevented most tulkus from becoming spoiled. Nowadays, however, young tulkus having considerable contact with Western people, culture, and electronic entertainment face greater disciplinary problems. This especially happens when visits to the West disrupt the stability of their home lives, interrupt their education, and introduce cultural conflict.

Traditional Tibetan Monastic Training

The spiritual education of both ordinary and tulku monks and nuns still retains its traditional form. The only difference is that formerly only tulkus and the most promising youngsters learned to write. Tulkus receive private tuition when they are young; the other children study in groups. In traditional Tibet, the position of nuns was inferior to that of their male counterparts. Only in recent times have steps been taken to bring their education and meditation training up to the standard of monks. There is still a long way left to go.

Up until the age of thirteen, education consists, for the most part, of learning to read and write, memorizing prayers and texts, and attending rituals. Buddhist prayers and texts are in the classical language, which is as intelligible to the average Tibetan as is Latin or Hebrew to the average Westerner. In almost all cases, the children receive no explanations and do no meditation. They are better able to advance in these areas at an older age, whereas in childhood their powers of memorization are at their peak.

The role of the teacher during the initial phase of education is to supervise by enforcing discipline and testing students each day. The children's youthful energy is channeled into screaming at the top of their lungs the texts they have memorized. All of them shout at the same time, with each one yelling something different. This helps them to develop the ability to concentrate despite any distraction. It also keeps them awake during study sessions that many find boring.

Teenage monks and nuns, including tulkus, study by means of debate. The debates are also extremely loud, punctuated by strong ritual gestures, and with several different debates taking place simultaneously, next to each other. Through them, the teenagers learn to think logically for themselves, to question everything, and to withstand defeat. Adolescents build their characters on the debate grounds.

Despite the universal advice that tantra practice is not for beginners and the long list of prerequisites for becoming a disciple of a tantric master, almost all Tibetan monks and nuns receive tantric empowerments at a tender age. If the students do any meditation, then, it consists of reciting sadhanas—ritual texts of tantra visualization. Because they lack the qualifications to study tantra, most have only vague ideas of what to do with their minds while reciting the texts. Similarly, many learn the tantra rituals and perform prostrations, but few are aware of their deeper significance. Most focus, instead, on building self-discipline from the practices, honoring their pledges to their teachers to repeat them each day, removing obstacles by the power of the rituals, and planting good instincts for future lives.

The Traditional Spiritual Life of Lay Tibetans

In ancient India, the main spiritual activity of lay Buddhist adults was to offer food to the monks and nuns who came to their homes on daily rounds for alms. Twice a month, the monasteries and nunneries would open their gates to laypeople, who would come to hear lectures in the form of moral stories. Both at home and at the monastic institutions, laypeople would also engage in devotional practices, such as lighting incense and making other offerings. Moreover, wealthy families would occasionally invite groups of monks or nuns to their homes. After serving a meal, the family would receive a short discourse from the senior monastic. Rarely, however, did the lay patrons learn the more profound teachings or receive detailed instructions on meditation, unless they were perhaps members of the royal family.

As in Tibet, a few laypeople studied with Buddhist tantric yogis, but they constituted a small minority. The custom of widely teaching meditation to Buddhist laypeople began only in the nineteenth century in Sri Lanka and then spread to Burma. Influenced by the Protestant model of lay congregations receiving religious instruction, it arose in these countries with the revival of Buddhism after missionary suppression under British colonial rule. The custom of teaching meditation to the general lay Buddhist public never spread to Tibet.

Tibetan monks and nuns never went to people's homes on alms rounds, perhaps because of the remoteness of the monastic institutions and the severe climatic conditions. Instead, laypeople occasionally went to the monasteries and nunneries to make offerings of butter and grain and to perform devotional practices such as circumambulating and making prostration. This custom still prevails in exile. The main spiritual practice at home for the vast majority of Tibetans was lighting butter lamps and incense, offering bowls of water, and reciting mantras. A *mantra* is a set of words or syllables to recite repeatedly; it is usually associated with a Buddha-figure. In premodern Tibet, after all, most laypeople were illiterate and therefore unable to read Dharma texts. Whatever knowledge they gained was through listening, watching, and repeating.

Neither in Tibet nor in exile do lay Tibetans have Dharma centers where they may learn Buddhism. Schools run by the Tibetan Government-in-Exile normally employ a monk to lead the children in daily prayers. They have not yet started to hire nuns. The monk, however, gives only rudimentary Buddhist teachings. Systematic study materials on Buddhism are unavailable in the colloquial Tibetan language. Only recently have a few Dharma talks by His Holiness the Dalai Lama appeared in print in Tibetan. Although Buddhist values permeate the society, much like Christian ones pervade the West, laypeople who know something deeper about Buddhism and who meditate are mostly former monks and nuns.

Great masters in premodern Tibet occasionally lectured to large audiences on the classic texts and gave tantric empowerments. Most of these took place in monasteries or nunneries, and few, if any, laypeople attended. Occasionally, however, masters conducted long-life ceremonies, gave empowerments, and explained basic teachings to the lay public. Most who attended did not even attempt to understand what was happening and did not subsequently engage in meditation. The prevalent attitude was that they were planting seeds of instinct for future lives, hopefully as monks.

Nowadays in exile, the reestablished monasteries and nunneries are no longer located in isolated areas as they were in Tibet. They are within or close to the lay communities. Consequently, most laypeople have daily contact with monastics, but still do not receive spiritual guidance from them. Tibetan Buddhist monks and nuns never developed the custom of engaging in community service such as teaching school or running orphanages, hospitals, or nursing homes. A few, however, serve in government. As in premodern Tibet, the major spiritual contact that laypeople have with monastics consists of inviting monks or nuns to perform rituals in their homes or commissioning these to be done at the monasteries or nunneries. The rituals are mostly for removing obstacles and bringing success to the sponsors' worldly affairs.

Great teachers occasionally explain texts and give empowerments to large crowds of both ordained and laypeople. They make a special effort to give general Dharma advice to the laypeople who attend, but the attitude of the public remains mostly as before. They go to receive "blessings" and to lay instincts for future lives. Tibetans do not have the custom of asking questions, particularly in public.

The Contrast with Western Spiritual Seekers

The situation is totally different with Westerners attracted to Tibetan Buddhism. Few start their Buddhist educations as children, other than those who attend the equivalent of Sunday school arranged by their Buddhist-convert parents. Almost all Westerners, then, come to Buddhism after having received a modern education and after having read some books on the subject. Because the books are in colloquial modern languages, Westerners can learn from them without a teacher. However, Westerners are usually weak in absorbing the material, since they neither memorize the texts nor debate every point.

Westerners go to Dharma centers, not monasteries or nunneries, and, as laypeople, they wish to learn the most profound teachings and to gain meditation experience now, in this lifetime. Although, like Tibetans, they receive tantric empowerments long before they are qualified to practice tantra, many want to receive the full instructions and to engage in the practices immediately, without waiting to gain the prerequisite skills. The attention span of most Westerners is short and, without periodic external stimulus, they quickly lose interest. Almost no one thinks of future lives or is satisfied with planting seeds of good instinct. Some Westerners, in fact, entertain the romantic fantasies that they are Milarepas—the famous Tibetan yogi who meditated in a cave and attained enlightenment in his lifetime. They forget, of course, the hardships that Milarepa underwent to receive teachings. Tibetans would never be so presumptuous.

With certain exceptions, the few Westerners who eventually become monks or nuns take robes only after much study and meditation practice. To gain access to the teachings, however, Westerners do not need to renounce family life or life as a single, nor do they need to take robes. Hardly any Western Buddhists live with their spiritual teachers as part of the household. Some, however, live at Dharma centers where their teachers may also reside, but separately from the students.

Coming mostly from egalitarian backgrounds, Western laypeople expect the same opportunities as monks or nuns receive. Further, they have no tolerance for sexual or any other form of discrimination. They wish to have all the texts available in their colloquial languages and not in a classical tongue. Even if they chant rituals in Tibetan, most will do so only if they know what they are reciting. Very few are willing to chant the scriptures, let alone to memorize them.

Unlike Tibetans, most Westerners are impatient with learning slowly. This derives from their leading busy lives. Few can spare more than one or two nights a week and an occasional weekend to go to Dharma centers. Many have little free time during the day to meditate. Accustomed to the speed of modern conveniences, they want instant, complete access to the teachings and quick results, especially when they need to pay for Dharma instruction. Tibetans would hardly share these expectations.

With these vast cultural differences between Westerners and Tibetans, no wonder that misunderstandings often arise when spiritual seekers and spiritual teachers come from different societies. Persons with deep understanding and full appreciation of the two cultures are very rare.

The Traditional Meaning of a Spiritual Teacher

The Rectification of Terms

Titles, particularly those in foreign languages, often mystify Western people. They frequently conjure romantic images that are inappropriate. This especially happens with the various titles for spiritual teachers, such as—in the Tibetan Buddhist tradition—guru, lama, tulku, rinpochey, geshey, and kenpo. These titles are baffling enough when applied to traditional Asian teachers. They become even more puzzling when converted Westerners go by them.

Classical Chinese philosophy teaches that difficulties often come because of confusion about terms. This insight aptly applies to issues of translation. Imprecise translation terms often give people wrong ideas, especially when the two languages involved are from widely divergent cultures. If terms actually convey their intended meanings, then people trying to embody the principles represented by the words can endeavor to act in the intended ways. Confucius therefore called for a "rectification of terms." If people know how a ruler and a subject, or a parent and a child, need to act and what is the proper relationship between the two, they can try to follow that model. Success in their efforts will bring harmony to society. On the other hand, if social roles become confused and people do not follow proper guidelines, chaos and disaster will easily follow. We may extend this principle to a spiritual teacher and a spiritual seeker. If we are sloppy with our use of terms and let anyone call him or herself a guru or a disciple, we open the door to unfortunate relationships.

We need standards. Just as consumer groups keep vigilant watch on the quality of products, we need a similar approach regarding spiritual teachers. The hierarchic structure of Tibetan Buddhism differs greatly from that of an organized church. Neither the Dalai Lama nor the heads of the four traditions have the authority to dictate who are qualified teachers or to declare people incompetent. Moreover, nowadays, because of possible lawsuits in the West, we cannot expect either individuals or boards of authority to take responsibility for guaranteeing other people's ethical conduct.

In his book, *Personal Instructions from My Totally Excellent Teacher*, the outspoken Nyingma master Peltrül indicated the only reasonable approach: spiritual seekers need to take responsibility themselves. Charlatans and scoundrels may present themselves as great teachers. They may even have professionals launch effective advertising campaigns for their books and lecture tours. Nevertheless, it is up to the public to choose whether or not to become their followers. If we know the standards, we will not let imitations fool us. We will only be satisfied with authentic masters.

The Derivation of the Words Guru and Lama

To gain insight into the subtle connotations of Buddhist technical terms, we need to look to the etymology of each of their syllables. In the case of Sanskrit, each syllable and sometimes even each letter of a word may imply other terms that contain that syllable or letter. In the case of Tibetan, each syllable of a word may either constitute a word on its own or be a syllable in another term. The explanatory tantra, *A Vajra Garland*, for example, indicated the most advanced steps of the tantra path encoded in this manner in the first forty Sanskrit syllables of *The Guhyasamaja (Assembly of Hidden Factors) Tantra*. Therefore, as a first step toward implementing a rectification of terms, let us apply this traditional Buddhist analytical tool to the various Sanskrit and Tibetan words for a spiritual teacher.

The most well-known Sanskrit term for a spiritual teacher is *guru*. Although in several Western countries the word *guru* negatively connotes the head of a cult, the term literally means someone weighty or heavy. This does not mean that gurus are necessarily fat, although many are in fact overweight. Nor does it mean that gurus provide oppressively serious company. Most Buddhist teachers, especially Tibetan ones, have great senses of humor. His Holiness the Fourteenth Dalai Lama, for example, laughs and jokes whenever something strikes him funny, even when teaching the most profound subjects. The connotation, instead, as the founder of the Sakya Tsar tradition, Tsarchen, explained in *A Commentary on [Ashvaghosha's] "Fifty Stanzas [on the Guru]"*, is that gurus are weighty with qualifications. *Gu* is short for *guna*, good qualities, and *ru* stands for *ruchi*, a collection.

Moreover, gurus are weighty in the sense of having a substantial presence. Anyone in the room with a true guru, if at all sensitive, can feel that the person's outstanding qualities far surmount those of anyone else. As *gu* also stands for *guhya*, hidden, and *ru* for *rupa*, body, the full scope of qualities that gurus embody far exceeds imagination. Thus, gurus are sublime beings, since *u* stands for *uttara*, meaning supreme.

The Tibetans translated *guru* as *lama* (*bla-ma*). *La* means unsurpassable or sublime, while *ma* means mother. Lamas resemble mothers in that they have given birth internally to what is sublime. In other words, lamas are people who are extraordinarily advanced in spiritual development. Moreover, lamas help others to give birth to their own achievements of similar states. The word *lama*, however, connotes far more.

As that which is unsurpassed, *la* refers to *bodhichitta*—a heart fully focused on enlightenment and totally dedicated to achieving it to benefit others. It derives from love and compassion. Enlightenment is the highest level of spiritual self-development possible, reached with the elimination of every negative trait and with the realization of every positive quality. Its actualization is equivalent to Buddhahood and brings the ability to help others as fully as is possible. *Ma* connotes wisdom, which is the mother of all spiritual attainments. Lamas, then, combine totally dedicated hearts with wisdom and are able to lead others to similar achievements. In possessing these outstanding features, lamas are weighty with good qualities.

As gurus, lamas are also substantial persons whose presence impresses, uplifts, and inspires others. Another usage of *la* connotes this ability and reveals deeper levels of its significance.

La *as a Cosmic Force*

The early Tibetans used *la* in a sense similar to the Old Turkic word *qut*. According to the beliefs of the Old Turkic people of Central Asia, qut is a cosmic force linking the earth with the infinite sky. A holy mountain in Mongolia serves as its anchor. Whoever rules this mountain embodies its qut. Consequently, the person gains the power and charisma to unify the Turkic tribes and to become the Great Khan (the grand ruler). Thus, as an integrative force, qut empowers greatness and majesty. It allows a ruler to bring his often-warring people together and to organize them into a powerful nation.

The concept of qut, as *la*, came into the Tibetan cultural sphere via Central Asian astrology. In this context, *la* is the life-spirit force within each person that empowers or enables the individual to organize and to keep together his or her affairs. Astrological calculations can indicate the strength of this force during particular periods. When people's life-spirit force is strong, they become as stable as a mountain. When it is weak or stolen by harmful forces, they lose the ability to function normally.

Another dimension of *la* derives from its usage in the *Kalachakra* (cycles of time) teachings. There it appears as part of the subtle energy-system of the body. Among the components of this system is a life-spirit drop. This subtle creative drop or spark of energy (*tigley, thig-le*; Skt. *bindu*), also called *bodhichitta* in Sanskrit, passes to different spots in the body each day during a month-long cycle. Life-spirit energy gathers around it, rendering the spot in which the drop is located the most potent point in the body that day for medical treatment with acupuncture or cauterization.

The early Tibetans translated *bodhichitta* here as *la*, undoubtedly because of the similarity between the life-spirit drop in Indian physiology and the life-spirit force in Central Asian astrology. A further rationale for this choice was perhaps that bodhichitta, in its meaning as a totally dedicated heart, reigns as the unsurpassed method for attaining enlightenment. Since *la* also means unsurpassable, it can serve as a synonym for bodhichitta according to the principles of Sanskrit and Tibetan poetics.

The Full Original Meaning of Lama

Putting together the various meanings of *la* gives a fuller picture of some of the outstanding qualities that lamas possess and can lead others to attain. Lamas have the force to tame their wild behavior and disturbing emotions so that they become as stable and substantial as mountains. With this force, lamas can organize their lives to benefit all.

This life-spirit force is a dedicated heart of bodhichitta, which grants lamas the charismatic power to affect the most beneficial and healing changes in others. Further, by the force of their spiritual development, lamas possess the power to tame wild disciples and to help them to organize their lives most meaningfully. This power derives from heart-felt love and compassion. These aspects of *la* constitute the "method" side of a lama's attainment.

Ma, as mother, refers to the wisdom embodied in *The Prajnaparamita Sutras*, the scriptural texts in which Buddha taught far-reaching dis-criminating awareness (*sherab, shes-rab*; Skt. *prajna*), the "perfection of wisdom." These texts and their contents are often called the "mother of all Buddhas," since mastery of them gives birth to enlightenment. Lamas are those with mastery of the scriptures and their contents. They combine their wisdom with all aspects of method. Like good mothers, lamas nurture disciples and raise them to be mature spiritual adults.

The original meaning of the term *lama*, then, is a highly advanced spiritual teacher. Such persons are fully capable of guiding disciples along the entire Buddhist path, all the way to enlightenment, by vir-tue of the qualities implied by the connotations of guru, *la*, and *ma*. The classical textual presentation of how to relate to a spiritual teacher refers to the optimal relationship with such a person. To rectify prob-lems in student-teacher relationships, spiritual teachers need to live up to this meaning of the titles *guru* and *lama*.

Other Uses of the Word Lama

Tibetan Buddhism developed four major traditions—Nyingma, Kagyü, Sakya, and Gelug—and spread beyond Tibet to the other Himalayan regions, Mongolia, much of northern China, Manchuria, parts of Siberia, and several other Central Asian cultures. Because of this diversity, the word *lama* gradually acquired other meanings. One source of confusion about so-called guru-devotion comes from think-ing that the practice applies to lamas in different senses of the word. A survey of the other types of lamas may help with the rectification of terms.

Many serious practitioners of the Kagyü and Nyingma traditions enter a three-year meditation retreat. During this period, they train in the major Buddha-figure (*yidam, yi-dam*) systems of their lineage.

Spending several weeks or months on each tantra system, they master its rituals and familiarize themselves with its meditation practice. The heads of some subdivisions of these lineages have recently started the custom of granting *lama* as a title to the most proficient graduates of a retreat. In the Gelug tradition, monks who successfully complete rigorous training at one of the tantric monastic colleges near Lhasa are called *tantric lamas* (*lama gyüpa, bla-ma rgyud-pa*). Such monks, however, do not use *lama* as a title, nor do people address them as "lama."

In both these cases, *lama* signifies a ritual master. Although such lamas have trained in meditation, they have not necessarily achieved any spiritual attainments. Nor are they necessarily qualified to lead others through the Buddhist path. Nevertheless, they can perform the rituals correctly and can instruct others to do the same. Among the Tibetans, such lamas serve somewhat like village priests. They travel from village to village and perform rituals for people in their homes. These rituals help to bring prosperity, health, and good fortune to the families, and help to remove any obstacles to success.

Whether lamas are highly realized spiritual teachers or simply ritual masters, they may be monks, nuns, or laypeople. In Ladakh, however, and among most Mongol groups during the precommunist era, *lama* became a synonym for *monk*. This resembles the Indian custom of calling Buddhist monks by the honorific *guru-ji*. Irrespective of a monk's level of scriptural education, ritual training, or spiritual attainment, he is still a lama in this sense of the word.

During the communist period in the Soviet Union and in the Mongolian People's Republic, the authorities forced the Buddhist monks to disrobe and to break their vows. There had never been any nuns. For propaganda purposes, however, Stalin eventually allowed a few monasteries to reopen and a few former monks to perform rituals there. These people were usually laymen who wore robes during the day like uniforms at work and shed them at night when they returned home to their wives and children. They were also called lamas. Even now in the postcommunist era, such people still bear the name *lama*. Often they counsel others by relying on astrological or divinatory means.

People who are lamas by virtue simply of being ritual masters, monks, or lay performers of monastic rituals command respect. Even if their levels of spiritual development are not particularly advanced, their training, their vows, or the services they provide makes them worthy of esteem. Nevertheless, those who are lamas in merely one of these honorific senses are not the persons to whom the classical disciple-mentor relationship refers.

Reincarnate Lamas: Tulkus and Rinpocheys

Another common use of the word *lama* is in reference to reincarnate lamas, tulkus. Although tulkus are the reincarnations of highly advanced tantric practitioners, such practitioners need not necessarily have been great spiritual teachers, nor monks or nuns. They may have been lay meditators, for instance, who lived alone as hermits in caves. To start a line of tulkus requires usually only four conditions: (1) foreknowledge that recognition of one's future incarnations will be beneficial to others, (2) well-developed bodhichitta as the motivation, (3) sincere prayers to take rebirth in a form, beneficial to others, which will be recognized as a tulku, and (4) a certain degree of mastery of the first stage of the highest class of tantra.

Here and elsewhere in the book, we shall use the term *highest tantra* to refer both to *anuttarayoga* in the Gelug, Kagyü, and Sakya systems and to the unit formed by *mahayoga, anuyoga,* and *atiyoga* (*dzogchen, rdzogs-chen*; the great completeness) in the Nyingma tradition. On the first level of highest tantra, the generation stage, practitioners generate vivid visualizations to simulate the process of death, the in-between state (*bardo, bar-do*), and rebirth.

Followers of great teachers who have reached some level of attainment on the generation stage, and who have thus performed the prescribed meditations at death, first consult a distinguished Tibetan master famous for extrasensory perception. In the case of highly advanced tantric practitioners who were not noted as teachers, Tibetan masters may make investigations without their being requested. Through various means of divination, including dream analysis, the master determines whether or not the person in question has intended to start a line of tulkus. If so, the master further determines if finding the present incarnation will have special benefit.

The devotion of a teacher's followers and their enthusiasm for finding the reincarnation of their mentor are not sufficient reasons for commissioning a search. Some of the most famous lamas, such as Tsongkapa, did not start a line of tulkus. Further, some lamas, such as several successive incarnations of Shamar Rinpochey within the Karma Kagyü tradition, were not recognized during their lifetimes due to political reasons.

Once a great master has sanctioned a search for a tulku and, through further divination, given some indication of the identity of the child and where to look, the followers of the teacher in question, or a group commissioned by the sanctioning master, begin their quest. After locating two or three promising candidates of the appropriate age, they consult once more the master who directed the search. Based on indications that the children may have given of their identities, such as recognition of persons and possessions from the previous lifetime, and further divination, the master makes the final choice.

Young tulkus usually leave their families of birth shortly after recognition and, if their predecessors were monks or nuns and noted teachers, they grow up in the predecessors' private monastic homes (*labrang*, *bla-brang*). If the predecessors were not monastics or if, as monastics, they were not noted teachers and thus did not have private homes, the children still enter monastic institutions and their families or patrons sponsor the construction of houses for them. To celebrate their return, the predecessors' monastic estates or the young tulkus' families or patrons make large donations to the reincarnates' affiliated monastic institutions and extensive offerings to their monks and nuns The children inherit all former possessions and receive special education and training.

The tulku system has not been foolproof. Occasionally, even the greatest masters have admitted that they might have made mistakes in their recognition. Moreover, corruption sometimes has blemished the system when masters have acceded to political pressure or bribery to recognize certain candidates. Monastic institutions with famous teachers who attracted large donations sometimes have even declared and recognized new lines of tulkus because of their wish to continue receiving contributions.

Over a thousand lines of tulkus have been reincarnating among Tibetans, Mongols, Bhutanese, and the various Indian Himalayan people. In recent decades, several dozen have taken rebirth as Westerners or Chinese. People generally address reincarnate lamas with the honorific title *Rinpochey* (*rin-po-che*), which means Precious One. Not all rinpocheys, however, are tulkus. Current and retired abbots and abbesses also receive the title. Moreover, as signs of respect, many disciples call their spiritual mentors "Rinpochey," even if the teachers are neither tulkus nor abbots or abbesses.

The word *tulku* means a network of emanations (Skt. *nirmanakaya*, emanation body). Not only do fully enlightened Buddhas generate and appear as an array of emanations, so do advanced practitioners of the highest class of tantra. The array they generate is called a network of pathway-level emanations. The founders of lines of tulkus, then, may have achieved any level of spiritual attainment ranging from part of the generation stage to Buddhahood. Thus, they do not even need to have attained straightforward nonconceptual perception of reality (voidness, emptiness, the absence of impossible ways of existing). In short, only a tiny fraction of the founders of tulku lines comprises enlightened beings.

For this reason, the majority of tulkus still have negative karmic potentials in addition to a vast network of positive instincts (collection of merit). Depending on the circumstances of their upbringing and the societies in which they live, different potentials come to the fore and ripen in each lifetime. Thus, some tulkus may act in completely unenlightened ways. Nevertheless, by the force of the death-juncture meditation and prayers of the founders of their lines, their next incarnations may still be as rinpocheys, located and recognized by the masters who have determined that to do so would have special benefit. This may occur even if the tulkus in question failed to perform death-juncture meditation when they died.

Lamaism and the Traditional Social Role of Tulkus

A complex social system arose in Tibeto-Mongolian cultural regions surrounding the institution of tulkus. The reincarnate lamas became somewhat like local feudal lords and owned vast tracts of land around their monasteries and nunneries. Many peasants worked these lands, giving part of the produce to support the rinpocheys' households and the monastics under their guidance.

Despite inevitable abuses of the system, most people regarded this arrangement as a way to create positive potential (merit) for themselves and their families. The tulkus provided spiritual and social leadership. They served as the embodiments of regional identities and the focal points around which to consolidate and express regional or tribal loyalties. People had enormous faith and treated their local tulkus reverentially with highly elaborate protocol. To outsiders, it appeared almost as if they worshipped their lamas. Perhaps some did, since many considered their rinpocheys as having supernatural powers.

To differentiate this form of Buddhism from traditional Chinese Buddhist schools, the late-seventeenth-century Manchu rulers of China coined the word *lamajiao* (Lamaism). They called the Chinese forms of Buddhism simply *fojiao* (Buddhism). Making this distinction was undoubtedly part of their policy to try to gain the political allegiance of the Tibetans and Mongols in their empire. They did this by trying to impress on the two ethnic groups their fellowship with the Manchu people established by virtue of a common religion, distinct from that of the Han Chinese. Many early Western scholars adopted this custom and perpetuated the artificial distinction.

Further, the Manchus forced certain lines of tulkus to serve in the imperial government as local administrators and tax collectors. To exploit even more the people's reverence and obedience to the politically useful lamas, the Manchus called all tulkus *hefo* in Chinese, meaning "living Buddhas." Some Western scholars and journalists still follow this convention, creating even more confusion about lamas.

In short, as His Holiness the Fourteenth Dalai Lama stressed at the 1988 conference of tulkus in exile, just because tulkus bear famous names does not mean that they qualify now as spiritual mentors. It merely signifies that they are the reincarnations of great spiritual masters and have been born with enormous amounts of positive potential. Tulkus need to prove themselves as mentors now, through their attainments in this lifetime.

Because of inherited potentials, reincarnate lamas naturally command respect. Nevertheless, circumstances may not allow full activation of those potentials or may not be conducive for their optimal use. For example, because a rinpochey may still be a child, the potentials may enable the boy or girl merely to advance quickly. Occasionally, excessive reverence shown by followers may act as the circumstance merely for success in power politics or empire building. In some cases, inordinate deference, lavish gifts, and high expectations may even spoil young rinpocheys or activate negative potentials for them to rebel when older. Differentiating the term *reincarnate lama* from *lama*—either in its meaning as a spiritual mentor or as a living Buddha—can help prevent disappointment.

"God-Kings"

Over the centuries, Tibetan spiritual leaders recognized several of the most politically influential tulkus as emanations of Buddha-figures. The Dalai Lamas and Karmapas, for example, were emanations of Avalokiteshvara; the Sakya heads were Manjushri; and the Panchen Lamas and Shamar Rinpocheys, Amitabha. The custom extended beyond religious figures to include the early Tibetan kings as Avalokitesh-vara; Confucius and the Manchu emperors of China as Manjushri; Chingghis Khan and his descendents as Vajrapani; the czars of Russia as Tara; and Queen Victoria as Pelden Lhamo.

Political considerations may have influenced this development. Avalokiteshvara, Manjushri, and Vajrapani are the Buddha-figures whom Tibetan Buddhists regard as holding the responsibility to safeguard the welfare respectively of Tibet, China, and Mongolia. Therefore, according to the Tibetan way of thinking, the legitimate rulers of each of these lands must be emanations of its guardian Buddha-figure. This accounts for the identities of the early Tibetan kings, the Dalai Lamas, the Manchu emperors of China, and the Mongol Khans. The name *Manchu*, in fact, according to some scholars, derives from Manjushri.

The custom of identifying politically influential lamas with Buddha-figures began as early as the thirteenth century, when the second Karmapa, as Avalokiteshvara, was a candidate for becoming the ruler of Tibet. Kublai Khan, however, the first Mongol emperor of China, awarded this role to the Sakya heads. As Manjushri, the Sakya heads helped to unify the Mongol Empire by serving as the spiritual heads for Chinese Buddhists as well as for Tibetans and Mongols.

Avalokiteshvara belongs to the Buddha-family of Amitabha. Thus, the lines of Panchen Lamas and Shamar Rinpocheys were emanations of Amitabha, because their founding figures were the mentors respectively of the Dalai Lama and Karmapa of their times. Further, Tara and Pelden Lhamo are the traditional helper and protector associated with Avalokiteshvara. Thus, when the Thirteenth Dalai Lama sought Russian and British protection against the Chinese at the start of the twentieth century, he addressed the rulers of these lands with the honorific names of these Buddhist figures and thereby indirectly indicated their natural roles.

For Tibetans, the Dalai Lama *is* Avalokiteshvara. He safeguards their country and its religion and culture. The Dalai Lama, then, not only embodies the Buddha-figure representing compassion; he embodies Tibet and Tibetan Buddhism. As such, he serves as the symbol of hope for all Tibetans to preserve their nation and way of life during the difficult times of Chinese military occupation. Although Western authors and journalists ascribe the term "god-king" to the Dalai Lama, he is not a god in any Western sense of the word.

Tibetan Humor

Tibetan spiritual mentors often possess mischievous senses of humor. As a playful way of showing warm regard, they sometimes call their Western disciples "Lama," "Rinpochey," or even "Dharma-Protector." Occasionally, some of these Westerners do not understand the Tibetan sense of humor and publicize that they have been officially recognized. Since most Tibetans are too polite to give public disclaimers, confusion and even abuse of power have occasionally arisen from what began as an innocent joke. Analogously, some Western parents might affectionately call their children "real devils." For such a child, later in life, to assume the title *Devil* would be clearly absurd.

Spiritual Friends

The word commonly translated as *guru* in the expression *guru-devotion* is actually neither guru nor lama. Instead, it is *kalyana-mitra* in Sanskrit and *geway-shenyen* (*dge-ba'i bshes-gnyen*) in Tibetan, abbreviated as *geshey* (*dge-bshes*). The term appears in this expression exclusively within the context of the *Mahayana* (vast vehicle) teachings for attaining enlightenment, and translators usually render it in either language as *spiritual friend*. Let us look closer at the implications of the original terms to help avoid any misunderstanding.

Many translators use *virtuous* as the English equivalent for *kalyana* or *gewa*, the component for *spiritual* in this expression. A "virtuous friend," a "friend of virtue," and a "friend who leads others to virtue," however, all carry the subtle flavor in English of someone prim, stiff, and self-righteous. *Constructive* might perhaps be a more appropriate translation. In Buddhism, constructive behavior is to act, speak, and think in ways that build habits which, in the long term, lead to personal happiness. Spiritual friends, then, are constructive friends, friends of what is constructive, and friends who lead others to constructive behavior.

To grasp the deeper implications of being a spiritual friend requires understanding the Buddhist concept of constructive behavior. The Tibetan schools base their ethical systems on two Indian works, *A Treasure-House of Special Topics of Knowledge* by Vasubandhu and *An Anthology of Special Topics of Knowledge* by his brother Asanga. The combination of their explanations provides a fuller picture.

Constructive actions are those that are motivated by constructive states of mind. Such mental states consist of complexes of positive attitudes and qualities. They contain confidence in the benefits of being positive and a sense of values from respecting positive qualities and persons possessing them. Discriminating awareness that destructive behavior leads to unhappiness, a sense of scruples that allows restraint from brazenly negative behavior, and a sense of fitness to be able to refrain from such action also accompany them. Moreover, constructive states of mind come from having a sense of self-pride and concern for not disgracing one's spiritual teachers, family, or nation by acting destructively. An absence of certain negative components also characterizes constructive mental states. They lack greed, attachment, hostility, naivety, and other disturbing mental factors such as flightiness, dullness, recklessness, and laziness.

In short, constructive mental states have strong conviction of ethical principles and have the ability to follow them. Such conviction and ability naturally bring restraint from destructive behavior. As spiritual friends, spiritual mentors are teachers with constructive states of mind, which lead to constructive manners of acting, speaking, and thinking. Moreover, they are able to inspire and teach disciples to think and behave similarly.

The term *constructive* also refers to the ultimate spiritual attainments —liberation from the recurring problems of uncontrollable rebirth (Skt. *samsara*) and, beyond that, enlightenment as a Buddha. The attainment of either of these states is ultimately constructive. However, since *kalyana-mitra* here is a Mahayana term, the constructive state to which spiritual friends lead disciples is specifically enlightenment.

The Buddhist Concept of Friendship

The second component of the term *spiritual friend*, *mitra* in Sanskrit, is the common word for *friend*. As the root of the word *maitri*, meaning love, its connotation derives from the Buddhist definition of love. Love is the wish for others to be happy and to have the causes for happiness. As a selfless wish, it does not imply clinging attachment to the people one loves or desire for anything in return, not even reciprocal love, affection, or appreciation. Nor does it imply needing the objects of one's love for emotional security or a sense of self-worth. A friend, then, is someone with a purely altruistic attitude, not someone who, for neurotic reasons, compulsively tries to please others or to make them happy.

The Buddhist tradition further defines a friend as someone in whose presence, or in thinking of whom, one would feel ashamed to act, to speak, or to think destructively. In this sense, a true friend is actually a spiritual friend, someone who helps others to be constructive. Constructive behavior, after all, is the cause of happiness, which is the primary wish a friend holds for someone. In contrast, a misleading friend draws others away from constructive behavior and causes them either to waste their time or to act, speak, or think destructively. Such behavior leads to the experience of suffering and unhappiness, the opposite result of that wished for by love.

Shenyen, the Tibetan translation here for *mitra*, means literally relative-friend. In many Asian cultures, people address elders in a friendly manner by calling them "uncle" or "aunt." Those equal in age, they call "brother" or "sister," and they address any child as "son" or "daughter." Thus, a friend automatically becomes part of one's family. This carries only a positive connotation, namely that the person joins the ranks of those with whom one has a close, loving, and harmonious relationship.

Most Asians live in large extended families, with several generations residing their entire lives under a single roof. Often, a wall surrounds the home to protect the family from harm. Being with family and relative-friends implies feeling safe, physically and emotionally, with confident trust of never being attacked, abused, or led astray. Similarly, spiritual mentors and disciples form spiritual families and feel totally at home with each another. Moreover, being a member of a traditional Asian family, much like being a member of a traditional Mediterranean one, nurtures and supports one's life-spirit force. Being a member of a mentor's spiritual family functions similarly. It gives the strength to organize and maintain a vigorous and healthy spiritual life.

Although spiritual mentors may be older, younger, or the same age as their disciples, the teachers are always the spiritual elders. The common Tibetan word for teacher, *gegen* (*dge-rgan*), often used in its abbreviated form *gen* (*rgan*) as a familiar term of address, in fact means a spiritual elder. Again, *spiritual* here is a loose translation of the word for constructive. As spiritual elders, mentors command the greater deference, although of course both sides deeply respect each other. Disciples respect the teachers' realized qualities, while teachers respect the disciples' potentials.

Spiritual friendship, then, in the strict sense of the Buddhist technical term, does not imply that the two people involved are equal like two buddies would be. In a Western friendship, both parties are called friends, whereas here only the spiritual mentor is called the spiritual friend. Although fellow Dharma students or fellow disciples may be spiritual friends in the Western sense of friends, they are not each other's spiritual mentors or guides. Even if being with one another leads both of them to think and to act constructively, fellow students cannot lead each other to enlightenment as Buddhas. At best, they may accompany one another.

The closest Western analogy to a spiritual friend in the Buddhist sense is perhaps a platonic friend in its classical meaning. A platonic friend, as a more mature and experienced person, is a teacher and mentor with whom a relationship uplifts and leads a younger person to the highest level of spiritual ideal. A lack of romance, sex, and base emotion characterize the loving relation between the two. Unlike ancient Greek thought, however, Buddhism does not conceive of the relationship in the context of spiritualized, ideal beauty, goodness, and truth. Instead, it formulates the relationship in terms of familial closeness and aims it at the attainment of enlightenment.

Gesheys and Kenpos

Geshey, the abbreviated form of the Tibetan term for a spiritual friend, originally was a title used in the Kadam tradition for great spiritual teachers. Simplicity, humility, and hidden greatness characterized the Kadampa gesheys. Especially noted for their teachings on *lojong* (*blo-sbyong*), cleansing of attitudes (mental training), they embodied everything that they taught.

The Gelug tradition reunited the fragmented Kadam lineages, reformed corruptions, and continued as its successor. Subsequently, the Fifth Dalai Lama borrowed the title *Geshey* and used it to replace previous titles for the degree granted at the successful conclusion of the Gelug monastic education system. Currently, the term retains that usage. So far, only monks have received this degree, although in exile nuns and laypeople have begun to study for it.

Becoming a geshey requires memorizing texts, studying them for more than twenty years with logic and debate, and passing several levels of intensive examinations. It does not require incorporating the meaning of the texts into one's self-development, nor does it imply experience and proficiency in meditation. The title *Geshey*, then, resembles a Ph.D. Like its Western counterpart, it does not guarantee the teaching skills or character of its holder. Many gesheys, of course, possess those skills and are spiritually realized. Their titles, however, merely indicate scholarly expertise.

The same pertains to the title *Kenpo* (*mkhan-po*), meaning a learned one. Equivalent to a geshey degree, it is granted by Kagyü and Nyingma monasteries to successful graduates of their education systems. Those who complete Sakya monastic education also receive a geshey degree. They normally use geshey as a title, however, only when they travel outside the monasteries to teach. Within the monasteries, monks usually call them "kenpo." *Kenpo* also means an abbot of a monastery. All Tibetan traditions call abbots "Ken Rinpochey."

If a geshey or kenpo has qualifications merely like those of a professor, the person certainly commands respect for his knowledge and learning. As in the case of lamas and rinpocheys, however, gesheys and kenpos are not necessarily spiritual mentors capable of leading disciples to enlightenment. Only those who live up to the original meaning and implication of their titles have that skill.

Summary

For spiritual teachers to be and to act as spiritual mentors, they need to be weighty with positive qualities and need to combine compassion and bodhichitta with a deep understanding of reality. Moreover, they need to have the power to uplift and to inspire disciples to achieve the same. They need to be spiritual friends in the sense that they act, speak, and think constructively in ways that never cause long-term harm, but only ultimate benefit. These ways are always free of greed, attachment, anger, or naivety as their motivation. Instead, they arise from love and compassion and come from wisdom. Further, spiritual mentors lead disciples to constructive behavior, like friends who have become trusted, close family members. Ultimately, spiritual mentors lead disciples to liberation and enlightenment.

When spiritual teachers have the additional qualities associated with the secondary meanings of *lama*, they may be even more effective mentors for inspiring disciples. For example, if laypeople acting as spiritual mentors serve in monastic settings, potential disciples gain more confidence in their commitment and authority than if they serve outside that setting. If, in addition, spiritual mentors are monks or nuns, they set potent examples. *The Abbreviated Kalachakra Tantra* explains the reason: people upholding monastic vows automatically command respect as representatives of the *Sangha* Refuge—those with straightforward, nonconceptual understanding of reality. Although such persons may be lay or ordained, the community of monks and nuns represents the Sangha as an object of respect. The use of *Sangha* as an equivalent for the congregation of members either of a specific Dharma center or of a group of centers is purely a Western convention.

Further, if spiritual mentors are masters of ritual who have completed three-year meditation retreats or have trained at one of the tantric colleges, people feel that this certifies their qualifications. The same is true if they have successfully completed formal monastic education and received geshey or kenpo degrees. Finally, if authorities have recognized spiritual mentors as the reincarnations of great tantric masters, many people automatically have strong faith in their abilities.

On the other hand, people may be merely monks, nuns, laypeople serving in monastic settings, ritual masters, monastic degree holders, recognized reincarnations, or some combination of these. Such persons certainly deserve respect and may be able to teach many things. Nevertheless, without the further qualifications indicated by the full original meanings of *guru*, *lama*, and *spiritual friend*, they are not spiritual mentors and guides capable of leading disciples all the way to enlightenment. We may avoid disillusionment and possible spiritual harm if we rectify terms.

~3
The Traditional Meaning of a Spiritual Seeker

MANY PEOPLE may consider themselves spiritual seekers and may even study with spiritual teachers at Dharma centers. The most committed type of spiritual seeker, however, is a disciple of a spiritual mentor. Problems in relating to spiritual teachers often arise because of students prematurely considering themselves to be someone's disciples—whether or not the person chosen is a qualified mentor—and then trying to follow the traditional protocol for a disciple-mentor relationship. To begin to dispel this confusion, let us continue our rectification of terms by examining the Sanskrit and Tibetan words usually translated as *disciple*.

The Implications of the Sanskrit Terms for a Disciple
The main Sanskrit terms for a Buddhist disciple are *shaiksha*, *shishya*, *vaineya*, and *bhajana*. A *shaiksha* is someone who offers him or herself for *shiksha*, training by a spiritual mentor. Specifically, this means receiving three types of "higher training"—in ethical self-discipline, concentration on constructive objects, and discriminating awareness of reality.

Training in ethical self-discipline means learning to restrain from acting, speaking, or thinking destructively. It also entails engaging in constructive behavior and positive ways of thinking and feeling. As with the explanation of spiritual friends and spiritual mentors, *constructive* implies behaving and thinking without disturbing emotions or attitudes, such as greed, attachment, hostility, or naivety. It also implies having confidence in the benefits of being positive and maintaining a sense of values derived from respecting positive qualities and persons possessing them. Thus, disciples train in methods for self-development, such as meditation, within a wholesome, ethical framework. Moreover, in the context of being a disciple of a Mahayana spiritual friend, *constructive* also signifies that the higher training aims for reaching enlightenment. Thus, while training to become Buddhas, disciples actively help others as much as they can.

The term *shishya* derives from the same root as the word *shasana*, meaning an indication of Buddha's attainments. Through his way of being and his spoken words later recorded as scriptural texts, Buddha indicated his enlightenment to others and taught methods for attaining it. Correspondingly, disciples learn the three types of higher training from a spiritual mentor through observing the person's character and demeanor and through listening to his or her explanation of the scriptural teachings. Similarly, disciples combine experiential and theoretical knowledge, to bring about constructive transformations of their personalities and manner.

Vaineya implies someone who trains in *vinaya*, the methods for "becoming tame." Through vinaya training, disciples gain ethical self-discipline through keeping the vowed restraints of Buddhist laypeople or monastics. By formally taking vows to tame their unruly patterns and to behave and think more constructively, disciples demonstrate a deep level of commitment to the process of self-development.

Bhajana means a receptacle or container. Disciples serve as receptacles for receiving and holding the Dharma teachings. Specifically, they serve as vessels for containing the three types of higher training and either lay or monastic vows. To be proper vessels, disciples require a certain level of maturity before establishing a relationship with a mentor. They need open-mindedness to receive training and vows, stability to maintain the continuity of each, and freedom from strong psychological problems so that they can observe the two purely.

The term *chela*, commonly used for a Hindu disciple who leaves household life to live and study with a *sadhu* (a homeless spiritual devotee), means someone who dresses in the rags of an ascetic yogi. The Tibetan translation *raypa* (*ras-pa*), however, lost the connotation of a disciple. Instead, it became a term for a tantric yogi who dresses in the scant rags of an Indian ascetic, for example Mila-raypa (Milarepa).

Tibetans translated both *shaiksha* and *shishya* as *lobma* (*slob- ma*), *vaineya* as *dülja* (*gdul-bya*), and *bhajana* as *nö* (*snod*). The Tibetan terms carry mostly the same nuances as the Sanskrit equivalents, but in certain cases add more richness. The syllable *ma* in *lobma*, for example, connotes wisdom, another word for discriminating awareness, as it does in *lama*. Disciples train to discriminate for themselves what is constructive from what is destructive and fantasy from reality. *Nö* is often coupled with *chü* (*bcud*), meaning the refined essence of something. Disciples serve as proper vessels for receiving and holding the refined essence that a mentor can offer—the enlightening methods for becoming a Buddha.

In short, if spiritual mentors are constructive persons who lead others to behave and to think constructively in order for them to attain enlightenment, disciples are those who are led to enlightenment by such persons through training in constructive behavior and thought.

The Meaning of Being a Teacher's Getrug

Getrug (*dge-phrug*), an additional Tibetan term for disciple, corroborates the previous explanations. *Ge* means constructive and *trug* means a child. A *getrug* is a child raised by a spiritual mentor to be constructive—along the way as an increasingly balanced, ethical, and positive person, and ultimately as a Buddha. *Child* does not necessarily refer to the disciple's age. It means a minor with respect to the spiritual path.

In addition to its etymological meaning, the term *getrug* has another connotation. The term may also signify someone who has lived in a teacher's home since childhood and is included in the finances of the household. Often, getrug are younger relatives. The two meanings of *getrug* do not necessarily overlap. Spiritual disciples may not be included in the finances of their mentors' households and those included may hardly receive any formal spiritual training, for example the cook.

The Starting Point for Becoming a Disciple

To understand correctly what being a disciple means in the Buddhist context requires knowing at which stage on the spiritual path one may appropriately become a disciple. Although the classical texts agree on the necessity for spiritual teachers at every stage along the path, spiritual seekers begin the journey long before becoming disciples of qualified mentors. Much confusion has arisen about this point because Kadam masters, such as Sangwayjin, explained the disciple-mentor relationship as the "root of the path" and presented the topic at the start of their graded-path (*lamrim, lam-rim*) texts. Subsequently, Tsong-kapa and all later Gelug masters followed suit. The placement of this topic in the outline of their texts, however, does not mean that seekers need to enter a disciple-mentor relationship as the first step on their spiritual paths. Let us examine what these masters meant.

In *The Essence of Excellent Explanation of Interpretable and Definitive Phenomena*, Tsongkapa explained that the classification system of three Dharma cycles (three turnings of the wheel of Dharma) does not indicate a temporal sequence of teachings. It indicates, instead, a division scheme made according to subject matter. The first cycle's topic, the "four noble truths," serves as the basis for the teachings classified in the second two cycles. Similarly, Sangwayjin's placement of the disciple-mentor relationship as the first major topic in *An Extensive Presentation of the Graded Stages of the Path* does not indicate its temporal position on the path. It merely indicates its essential role as the stable foundation for developing the graded stages of spiritual motivation in their fullest forms.

In *The Gateway for Entering the Dharma*, Sönam-tsemo, the second of the five Sakya founders, explained that before building a relationship with a spiritual mentor, seekers need to recognize and acknowledge suffering in their lives and to develop the wish to overcome it. In other words, they need a rudimentary level of "renunciation." In addition, they need knowledge of Buddha's teachings about what to practice and what to avoid in order to reduce and eliminate the suffering they wish to overcome. Only then are seekers ready to establish a serious relationship with a spiritual mentor, to help them achieve their goals.

Spiritual mentors, however, are teachers who help disciples to reach enlightenment. Therefore, before establishing a disciple-mentor relationship, seekers also need initial interest in becoming Buddhas for everyone's sake. This is clear from the writings of the Indian master Atisha, the formulator of the graded path and fountainhead of the Kadam tradition. In *An [Auto-]Commentary on the Difficult Points of "A Lamp for the Path to Enlightenment*,*"* Atisha first mentioned the disciple-mentor relationship in the context of developing bodhichitta. Moreover, developing a Mahayana motivation of bodhichitta presumes at least a beginning level of safe direction (refuge) in the Buddhas, the Dharma, and the highly realized Sangha community.

The Fifth Dalai Lama made these points explicit in his graded-path text *Personal Instructions from Manjushri*. There, he argued for the necessity and propriety of taking safe direction and developing bodhichitta before establishing a disciple-mentor relationship. Following this argument, the Second Panchen Lama, in *A Speedy Path*, changed the order of Tsongkapa's *Grand Presentation of the Graded Stages of the Path*. To reflect the actual order of spiritual development, he placed the preliminary practices before the discussion of the disciple-mentor relationship. The preliminaries include taking safe direction and enhancing one's bodhichitta motivation. Thus, the Kadam/Gelug understanding of the graded path is consistent with the frequent Kagyü and Nyingma explanations that establishing safe direction, bodhichitta, and then a healthy disciple-mentor relationship is the sequence of essential preliminaries for Buddhist spiritual advancement.

Tsongkapa further explained that each stage of self- development along the graded path is a stepping-stone on the way to enlightenment. Thus, although seekers need already to have recognition of suffering, renunciation of it, knowledge of what to practice and avoid, safe direction, and bodhichitta before becoming disciples, they need merely to have the five as a spiritual orientation. The initial level of intensity of the five that seekers possess acts as a stepping-stone for proceeding further, now as disciples of spiritual mentors, and is hardly the end of the development of them along the way. Thus, although having safe direction and bodhichitta implies striving toward liberation and then enlightenment, having the two as merely a spiritual orientation does not imply comprehending and accepting on a visceral level the full implication of attaining these goals.

The Necessity of Correct Understanding and Conviction in Rebirth for a Disciple to Aim Sincerely for Liberation and Enlightenment

To strive toward liberation and then enlightenment, with a full comprehension and visceral acceptance of what these goals imply, comes only after comprehending and viscerally accepting the Buddhist explanation of rebirth. In Buddhism, rebirth does not imply the existence of a permanent soul that goes to an eternal afterlife or that passes from one incarnation to the next, facing progressive lessons that are given to it to learn. The Buddhist understanding implies, instead, an infinite continuity of individual experience, without an unchanging, singular entity, independent from body and mind, which is really "me" and which continues from one life to the next. The continuity proceeds from one lifetime to the next either uncontrollably driven by disturbing emotions and attitudes and by compelling impulses (Skt. *karma*) or consciously directed through the force of compassion. The Buddhist explanation is sophisticated and extremely difficult to understand.

Liberation means freedom from the suffering of uncontrollably recurring rebirth (Skt. *samsara*) and its causes, while enlightenment brings the ability to help others gain similar freedom. How can disciples sincerely strive for liberation from uncontrollable rebirth without correctly understanding what rebirth means according to Buddhism and without conviction that they have been experiencing it uncontrollably, without a beginning, and will continue to do so, unless they do something about it? How can they strive for enlightenment without certainty that everyone else also experiences the suffering of samsara?

The Necessity of Correct Understanding and Conviction in Rebirth for a Disciple to Reach Even the First Stage of Spiritual Development

Correct understanding and conviction in the Buddhist explanation of rebirth is necessary for reaching even the first stage of spiritual development once one has entered a disciple-mentor relationship. For example, in *A Lamp for the Path to Enlightenment*, Atisha identified three distinct stages of self-development that disciples reach while progressing along the graded path to enlightenment. Disciples attain the initial stage when they aim for favorable rebirths because of wishing to avoid the suffering of unfavorable ones. Clearly, they will only aim for favorable rebirths if they are sincerely convinced that future lives exist and that they will experience them after death. They attain the second stage when they aim for liberation from uncontrollable rebirth altogether, whether favorable or unfavorable, and the third when their goal is enlightenment.

The spiritual context of the initial aim of Buddhist disciples differs greatly from that of followers of other traditions who pray to go to heaven after they die and to remain there for eternity. To continue working, beyond this lifetime, toward liberation and enlightenment requires gaining rebirths with circumstances that are conducive for spiritual practice. Thus, gaining favorable rebirths is only a provisional goal for Buddhist disciples.

All subsequent Tibetan formulations of the stages of the path concur with Atisha about the initial level. For example, Sachen, the senior of the five Sakya founders, popularized Manjushri's revelation to him of *Parting from the Four [Stages of] Clinging*. In this formulation, the first stage of spiritual life entails parting oneself from clinging to the wish to benefit this lifetime. The four themes of Gampopa, the father of the twelve Dagpo Kagyü lines, echo this view. The first theme, turning one's mind to the Dharma, also requires switching the major focus of attention from this lifetime to future ones. The consensus is clear.

The Place of Conviction in Rebirth in Entering a Disciple-Mentor Relationship

Although a correct Buddhist understanding of rebirth and conviction in its existence are necessary for reaching even the initial level of the graded path to enlightenment, the question remains whether or not conviction in rebirth is a prerequisite for becoming a disciple of a spiritual mentor. I would argue that merely intellectual understanding, openness to the idea, and tentative acceptance are required, but not full conviction, despite the fact that conviction is traditionally assumed. As the place of conviction in rebirth is controversial in Western Buddhism, let us examine the reasoning behind this assertion.

According to the presentation of the graded path, disciples begin training in the initial scope teachings while still obsessed and worried about their material welfare, emotional happiness, and interpersonal relationships in this life. By meditating on the rarity of attaining a human life and on death and impermanence, they overcome that obsession. When their main concern is to gain welfare, happiness, and positive relationships in future lives—but only as provisional goals on the way toward liberation and enlightenment—disciples reach the initial level of spiritual development.

If spiritual seekers had no need to accept rebirth before becoming disciples, but needed to gain conviction in its existence as part of their training to reach the initial level of development, explanations and proofs of past and future lives would appear in the graded-path texts. The logical place for such material is after the discussion of death and impermanence and before the presentation of karma. Its absence there suggests that the intended audience—seekers imbued in the traditional Tibetan worldview—had no need for this material. Only advanced textbooks of logic contain explanations and proofs of rebirth and these are to refute the obscure beliefs of an ancient Indian school of materialists.

Most Tibetans accept rebirth as a reality, although their understanding of it may be vague. When a relative dies, for example, Tibetans regularly request prayers and rituals to help the departed attain a favorable rebirth. Westerners who seek relationships with spiritual teachers, however, typically share few of the cultural assumptions made in the classical Buddhist texts. Despite the Biblical teachings about heaven and hell, most question the existence of an afterlife. Even if Westerners believe in rebirth, they often understand the phenomenon to occur in the manner in which Hindu or New Age texts explain it, which differs significantly from the Buddhist explication. Therefore, they need a correct Buddhist explanation and certainty about its validity before they can reach the initial level of the graded path. If, for most Westerners, conviction in rebirth develops only in stages, where on the spiritual path does consideration of the existence of rebirth as understood in Buddhism logically need to begin?

In the case of renunciation, safe direction, and bodhichitta, seekers need an initial, stepping-stone level of the three as their general spiritual orientation before entering a disciple-mentor relationship. After establishing the relationship, they develop them fully during the course of their training. Correct understanding and conviction in the Buddhist explanation of rebirth are likewise fundamental to a Buddhist spiritual orientation. Therefore, it seems reasonable to assert that potential disciples similarly need an intellectual understanding of rebirth as Buddhism explains it, and either a tentative acceptance of its reality or at least an open mind toward the possibility of its existence, before committing themselves to the Buddhist path. Conviction comes afterwards, before reaching the initial level of spiritual development, through further study and thought about the logical proofs and documented evidence of rebirth.

Entering a Disciple-Mentor Relationship While Aiming for Spiritual Goals Only in This Lifetime or Also for Future Generations

Another important question is whether or not Western seekers, to become Buddhist disciples, need concern for fortunate rebirths as their starting motivation, even if their acceptance of the existence of rebirth is still only tentative. I would argue that this does not necessarily need to be so. Sönam-tsemo stated that the prerequisite for becoming a disciple is merely to recognize some level of suffering in one's life and to have the determination to be free of it. He did not specify the scope of suffering one needs to address.

Moreover, in *The Three Principal Aspects of the Path*, Tsongkapa differentiated two levels of renunciation, depending on the scope of suffering from which one determines to be free. Following the model of Sachen's *Parting from the Four [Stages of] Clinging*, Tsongkapa formulated the two levels in terms of turning first from thoughts of only this lifetime and then from thoughts of only future lives. If disciples advance through progressive stages of renunciation in general, it is reasonable to assert that within a specified stage they also advance through progressive steps.

Most Western seekers recognize the problems that arise from obsession with instant gratification of material and emotional desires. In renouncing that suffering and turning to the Buddhist path, they may be willing to commit themselves first to working for ecologically sustainable material welfare, emotional well-being, and good relationships in the future. The future may include the later part of their lives or, with expanded scope, it may extend to the lifetimes of future generations. However, while having only an intellectual understanding and tentative acceptance of rebirth, Western seekers cannot sincerely work for happiness in future lives as a realistic option in case they do not succeed in reaching their goals before they die.

Similarly, in renouncing the suffering that comes from obsession with instant gratification of desires, Western seekers may be willing to commit themselves to working toward liberation and enlightenment. However, until they gain firm conviction in rebirth as understood in Buddhism, they can sincerely aim for liberation and enlightenment only in this lifetime, not in future lives.

I would argue that renouncing the suffering that comes from obsession with instant gratification of desires is sufficient for entering a Buddhist disciple-mentor relationship. I would further assert that provisionally aiming for happiness later in life, or also for future generations, or for liberation and enlightenment only in this lifetime, is sufficient motivation thereafter, until one gains conviction in the Buddhist explanation of future lives. Moreover, I would further assert that, for most Western disciples, aiming for these provisional goals is pragmatically necessary as a preliminary stage for making the classical graded path accessible. Certain stipulations, however, are required.

Stipulations for a Beginner Disciple to Aim Provisionally for Nontraditional Goals

By restraining from destructive behavior and disturbing emotions and attitudes, disciples may experience sustainable welfare, happiness, and good relationships later in life, but there is no guarantee. Many additional factors may affect what happens, such as being killed in an accident before experiencing the fruits of their efforts. Similarly, there is no certainty that future generations will gain happiness as the result of their constructive steps. Much depends on the behavior and attitudes of future generations themselves. Thus, while striving to eliminate difficulties later in life or also for future generations, beginner disciples need to understand and acknowledge the impossibility of solving all problems with this limited scope. The best they can hope for is some improvement.

By totally eliminating disturbing emotions and attitudes, disciples may gain liberation in this lifetime, and by additionally eliminating their instincts, they may also reach enlightenment. However, since these goals are extremely difficult to attain, it is quite probable that they will not achieve them in this lifetime. Thus, while striving toward liberation and enlightenment in this life, disciples need to understand and acknowledge that most likely they will only be able to make strides in that direction before they die.

In short, so long as beginner disciples understand and tentatively accept future lives as explained in Buddhism and avoid unrealistic expectations for success, I would argue that they might reasonably strive for spiritual goals only in this lifetime, or also for future generations. In addition, however, they would need to regard these goals as mere stepping-stones until they gain firm conviction in the Buddhist understanding of rebirth. Only with firm conviction may disciples actually progress through the graded levels of motivation outlined in the traditional texts.

One might object that the assertion of these provisional goals violates the logical consistency of the graded path. According to the classical presentation, one of the prerequisite causes of taking safe direction is dread of experiencing the suffering of unfavorable rebirths. If potential disciples need a spiritual orientation of safe direction and yet typical Western seekers hardly dread unfavorable rebirths because they lack conviction in rebirth, how can they have safe direction as their spiritual orientation? I would argue that dread of experiencing emotional problems becoming worse in this lifetime, or also becoming worse for future generations, could serve as a stepping-stone level of incentive prior to having the prescribed motivation. Either of the two could serve as provisional motivations, but with the stipulation that the seeker has a correct understanding of rebirth as explained in Buddhism and a tentative acceptance of its existence.

The Difference between Becoming a Disciple of a Spiritual Mentor and Becoming a Client of a Therapist

Consider someone wishing to gain emotional happiness and good relationships for the rest of his or her life. Becoming a disciple of a spiritual mentor to achieve this goal in many ways resembles becoming a client of a therapist for the same purpose. Both arise from recognizing and acknowledging suffering in one's life and wishing to alleviate it. Both entail working with someone to recognize and understand one's problems and their causes. Many forms of therapy, in fact, agree with Buddhism that understanding serves as the key for self-transformation.

Further, both Buddhism and therapy embrace schools of thought that emphasize deeply understanding the causes of one's problems, traditions that stress working on pragmatic methods to overcome these factors, and systems that recommend a balanced combination of the two approaches. In addition, both Buddhism and many forms of therapy advocate establishing a healthy emotional relationship with the mentor or therapist as an important part of the process of self-development. Moreover, although most classical forms of therapy shy away from using ethical guidelines for modifying clients' behavior and ways of thinking, a few postclassical schools advocate ethical principles similar to those in Buddhism. Such principles include being equally fair to all members of a dysfunctional family and refraining from acting out destructive impulses, such as those of anger.

Despite similarities, at least five significant differences exist between becoming a disciple of a Buddhist mentor and becoming a client of a therapist. The first difference concerns the emotional stage at which one establishes the relationship. Potential clients generally approach a therapist when they are emotionally disturbed. They may even be psychotic and require medication as part of the treatment. Potential disciples, in contrast, do not establish a relationship with a mentor as the first step on their spiritual paths. Prior to this, they have studied Buddha's teachings and begun to work on themselves. As a result, they have reached a sufficient level of emotional maturity and stability so that the disciple-mentor relationship they establish is constructive in the Buddhist sense of the term. In other words, Buddhist disciples need already to be relatively free of neurotic attitudes and behavior.

The second difference concerns the interaction one expects in the relationship. Potential clients are mostly interested in having someone listen to them. Therefore, they expect the therapist to devote concentrated attention to them and to their personal problems, even within the context of group therapy. Disciples, on the other hand, normally do not share personal problems with their mentors and do not expect or demand individual attention. Even if they consult the mentor for personal advice, they do not go regularly. The focus in the relationship is on listening to teachings. Buddhist disciples primarily learn methods from their mentors for overcoming general problems that everyone faces. They then assume personal responsibility to apply the methods to their specific situations.

The third difference concerns the results expected from the working relationship. Therapy aims for learning to accept and to live with the problems in one's life or to minimize them so that they become bearable. If one approaches a Buddhist spiritual mentor with the aim of emotional well-being for this lifetime, one might also expect to minimize one's problems. Despite life's being difficult—the first fact of life (noble truth) that Buddha taught—one could make it less difficult.

As stated earlier, making one's life emotionally less difficult, however, is only a preliminary step for approaching the classical Buddhist path. Disciples of spiritual mentors would at least be orientated toward the greater aims of favorable rebirths, liberation, and enlightenment. Moreover, Buddhist disciples would have an intellectual understanding of rebirth as explained in Buddhism and at least a tentative acceptance of its existence. Therapy clients have no need for thinking about rebirth or about aims beyond improving their immediate situations.

The fourth major difference is the level of commitment to self-transformation. Clients of therapists pay an hourly fee, but do not commit themselves to a lifelong change of attitude and behavior. Buddhist disciples, on the other hand, may or may not pay for teachings; nevertheless, they formally change their direction in life. In taking safe direction, disciples commit themselves to the course of self-development that the Buddhas have fully traversed and then taught, and that the highly realized spiritual community strives to follow.

Moreover, Buddhist disciples commit themselves to an ethical, constructive course of acting, speaking, and thinking in life. They try, as much as is possible, to avoid destructive patterns and to engage in constructive ones instead. When disciples sincerely wish liberation from the recurring problems of uncontrollable rebirth, they make an even stronger commitment by formally taking lay or monastic vows for individual liberation (Skt. *pratimoksha* vows). Disciples at this stage of self-development vow for life to restrain at all times from specific modes of conduct that are either naturally destructive or which Buddha recommended that certain people avoid for specific purposes. An example of the latter is monastics abandoning lay dress and wearing robes instead, to reduce attachment. Even disciples who aim to avoid unfavorable rebirths or to minimize emotional difficulties in this lifetime, or also for future generations, might take liberation vows with any of these three provisional objectives before developing the prescribed motivation.

Clients of therapists, on the other hand, agree to follow certain rules of procedure as part of the therapeutic contract, such as keeping to a schedule of fifty-minute appointments. These rules, however, pertain only during treatment. They do not apply outside the therapeutic setting, do not entail refraining from naturally destructive behavior, and are not for life.

The fifth major difference between disciples and therapy clients concerns the attitude toward the teacher or therapist. Disciples look to their spiritual mentors as living examples of what they strive to attain. They regard them in this way based on correct recognition of the mentors' good qualities and they maintain and strengthen this view throughout their graded path to enlightenment. Clients, in contrast, may conceive of their therapists as models for emotional health, but they do not require correct awareness of the therapists' good qualities. Becoming like the therapist is not the aim of the relationship. During the course of treatment, therapists lead their clients beyond projections of ideals.

Inappropriate Usage of the Term Disciple

Sometimes, people call themselves disciples of spiritual teachers despite the fact that they, the teacher, or both fall short of fulfilling the proper meaning of the terms. Their naivety often leads them to unrealistic expectations, misunderstandings, hurt feelings, and even abuse. Becoming an object of abuse, in this context, means being exploited sexually, emotionally, or financially, or being manipulated by someone in a show of power. In our effort to rectify terms, let us examine three common types of pseudo-disciples found in the West who are especially susceptible to problems with spiritual teachers.

Some people come to Dharma centers looking for fulfillment of their fantasies. They have read or heard something about the "mysterious East" or about superstar gurus, and wish to transcend their seemingly unexciting lives by having an exotic or mystical experience. They meet spiritual teachers and instantly declare themselves to be disciples, especially if the teachers are Asian, and even more so if they are robed. They are prone to similar behavior with Western teachers who have Asian titles or names, whether or not the persons wear robes.

The quest for the occult often destabilizes the relationships such seekers establish with spiritual teachers. Even if they declare themselves disciples of properly qualified mentors, they often leave these teachers when they realize that nothing supernatural is happening, except perhaps in their imaginations. Moreover, the unrealistic attitudes and high expectations of "instant disciples" often cloud their critical faculties. Such persons are particularly open to deception by spiritual charlatans clever in putting on a good act.

Others may come to centers desperate for help to overcome emotional or physical pain. They may have tried various forms of therapy, but to no avail. Now, they seek a miracle cure from a magician/healer. They declare themselves disciples of anyone who might give them a blessing pill, tell them the special prayer or mantra to repeat, or give them the potent practice to do—like making a hundred thousand prostrations—that will automatically fix their problems. They especially turn to the same types of teachers that fascinate people who are in quest of the occult. The "fix-it" mentality of miracle-seekers often leads to disappointment and despair, when following the advice of even qualified mentors does not result in miraculous cures. A "fix-it" mentality also attracts abuse from spiritual quacks.

Still others, especially disenchanted, unemployed youths, come to Dharma centers of cultish sects in the hope of gaining existential empowerment. Charismatic megalomaniacs draw them in by using "spiritual fascist" means. They promise their so-called disciples strength in numbers if they give total allegiance to their sects. They further allure disciples with dramatic descriptions of fierce protectors who will smash their enemies, especially the followers of inferior, impure Buddhist traditions. With grandiose stories of the superhuman powers of the founding fathers of their movements, they try to fulfill the disciples' dreams of a mighty leader who will lift them to positions of spiritual entitlement. Responding to these promises, such people quickly declare themselves disciples and blindly follow whatever instructions or orders authoritarian teachers give them. The results are usually disastrous.

The Realistic Attitude of an Authentic Disciple

Authentic disciples are relatively mature and sober spiritual seekers whom mentors train in ethical discipline, concentration, and awareness in order to improve the quality of this lifetime, while they are working to gain conviction in rebirth as Buddhism explains it, and then to gain favorable rebirths, liberation, and ultimately enlightenment. They do not expect occult phenomena, miracle cures, or existential empowerment from spiritual mentors. To fulfill the meaning of the term *disciple*, then, spiritual seekers need realistic attitudes. Such attitudes derive from a proper understanding of the progressive goals their training can bring. Thus, authentic disciples avoid aiming for too little or too much on each stage of the graded path.

On the preliminary level, authentic disciples avoid aiming for ecologically sustainable material welfare, emotional happiness, and good relationships in this lifetime as the final goals of their spiritual paths. Moreover, disciples do not expect that with such an aim they can escape experiencing further problems in this life.

On the initial level, authentic disciples avoid aiming for fortunate rebirths as an excuse for ignoring emotional problems in this life. Further, disciples do not conceive of a fortunate rebirth as an eternal paradise.

On the intermediate level, authentic disciples avoid aiming for liberation merely from emotional problems, without including freedom from the recurring problems of uncontrollable rebirth. Moreover, disciples do not conceive of liberation as a total annihilation of their existence, free from ever appearing again in the world to benefit others.

Finally, on the advanced level, authentic disciples avoid aiming for an enlightenment that does not entail liberation from the recurring problems of uncontrollable rebirth. Further, disciples do not conceive of enlightenment as a form of omnipotence, with the power to cure all beings instantly of their problems.

In short, just as not everyone who teaches at a Buddhist center is an authentic spiritual mentor, similarly not everyone who studies at a center is an authentic spiritual disciple. The call for a rectification of terms requests precise usage of both the terms *mentor* and *disciple*. Full implementation of the policy requires spiritual honesty and lack of pretense.

~4

The Different Types of Spiritual Teachers and Spiritual Seekers

Premises

PEOPLE AT DHARMA CENTERS often have difficulty relating to spiritual teachers, even properly qualified ones. Some may feel nothing toward the resident teacher, even if the person is a geshey or a lama. Others may be unimpressed with a famous teacher who visits, though everyone else treats the person with extreme devotion. They find confusing the teaching that they must regard spiritual teachers as Buddhas. They may think that they need to regard all teachers in this way and that they need to do so from the start. Consequently, they feel that they are doing something wrong.

The first step for unraveling the problem is to acknowledge certain empirical facts about student-teacher relationships. (1) Almost all spiritual seekers progress through stages along the spiritual path. (2) Most practitioners study with several teachers during their lifetimes and build up different relationships with each. (3) Not every spiritual teacher has reached the same level of accomplishment. (4) The type of relationship appropriate between a specific seeker and a specific teacher depends upon the spiritual level of each. (5) People usually relate to their teachers in progressively deeper manners as they advance along the spiritual path. (6) Because the same teacher may play different roles in the spiritual life of each seeker, the most appropriate relationship each seeker has with that teacher may be different. The presentation in this book follows from these premises.

Terminology

The six points listed above are suggested by a distinction that Gampopa made in *A Precious Ornament for Liberation*, based on the Prajnaparamita literature. During the course of progressing to enlightenment, spiritual seekers become capable of receiving and understanding instruction from teachers who are increasingly more sophisticated in their realization of voidness. Thus, both spiritual teachers and seekers divide into levels. Here, we shall differentiate levels of spiritual teachers according to other criteria: the increasingly broader contents, perspective, and intent of the instruction that they impart. Further, in conjunction with each type of spiritual teacher, we shall formulate a corresponding spiritual seeker.

To clarify the discussion, let us adopt certain conventions. Let us call someone who conveys information about Buddha's teachings from a withdrawn perspective a "Buddhism professor." A person who not merely sits in the audience, but who actually studies with such a Buddhism professor would be a "student of Buddhism." Someone, on the other hand, who imparts the teachings from the point of view of their practical application to life, based on personal experience, we shall name a "Dharma instructor." Someone who learns practical Buddhism from a Dharma instructor would be his or her "Dharma pupil." A person who trains others in the pragmatic aspects of meditation or ritual practice, we shall call a "meditation or ritual trainer." The corresponding spiritual seeker would be a "meditation or ritual trainee."

We shall use "spiritual mentor," in the Mahayana sense, for someone who leads others along the graded path to enlightenment. Someone whom a spiritual mentor leads along the graded path would be his or her "disciple," starting with a seeker who wishes first for spiritual goals only in this lifetime, or also for future generations. Among spiritual mentors, someone who confers Mahayana safe direction or either lay or monastic vows, we shall call a "refuge or vow preceptor." Someone who receives refuge or liberation vows from such a preceptor would be a member of the person's "refuge or vow progeny."

A mentor who teaches the methods for developing bodhichitta and who leads a seeker along the bodhisattva path, we shall name a "Mahayana master." Someone whom he or she guides would be a "Mahayana disciple." Further, a Mahayana master who leads disciples to enlightenment through the methods of tantra, we shall designate a "tantric master." Corresponding to a tantric master would be a "tantric disciple." Further, the teacher who turns a seeker's heart and mind most strongly to the Dharma we shall refer to as a "root guru." "Spiritual teacher" and "spiritual seeker" will be used as general terms.

Classical textual presentations of the relationship between a spiritual seeker and a spiritual teacher speak only about specific categories of mentors and disciples. They do not pertain to prior levels of teachers or seekers. On the one side, they concern spiritual mentors who are primarily Mahayana masters, tantric masters, or root gurus—all three of whom are gurus, lamas, and spiritual friends. On the other side, they deal mainly with either Mahayana or tantric disciples. The relationship between a refuge or vow preceptor and his or her refuge or vow progeny usually appears in a separate context: the discussion of monastic discipline. The emphasis there is almost exclusively on the relationship with a preceptor for monastic vows.

Buddhism Professors

Many people interested in Buddhism do not have spiritual teachers to guide them. They may study Buddhism merely from books, tapes, videos, or from the Internet. His Holiness the Fourteenth Dalai Lama has affirmed the propriety of learning in this way. Appropriate topics include impermanence, karma, compassion, and voidness. Most Westerners, in fact, initially develop interest in the Dharma and gain their introductory knowledge from books—not only from works on Buddhism, but also from New Age books and from fictional and nonfictional accounts of Tibet. Even seeing popular films on Tibetan themes can spark people's interest.

Books, tapes, and videos, however, cannot answer questions. No matter how interactive a computer program may be, it too cannot provide all the answers. Only a live teacher can do that. Therefore, for most people the next step after gaining some information about Buddhism is to attend a few lectures.

Some may take a course with a Buddhism professor at a university, to learn more facts about the subject. Knowledge of the history of Buddhism, the influence on it from political developments, and the cultural adaptations that came with its spread helps to dispel romantic illusions. It provides the background and intellectual tools for sifting through massive amounts of material to pinpoint the essence. Buddhism professors may also educate students in the contents of Buddha's teachings. They usually do this in a removed manner, as when objectively conveying the contents of any world religion.

Well-educated teachers, gesheys, or kenpos at Dharma centers may also impart the contents of Buddha's teachings in the same manner as do university professors. Such teachers may also explain how to apply the Dharma to life, but students of Buddhism pay little attention. They listen merely to gain information. Thus, for students of Buddhism, even gesheys or kenpos are merely Buddhism professors. If, as seekers, we wish to study Buddhism as a method for spiritual self-development, we need to work with a teacher as a Dharma instructor.

Dharma Instructors

The distinction between Buddhism professors and Dharma instructors derives from three progressive levels of discriminating awareness differentiated in Buddhism. (1) Discriminating awareness of correct information derives from listening to lectures by trustworthy teachers or from reading books by reliable authors. (2) Discriminating awareness based on correct intellectual insight derives from thinking about the correct information thus received. (3) Discriminating awareness based on correct experiential insight derives from meditating on a correct intellectual understanding. Spiritual teachers may instruct seekers based on one or more of the three levels of correct awareness.

Buddhism professors teach information gained from texts or from Western scholarly research. In addition, they may have tried to figure out the meaning of the teachings intellectually and thus may also teach from intellectual insight and understanding. Dharma instructors also have some level of scriptural knowledge and teach accordingly. In addition, however, they explain from experiential insight and understanding, gained from putting the teachings into practice and from trying to apply them to life. Buddhism professors may also have experiential insight, but they do not usually convey these insights to others.

Dharma instructors may be older spiritual seekers at Dharma centers with more knowledge and experience than the others have. More advanced than that, instructors may be resident teachers or may be visiting ones on tour. They may have university degrees in Buddhist Studies or monastic degrees, although neither is prerequisite. As Dharma pupils, we may learn how to apply Buddhist practices to life from any of these types of Dharma instructors.

Meditation or Ritual Trainers

Seekers who wish to go beyond intellectual knowledge of the Buddhist methods for self-transformation need to train in the practices. The training involves meditating and, for certain aspects of the teachings, performing ritual practices. Meditation involves either generating a beneficial state of mind or settling the mind into its natural wholesome state. Through frequent repetition, the state of mind becomes habitual and forms an integral part of one's personality. Ritual practice adds physical and verbal forms to meditation and creates a bond with tradition. It may entail arranging a shrine, making offerings, doing prostrations, chanting texts, or using the traditional ritual implements of vajra, bell, and hand drum. The sense of continuity and of belonging to a group of practitioners, past and present, performing the same rites brings with it a feeling of support, security, and confidence.

Several people at a Dharma center may be able to train us in the basic aspects of meditation and ritual. These include, again, older spiritual seekers and both resident and visiting Dharma instructors. Some centers have specialists as meditation or ritual trainers for beginners. These persons may have completed three-year retreats. They may not necessarily be able to instruct us in more than the elementary Dharma teachings, but have experience and competence in training people in the initial stages of meditation or ritual, or both.

Spiritual Mentors

The Buddhist teachings differentiate between flash insights (*nyam, nyams*) and stable realizations (*togpa, rtogs-pa*). A flash insight does not make a significant change in one's life, but may lead in that direction. A stable realization, on the other hand, whether it be partial or complete, actually produces a noticeable improvement that lasts. The distinction we are drawing here between Dharma instructors and spiritual mentors derives from this difference. Dharma instructors may have either insight or realization, whereas spiritual mentors need to have some level of stable realization.

A further distinction derives from the two ways in which Buddha conveyed to others what he had attained. He communicated his enlightenment verbally and through the effects of his realizations. Buddhism professors and Dharma instructors teach primarily through verbal instruction. For spiritual teachers to guide seekers fully, however, they need also to embody the teachings, integrated into their personalities. Only then, as spiritual mentors, can they truly inspire and teach disciples by their living examples. Because of the obvious personal development of mentors, spiritual seekers feel confident in entrusting themselves as disciples to them, to help reach similar levels of self-transformation. Spiritual mentors, then, help disciples to develop their personalities.

Thus, once we have gained sufficient practical knowledge of the teachings from studying with Dharma instructors and sufficient familiarity with pragmatic aspects through working with meditation or ritual trainers, we may be ready to take the next step. We may be ready to become disciples of spiritual teachers and to relate to them as spiritual mentors. To be spiritual mentors, teachers need the qualities of gurus, lamas, and spiritual friends, irrespective of the actual titles they bear. They may have been our Buddhism professors, Dharma instructors, or meditation or ritual trainers. Our spiritual mentors may also be other teachers, not specifically associated with our universities or Dharma centers.

Moreover, to become the disciple of a spiritual mentor requires living up to the name *disciple*. Specifically, seekers interested in Buddhism need to make a formal commitment to the Buddhist path. This entails taking vows to restrain from unruly behavior and to train in constructive ways. In *Ocean of Infinite Knowledge*, Kongtrül, the encyclopedist of the Rimey (nonsectarian) movement, explained three types of spiritual mentor. The distinction derives from which of three sets of vows a disciple takes in the mentor's presence: pratimoksha, bodhisattva, or tantric vows. Buddhist vows entail a long-term commitment. In the Tibetan tradition, lay or monastic vows are for an entire lifetime, whereas refuge, bodhisattva, and tantric vows are for all one's lifetimes until enlightenment. Consequently, the disciple-mentor bond that crystallizes around these major commitments also carries a great level of seriousness.

Refuge or Vow Preceptors

Those who wish to commit themselves to the Buddhist spiritual path formally take safe direction in life from the Triple Gem: the Buddhas, the Dharma, and the Sangha. Full engagement also entails taking either lay or monastic vows for individual liberation. Committed lay Buddhists, for example, promise to restrain from either all or some of the following destructive actions: killing, stealing, lying, indulging in inappropriate sexual behavior, and taking intoxicants.

Taking safe direction and liberation vows marks the watersheds in a Buddhist spiritual life. Although the classical texts describe several extraordinary methods whereby certain disciples at the time of the Buddha received monks' or nuns' vows, nowadays people require the presence of spiritual elders. Although Kongtrül discussed vow preceptors specifically in the context of taking monastic vows, disciples also need to take refuge and lay vows in the presence of elders. Therefore, we shall extend the scope of Kongtrül's category of vow preceptors to include those in whose presence disciples take Mahayana refuge or lay vows. Since most Westerners following the Buddhist path remain householders, let us limit our discussion to these preceptors for "premonastic" vows.

In the context of Tibetan Buddhism, refuge or vow preceptors are necessarily Mahayana elders. Moreover, they need to be spiritual mentors who have kept their vows purely for a certain number of years, depending on the level of vow conferred. This qualification adds gravity and authenticity to the event, as preceptors formally link their progeny to the traditions tracing back to the immediate disciples of the historical Buddha.

Refuge and vow preceptors need not be the same persons. Although they become one of our teachers in the context of our taking vows, they do not need to serve in other ways as our spiritual mentors. Moreover, taking safe direction or liberation vows with a preceptor connects us with Buddhism in general. It does not commit us to the specific Tibetan tradition of the preceptor, since all Tibetan sects transmit the same Indian lineage of vows. We become simply Buddhist practitioners, laypeople, or monastics, and not members of the Nyingma, Sakya, Kagyü, or Gelug order.

Some spiritual seekers formally take safe direction while still only students of Buddhism, Dharma pupils, or meditation or ritual trainees. Some take this step even as newcomers to Buddhism, knowing hardly anything of the teachings. Often, they do so by a spur of the moment decision made under group pressure, moved by the charisma of the teachers offering the refuge ceremonies. Merely participating in a ritual, however, does not constitute taking safe direction. Nor does it make participants the disciples of the teachers conducting the ceremonies, nor members of their refuge progenies. Taking safe direction, in its full sense, requires that both the spiritual teachers and the seekers fulfill the qualifications for preceptor and progeny and for mentor and disciple. Especially essential is that the spiritual seekers have appropriate motivations—at minimum, dreading emotional ill-being later in life. Moreover, the seeker needs not only the confidence that the Triple Gem provides a safe direction to avoidance of these troubles, but also the full intention to put this positive direction into their lives and to keep the refuge commitments and vows.

The refuge ceremony forms a standard part of all tantric empowerments. Since Tibetan lamas often permit insufficiently prepared spiritual seekers to attend empowerments, they also permit insufficiently prepared persons to take safe direction. The traditional rationale is that, even if seekers lack the appropriate causes for taking safe direction, attending the ceremonies plants seeds of positive potential for future lives. The spiritual seekers need not understand anything that is happening. Attendance alone successfully plants seeds for the future, unless the persons have negative attitudes that would prevent them from receiving positive, or at least neutral impressions of the proceedings. Nonetheless, attending empowerment ceremonies in this way to plant seeds for the future, or to receive the "blessings," still does not make the lamas their refuge preceptors, let alone make them their tantric masters.

Mahayana Masters

Just as taking safe direction is the gateway to entering the Buddhist path in general, developing a bodhichitta motivation is the entrance to the Mahayana way. Furthermore, bodhichitta has two stages. The mere development of the motivation constitutes "aspiring bodhichitta": the aspiration to become a Buddha to benefit others as much as is possible. With "engaged bodhichitta," disciples commit themselves, with bodhisattva vows, to train intensively in the methods and wisdom that bring enlightenment and to help others now as much as they can.

When their aspiring bodhichitta intensifies to become engaged bodhichitta, disciples may take bodhisattva vows in several ways. Best is in the presence of the spiritual mentors who have taught them the Mahayana way. If they have made sincere efforts to reach these mentors, but for some reason cannot arrange to take bodhisattva vows with them, there is no need to postpone. When disciples are ready to engage fully in bodhisattva conduct, the absence of their mentors to conduct a ceremony does not pose a problem. In such cases, the Indian mentor Shantideva explained in *Engaging in a Bodhisattva's Deeds*, sincere disciples may also take bodhisattva vows in the presence of Buddha statues or paintings. If none are available, they may even take them before Buddhas and bodhisattvas visualized as present.

Kongtrül specified that Mahayana masters are spiritual mentors in whose presence disciples take bodhisattva vows. Nevertheless, since Atisha emphasized the need for mentors to explain bodhichitta and the bodhisattva way before conferring vows, we may extend the definition of a Mahayana master. In a broader sense, Mahayana masters are the spiritual mentors whose teachings on compassion and bodhichitta lead disciples to develop aspiring bodhichitta and then to take bodhisattva vows. Such mentors, when fully qualified, are able to guide disciples along the complete path to enlightenment. The English term *master*, here, has nothing to do with masters and slaves, but rather with the spiritual mentors' mastery of the methods leading to the highest level of evolution possible.

Tantric Masters

Mahayana disciples may travel the path to enlightenment through the methods of either *sutra* or *tantra*. The sutras contain Buddha's basic teachings on the methods for gaining positive qualities such as ethical self-discipline, concentration, compassion, bodhichitta, and understanding of voidness. In the tantras, Buddha presented advanced methods to supplement the sutra practices for reaching enlightenment more efficiently and rapidly. These methods focus on using the imagination to transform one's self-image through the model of a Buddha-figure. All Tibetan Buddhist traditions teach paths to enlightenment that combine sutra and tantra practice.

As mentioned earlier, the gateway for entering the tantra path in general is receiving an empowerment (*wang, dbang*; initiation) for a specific Buddha-figure from a spiritual mentor. The Buddha-figure may be part of a practice from any tantra class. The Nyingma tradition delineates six classes of tantra, while the other Tibetan traditions speak of four. The three highest classes of Nyingma tantra are equivalent to the other traditions' highest tantra class. If we to use the term *tantric master* in its most general sense, it refers to a spiritual mentor who confers an empowerment from any of these tantra classes. For example, in *Clarifying [Ashvaghosha's] "Fifty Stanzas,"* Dragpa-gyeltsen, the third of the five Sakya founders, occasionally used the term *tantric master* in this sense.

Kongtrül, however, defined tantric masters as the spiritual mentors before whom disciples take tantric vows during empowerments and before the visualizations of whom they renew or strengthen those vows during "self-empowerments" after they have completed tantric retreats. Only an empowerment into either the third (*yogatantra*) or the highest class of tantra entails taking tantric vows. Tantric vows include promises concerning how disciples will regard and treat their tantric masters. Thus, in a more technical sense, the term *tantric master* applies only to spiritual mentors of the two higher classes of tantra. Tsarchen, for example, used the term in this way in his commentary to Ashvaghosha's text.

According to *Difficult Points Concerning Helping and Showing Respect to a Guru*, an anonymous Indian commentary to Ashvaghosha's text introduced to Tibet by the Kagyü/Nyingma translator Gö Lotsawa, the instruction to see one's tantric master as a Buddha pertains specifically to highest tantra. Of all the teachings concerning the student-teacher relationship, this instruction causes the most confusion. Since highest tantra offers the clearest explanation of this teaching, we shall further restrict the term *tantric master* in accordance with its usage in this anonymous text and limit our discussion to highest tantra.

Restricting the meaning of the term in this way also accords with its usage in the context of the widespread tantric practice of *guru-yoga* (*lamey-neljor, bla-ma'i rnal-'byor*) as Naropa, the Indian forefather of the Kagyü lineage, codified it in *Actualizing through a Guru*. In tantric guru-yoga, disciples imagine receiving four empowerments through colored lights emanated from their tantric masters. The four empowerments are an exclusive feature of highest tantra. Therefore, similarly, we shall use the term *tantric guru-yoga* to mean *highest tantric guru-yoga*.

Since highest tantra focuses on harnessing internal energies for spiritual use, let us borrow the imagery of rockets to elucidate the role of tantric masters. The Buddha-figures for which disciples receive empowerment are like classes and models of spacecraft, here used for undertaking the spiritual "inner-space" journey to enlightenment. The skills they gain on the Mahayana sutra path provide the systems for flying the ships. For optimal travel once they have taken off with empowerments, they need to supplement their energy with subsequent boosts (*jenang, rje-gnang*; permission) and refueling of mantras (*ngagtu, sngags-btu*; gathering of mantras). Moreover, to follow the course of the highest tantra path, they need also to receive the energization (*lung, lung*; oral transmission) of the appropriate texts and directive thrusts (*ti, khrid*; discourse) explaining the subtle points of the meditation practices. Tantric masters supply disciples with all these spiritual provisions.

In discussing how to relate to tantric masters, Ashvaghosha explicitly mentioned only those mentors who confer empowerment. Tsong-kapa, however, clarified this point in his commentary to Ashvaghosha's text, *The Complete Fulfillment of Disciples' Hopes*. There, he asserted that the protocol followed with empowering mentors also applies to other tantric masters, for example those who explain the texts and give guideline instructions (*menngag, man-ngag*). This is because receiving explanations or instructions for a specific highest tantra practice requires previous empowerment and thus tantric vows.

Tantric masters, then, are spiritual mentors who empower, boost, refuel, energize, and give directive thrust to our highest tantra inner-space journeys. As perpetual sources of inspiration, they keep our engines running. Moreover, through continuing supervision and instruction, our tantric masters provide ground control and dependable guidance systems that enable us to reach our goals accurately and safely.

Our tantric masters may already be our Mahayana masters, or may be other spiritual teachers with whom we have only rare contact. Moreover, the same tantric master may give us empowerment, subsequent boost, refueling of mantras, energization, directive thrust, and guideline instruction for a particular Buddha-figure, or we may receive the six from separate masters.

Before we receive tantric empowerments, mentors may give us oral transmissions of the tantric preliminary practices (*ngöndro, sngon-'gro*) or of various mantras. They may also explain general tantra or even highest tantra theory in order to dispel our misconceptions. Receiving such an oral transmission or explanation, however, does not establish a tantric disciple-master relationship. The relationship stems from taking tantric vows at a full empowerment.

Root Gurus

Root gurus are the spiritual mentors who turn disciples' hearts and minds most ardently to the Buddhist path. They are the strongest sources of inspiration to sustain disciples throughout their spiritual journeys. The relationships with such teachers act as roots for all attainments.

The mentors who serve disciples as their root gurus are not necessarily the first spiritual teachers that the seekers encounter or the ones who give them the most Dharma instruction or meditation or ritual training. Nor are they necessarily the mentors with whom they take refuge or liberation vows. Most, however, come from among their tantric masters. The discussion of root gurus traditionally appears primarily in the context of highest tantra practice.

The Sakya tradition, in fact, equates the terms *spiritual mentor, tantric master*, and *root guru*. Such mentors serve as the roots of our paths because of the refuge, liberation, bodhisattva, and tantric vows we take in their presence during highest tantra empowerments, and because of the experiences and flash insights we gain during the procedures through their inspiration.

Progressing through Graded Relationships
with Spiritual Teachers

The Nyingma and Kagyü traditions distinguish two types of tantric practitioners: those who progress through graded stages and those for whom everything happens at once. Kaydrub Norzang-gyatso, tutor of the Second Dalai Lama, explained the distinction in *A Lamp for Clarifying Mahamudra to Establish the Single Intention of the Kagyü and Gelug Traditions*. The former follow graded steps throughout their spiritual paths, whereas the latter travel the final steps all at once as the result of enormous networks of potential built up by graded practice in previous lives. Although the Nyingma and Kagyü texts explain the path to enlightenment mostly from the viewpoint of those for whom everything happens at once, these types of disciple are extremely rare. The overwhelming majority of practitioners progress through stages.

Often when Westerners approach Tibetan Buddhism, they read some literature and, because they have not received deep explanations, confusedly identify themselves as practitioners for whom everything happens at once. Believing that they do not need to progress through stages even during the earlier phases of the path, they think they must immediately jump into the deepest, most advanced form of relationship with a spiritual teacher. Not understanding the qualifications, intent, and profound dynamics of such relationships, their naivety and lack of awareness bring them much confusion and pain.

Relationships with spiritual teachers need to be built slowly. This allows for the natural growth of trust on both sides. Students need confidence in teachers' qualifications in order to trust that they will not mislead them. Teachers need confidence that students are serious in order to trust that they will not misunderstand or misuse the teachings. One of the teachers' bodhisattva vows, after all, is to avoid teaching voidness to those not ready to understand it. In addition, one of their tantric vows is to avoid revealing confidential teachings to those unable to keep them private.

Therefore, if we wish to become disciples of tantric masters, we need to start as students of Buddhism professors or as pupils of Dharma instructors. Only with growing maturity may we safely enter relationships with spiritual teachers that are progressively more advanced. Our initial level spiritual teachers may be unqualified to become our tantric masters or even to become our spiritual mentors. Similarly, our tantric masters may have initially been our Buddhism professors. We avoid problems as long as both sides keep the roles straight and follow the mode of behavior appropriate to the level of relationship.

Summary

As spiritual seekers, we need to look to spiritual teachers in terms of what we wish to learn and are ready to absorb. We may wish to gain intellectual knowledge of Buddhism, Dharma instruction about applying the teachings to life, or pragmatic training in meditation or rituals. We may also wish for spiritual growth leading to emotional well-being in this lifetime, favorable rebirths, liberation, or enlightenment, or for the total self-transformation of tantra as the most efficient means for becoming Buddhas. The appropriate relationships with our teachers depend on our aim and our level of development. Moreover, spiritual teachers need to consider honestly what they can offer to spiritual seekers.

As Wönpo Sherab-jungnay, nephew of the founder of the Drigung Kagyü tradition, implied in *A Grand Commentary to [Drigungpa's] "Single Intention of the Sacred Dharma,"* most teachers, objectively speaking, have not yet reached liberation or enlightenment. Nevertheless, so long as spiritual teachers do not pretend that they have already achieved these goals, and so long as they are progressing unerringly toward them, they may help us to reach their current levels. Thus, if teachers do not pretend to be able to teach beyond their capacities and if spiritual seekers do not project onto teachers roles that exceed the persons' qualifications or onto themselves levels of development beyond their present stages, each side avoids many problems.

~5
The Need for Various Levels of Spiritual Teachers on the Sutra Path

IN *A Precious Ornament for Liberation*, Gampopa cited three analogies from the sutras to elucidate the need for a spiritual mentor. Just as a traveler needs a navigator for traversing an unknown route, an escort for making a dangerous journey, and an oarsman for crossing a mighty river, a spiritual seeker needs a mentor for treading the path to enlightenment. As a navigator, a spiritual mentor supplies correct information so that a disciple knows the way. As an escort, he or she remains close throughout the journey so that a disciple does not wander astray. As an oarsman, the person provides the energy that drives a disciple on to reach his or her goal. Although the topic of building a relationship with a spiritual teacher pertains to building one specifically with a Mahayana master and, especially, with a tantric master as a root guru, the three analogies may help us to understand the need for all levels of spiritual teachers. This understanding is particularly important for modern seekers with "do-it-yourself" mentalities.

The Need for a Buddhism Professor
When one journeys through unfamiliar lands, naivety regarding local conditions and customs may make particular styles of travel unrealistic. Guidebooks may be useful, but far more helpful are natives of the regions. With lifetimes of experience, they can correct wayfarers' mistakes. Similarly, when attempting to travel the Buddhist path seekers may pass through the unknown territory of traditional Asian spiritual disciplines. They need experienced Buddhism professors with lifetimes of study to recognize their immature ways of thinking. Like

navigators and escorts, such teachers keep them on course throughout their studies by correcting them, for instance when they think illogically or when they mistake their culturally specific assumptions for universal truths.

Both books and lectures may be either dry or interesting. However, because the living energy of a person far surpasses the static energy of a written page, a professor's excitement about a subject can more easily spark a passion in students for their studies. Similarly, for our progress in Buddhism to gain momentum, we need initial boosts of energy. Therefore, we need to rely on enthusiastic, lively professors, like oarsmen, to help us to power our spiritual journeys.

The Need for a Dharma Instructor

If spiritual seekers try to apply the Dharma methods to themselves without living models against which to gauge their progress, they may easily deceive themselves and wander astray. With distorted fantasies about Dharma practice and its results, their preconceptions may be bizarre. Therefore, in addition to studying with Buddhism professors, we need to rely on Dharma instructors to dispel these fantasies and to keep our spiritual practices grounded in reality.

Moreover, to work on ourselves requires confidence that change is possible. When Dharma instructors share with us their experiences of personally pursuing this course and we can see for ourselves the beneficial results, we gain confidence and inspiration. Thus, we need Dharma instructors to keep us moving on the path.

The Need for a Meditation or Ritual Trainer

Trying to learn meditation or ritual from manuals or from people lacking experience courts almost certain failure. As when wishing to learn gymnastics, we need expert trainers to show us how to follow the procedures properly. They need to work with us on regular bases to adjust our performance and to correct our mistakes. In addition, we need systematic "workouts" with meditation or ritual trainers to overcome the laziness that may keep us from practicing on our own or from going through complete regimes.

The Need for a Spiritual Mentor

Gampopa explained that the main need for building a relationship with a spiritual mentor is to enable seekers to strengthen and expand their networks of positive potentials and deep awareness (collections of merit and wisdom). Doing so allows them to gain emotional well-being in this lifetime and favorable rebirths, and eventually to rid themselves of the obstacles preventing liberation and enlightenment. Liberation from the recurring problems of uncontrollable rebirth comes from ridding themselves of disturbing emotions and attitudes (Skt. *klesha*, afflictive emotions), especially naivety about reality. Enlightenment comes from additionally eliminating the unconscious projection of impossible fantasies.

Gaining emotional well-being in this lifetime, favorable rebirths, liberation, and enlightenment requires radical transformations of our personalities and our ways of viewing the world. The insights and realizations necessary for making these improvements do not come easily. We need to open ourselves, both intellectually and emotionally, to new ways of thinking, acting, and communicating. We also need a great deal of inspiration and support to give us the courage and strength to change. For the deepest inspiration, the Nyingma codifier Longchenpa stated in *A Treasure-House of Precious Guideline Instruction*, one definitely needs a proper relationship with a spiritual mentor. Let us examine whether Longchenpa's statement is culturally specific or relevant also for modern skeptical seekers.

As Western spiritual seekers, many of us read Dharma books. We attend classes at Buddhist centers and even participate in guided group meditations. These may open our minds and may even inspire us. Yet, granted that self-development is always difficult and slow, most of us find that we do not make significant progress. This is because, by themselves, these activities can only open and inspire us to a limited extent. We may develop an intellectual understanding and tentative acceptance of rebirth, a spiritual orientation of safe direction and bodhichitta, and knowledge of what to practice and avoid for achieving our spiritual goals, but something more is needed. We need something that will move our hearts in positive ways and thus give us the courage and strength to drop our limited views and negative habits.

In this regard, modern Western spiritual seekers are no different from traditional Asian ones. For this reason, we need to build inspiring relationships with spiritual mentors nowadays as well. Nevertheless, we also need a sober, responsible approach in order to find qualified mentors who suit our dispositions and in order to ensure that the relationships we build with such mentors are healthy ones.

In what ways can inspiration from mentors help us on our spiritual paths? To answer this question, we need to understand what Buddhism means by *inspiration*. The Sanskrit term for inspiration, *adhishtana*, often translated as blessings, means an elevation or an uplifting. The Tibetan rendering, *chinlab (byin-rlabs)*, implies waves that bring magnificence. Implicit is that the uplifting leads to emotional well-being, to favorable rebirths, and to the magnificent states of liberation and enlightenment.

Further, according to *The Great [Sanskrit-Tibetan] Etymological Dictionary*, a source of inspiration uplifts people through its truth, its calmness, its wisdom, and the positive things that it offers. Thus, more than Dharma instructors, we need spiritual mentors in order to gain inspiration in the complete sense of the word. Fully qualified mentors inspire disciples with the authenticity of their realizations, with their calmness and its soothing effect, with their wisdom, and with both the positive qualities that they have to share and the wonderful opportunities they offer. Inspiration, then, in its spiritual sense, has nothing to do with becoming excited or moved to action by someone's fame, power, wealth, or sex appeal.

In *Graded Visualizations as a Thrust for Conviction and Appreciation of a Guru*, the Drugpa Kagyü master Pema-karpo gave a clear example of the inspiring effect of a spiritual mentor. When disturbing emotions and thoughts upset our minds, if we imagine our mentors in our hearts, warmly smiling at us, we become relaxed, our minds calm down, and we may begin to smile ourselves.

Studying and meditating under the guidance of spiritual mentors with whom we have built deep relationships have a noticeably stronger effect than doing so on our own or with teachers toward whom we feel little or nothing. The inspiration we feel makes the practices more effective. It activates our potential and stimulates our deep awareness so that we slowly gain insight and realization. Gradually, our mental and emotional blocks disappear and we become free of our problems and our inability to help others. Thus, the ritual practices of guru-yoga in all Tibetan traditions include requesting inspiration from one's visualized mentor to realize each step of the path to enlightenment and imagining the inspiration entering one's heart in the graphic form of brilliant light.

The enlightening process takes place, however, only in the case of healthy relationships between emotionally mature disciples and properly qualified mentors. It does not occur in exploitative relationships in which naive seekers are overdependent on demagogues or frauds. The mechanism for its success hinges on the issue of trust. Because properly qualified mentors are free of emotional problems, are only concerned to benefit others, and are fully competent to guide disciples properly, we eventually come to trust such persons. Our trust derives from having built up, over time, long-term relationships with them so that we are totally convinced of their integrity.

In the process of gaining trust in our mentors, we also come to trust in ourselves that we can improve by bonding with them. The security gained from this realization allows us to be receptive to their positive influence and to be open to change. The protection-wheel practice of the Drugpa Kagyü *ladrub* (*bla-sgrub*; Skt. *guru-sadhana*; actualizing through the guru) tradition clearly illustrates this point. Before meditation on voidness and tantric transformation of their self-images, practitioners imagine their tantric masters sitting and smiling radiantly before them in the form of Avalokiteshvara, the embodiment of compassion. The security of the warm and trusting relations with their mentors provides the protected emotional space within which to begin dropping neurotic compulsive ways.

In short, the primary need for spiritual mentors is for people to move our hearts so that we gain the necessary uplifting energy for reaching our spiritual goals. In moving our hearts in the proper direction throughout our spiritual journeys, spiritual mentors act like oarsmen, navigators, and escorts.

The Need for a Combination of Sources of Inspiration

Generating and sustaining a positive motivation to work on ourselves, like doing the work itself, require courage, commitment, and enormous energy. Recalling our previous efforts at self-improvement may depress us rather than move us to action. If, on the other hand, we think of others who have gained liberation and enlightenment, of those who are well advanced toward these goals, and of the attainments that each has attained, we may become inspired. In other words, taking a safe direction in life from the Triple Gem of the Buddhas, the Sangha, and the Dharma, we gain inspiration. Their inspiration energizes our motivation and moves us to work on ourselves.

Further, if our thoughts of self-improvement dwell only on bene-fiting ourselves, we may still lack sufficient energy despite receiving inspiration from the Triple Gem. However, when we focus on others, especially on those who are suffering, we receive further inspira-tion. Together with inspiration from the Triple Gem, the added boost strengthens our motivation. It enables us to make even the most radical changes in ourselves in order to be able to help others. Thus, Shanti-deva explained that positive potential for gaining Buddha-qualities comes from focusing equally on the Buddhas and on suffering beings.

Inspiration from the Triple Gem and sincere motivation inspired by others, however, are still not enough to enable us to overcome neurotic habits. We need to supplement the two with an additional, more pow-erful source of inspiration. Practical experience has confirmed that the most potent source is a strong and healthy relationship with a spiritual mentor. The inspiration gained has special strength because it derives from the dynamics of a living human relationship and because that relationship is with someone having exemplary qualities.

Everyday experience corroborates these points. Looking at photos or even at videos of either heroes or anonymous disaster victims never moves us as much as actually meeting the people. Further, just meeting the people is never as uplifting as is having personal relationships with them. Since the Buddhas and lineage masters are no longer physically present, they cannot move us as deeply as can fully qualified mentors. Moreover, since qualified mentors are free of irrational behavior and swings in mood, healthy relationships with them are easier to maintain than with most people we feel moved to help. Consequently, the inspi-ration received from mentors tends to be more even and lasting.

In short, to develop and sustain a strong motivation to work on our-selves requires inspiration from the Triple Gem, from those in need of help, and from our spiritual mentors. Like an alloy of metals that is stronger than any of its individual components, an alloy of sources of inspiration provides our motivation and us with the greatest strength. Each element in the mixture reinforces the others so that, in the end, the energy of the whole is greater than that of the sum of its parts.

How Sources of Inspiration Work Together

Gampopa, and later Sakya Pandita, the fourth of the five Sakya found-ers, used the analogy of the sun, a magnifying glass, and kindling to explain how sources of inspiration work together to provide disciples with spiritual strength. Sakya Pandita explained that without a magnifying glass to focus the rays of the sun, the heat of the sun by itself cannot bring kindling to the flame. Similarly, without a healthy relationship with a spiritual mentor to focus the waves of the Buddhas' enlightening influence (*tinley*, *'phrin-las*), these waves by themselves cannot spark disciples to enlightenment. Effects arise dependently from a combination of causes and conditions.

On their own, the Three Gems may be too distant and impersonal to move disciples to action. In fact, most practitioners on the early stages of the path find conceiving of, let alone relating to, their qualities nearly impossible. Therefore, we need something to help us gain access to their enlightening influence. Qualified mentors provide that access by indicating, through teachings and their way of being, the goals we wish to attain, those who have reached them, and those who are striving toward them. Since inspiration from these indications comes from living persons with whom we can relate, it acts like a magnifying glass to focus within us the enlightening influence of the Triple Gem.

The tantras explain that this enlightening influence works primarily in four ways. It calms disturbances, stimulates growth, gives control over difficult matters, and forcefully ends dangerous situations. Because of our trust, being with our mentors calms us down. Because of our openness, it stimulates our good qualities to blossom. Because of our respect, we gain control of ourselves in their presence. Because of our awe, we forcefully resist any destructive impulses when with them, no matter how compelling the impulses might be. Thus, the positive emotional dynamics of healthy relationships with spiritual mentors allow the enlightening influence of the Triple Gem to affect us.

Healthy relationships with mentors also help us to gain easier access to inspiration from loved ones in need of help. Because fully qualified mentors are emotionally stable, wise, and benevolent people, mature relationships with them uplift us greatly. The security and strength we gain enables us to open our hearts more easily to emotionally challenging people. Without inspiration from our mentors, even loved ones may sometimes upset us too much to move us to help them. Thus, the Sakya master Gorampa's *Discourse Notes on "Parting from the Four [Stages of] Clinging"* recommended guru-yoga as a preliminary for bodhichitta meditation.

The Relation between a Spiritual Mentor
and Buddha-Nature

Gampopa indicated the mechanism of how spiritual mentors, as oarsmen, may move disciples along the spiritual path. He explained that
Buddha-nature is the cause, and a healthy relationship with a spiritual mentor is the condition, for reaching enlightenment. Buddha-
nature refers to the network of innate qualities and aspects of each individual that allows him or her to become a Buddha. Inspiration from a
spiritual mentor acts as the condition for activating this network.

According to Maitreya's *Sublime Continuum*, Buddha-nature is a network of three kinds of factors. Abiding factors, such as the nature of
the mind, constitute the first category. They never change. Evolving
factors, the second kind, grow like seeds with proper conditions. They
include the mind's innate systems of good qualities, positive potentials, and deep awareness. The aspect of everyone's heart and mind
that allows him or her to be inspired is the third type of factor. Inspiration stimulates the realization of abiding factors and the activation of
evolving ones.

In the magnifying glass analogy, then, Buddha-nature would refer to
the kindling and to the fact that it can catch on fire. A mentor's inspiration would be like the condition needed for the kindling to burst
into flames. The result, however, would not be the disciples' immola-
tion, but their transformation to more enhanced states. Perhaps a closer
example would be the firing of clay into magnificent porcelain.

Many things, such as nature, music, and patriotism, may uplift our
spirits. They lack the ability, however, to inspire us to enlightenment.
The Ninth Karmapa, a great luminary of the Karma Kagyü tradition,
clarified this point in *Mahamudra Eliminating the Darkness of Ignorance*.
He explained that a healthy relationship with a spiritual mentor is
the determining condition (*dagkyen, bdag-rkyen*) for becoming a Buddha, like the sensory cells of the eyes are the determining condition
for visual perception. In other words, visual cognition not only arises
through the medium and power of the cells of the retina, but also,
because of them, occurs as an instance of seeing, rather than of hearing.
Thus, the medium's being rods and cones determines that the form of
cognition arising through it is vision. Similarly, enlightenment not only
arises through the medium and power of a healthy relationship with a
spiritual mentor, but also occurs as an instance of someone becoming

an ideal teacher. Buddhahood does not entail a person's becoming a perfect sunset or a musical masterpiece.

How Inspiration Activates Buddha-Nature

In *A Precious Garland for the Four Themes*, Longchenpa used Gampopa's four themes to clarify how inspiration from a spiritual mentor helps to bring enlightenment. Together with safe direction and bodhichitta, this inspiration moves disciples to take the Dharma as a path—the second of Gampopa's four themes. In other words, the amalgam of the three moves disciples to practice the Buddhist methods as a pathway leading to enlightenment. Taking the Dharma as a path, then, analogously describes the process whereby the firing of clay brings it to porcelain.

Terdag Lingpa, Nyingma teacher and disciple of the Fifth Dalai Lama, further clarified the process. In *A Precious Ladder*, he explained Buddha-nature as the cause and a mentor's inspiration as the condition for generating true pathways of mind—the fourth noble truth. True pathways of mind are activated states of evolving factors of Buddha-nature, such as compassion and deep awareness. Through inspiration and other supporting conditions, these factors reach full maturity and bring the total transformation of enlightenment.

Inspiration from Oral Transmission

As stated earlier, spiritual mentors act as navigators, escorts, and oarsmen to help propel disciples along the pathways of mind to enlightenment that the disciples generate within themselves. They do this through both obvious and subtle ways. One of the more subtle methods is by giving oral transmission of Buddha's texts. The transmission occurs through mentors' reading texts aloud or reciting them from memory, usually at top speed, to disciples who listen attentively. As the need for transmission may be difficult for Westerners to understand at first, let us look more closely at this facet of the disciple-mentor relationship. To appreciate its significance, we need to outline some of the major features of the Buddhist approach to spiritual education.

In *A Brief Indication of the Graded Stages of the Path*, Tsongkapa explained that the sutras are difficult to understand by themselves. They purposely contain much repetition, do not present their topics in a logical sequence, and seemingly contradict one another. This is because Buddha intended them for disciples of differing abilities and needs. Many people learn more easily from abstract pictures of topics painted in dabs and pieces rather than from linear explications. Moreover, the sutras did not appear in writing until several centuries after Buddha orally delivered them. Repetition within them ensured that important points would not be lost when preservation of the words depended solely on memory.

Further, the "root texts" that later Indian and Tibetan masters composed have a vague style with many *this*s and *that*s that do not have clear referents. They were purposely written this way to allow the texts to serve as roots for several interpretations according to different sets of theories. When disciples recite these texts from memory, they must fill in the levels of significance themselves and keep several levels simultaneously in mind.

To clarify the meaning of the sutras and these later texts, Indian and Tibetan masters compiled commentaries, subcommentaries, and treatises. In addition, the Tibetans organized outlines, logic manuals, and systematic comparative presentations of the Indian schools of philosophical tenets. Although these materials make learning easier, they are nothing more than study tools. To use the tools properly for gaining realization, disciples require guideline instructions from spiritual mentors. One cannot learn everything by simply reading a textbook.

When studying mathematics, students cannot learn if the teacher solves all the problems for them. Teachers can impart the principles and show how to apply them with a few examples, but the students learn by working out problems for themselves. The same holds true with the Buddhist material. As my root guru, Tsenzhab Serkong Rinpochey, explained, "If Buddha or the ancient masters wished to write more clearly, they would certainly have done so. They were not stupid or incompetent. They purposely wrote as they did to make us think. Their style forces us to put together the meaning with the help of a mentor's guideline instructions."

Even in imparting guideline instructions, spiritual mentors do not reveal everything at once. Instead, they give mere hints or present only fragments at a time. This teaching method ensures that disciples fit together the pieces of the puzzle themselves. It also encourages them to develop perseverance and patience. This, in turn, helps disciples to fortify their motivations. It weeds out those who are not serious and who are unwilling to put in the effort required to overcome their disturbing emotions and attitudes.

The term *guideline instructions* and its honorific equivalent *personal instructions* (*zhel-lung, zhal-lung*) are often translated as "oral instructions." This translation may be confusing. Although guideline instructions derive from the personal experience of spiritual mentors and mostly originate from oral discourses, some appear first in written form. Moreover, most of the instructions that were first delivered orally have also been put into writing. Living mentors may give their own guideline instructions, either orally or in writing; however, most mentors rely primarily on the guidelines given by previous masters from their lineage.

When spiritual mentors give their own guideline instructions in person, disciples find them extremely inspiring. Disciples may also be inspired to a certain extent by reading the commentaries and recorded guideline instructions of lineage mentors. Merely reading them, however, is insufficient for gaining deep understanding of their meaning and integration of it into their lives. Disciples need the stronger inspiration that comes from living mentors in order to activate their Buddhanatures so that they can make the Dharma into true pathways of mind leading to liberation and enlightenment. The formal mechanism for gaining inspiration to understand and integrate the meaning of the texts and traditional guideline instructions is through receiving their oral transmission, in other words their energization, from a spiritual mentor.

The custom of oral transmission arose in ancient times before people applied the written language to spiritual matters. Periodic group recitations of Buddha's words from memory ensured that additions, deletions, and errors did not corrupt them. Listening to the words chanted in perfect unison, disciples gained confidence that successive generations from the time of Buddha had transmitted them correctly. This confidence led disciples to trust that studying and digesting these words would put them on the authentic Buddhist path. Teachers later extended the custom of oral transmission to the commentaries and guideline instructions of the great Indian and Tibetan masters. Although texts existed in written form, copies were extremely rare.

The lines of oral transmission of most of Buddha's discourses, their commentaries, and the guideline instructions have continued without break up to the present. They play a central role in Tibetan Buddhism. In fact, the four Tibetan traditions and their subdivisions define themselves by the specific lineages that they transmit. Nevertheless, the lines of transmission are not mutually exclusive. Many schools share several lineages up to certain points in their histories.

Group chanting of Buddha's words still occurs in the monasteries and nunneries. Nowadays, however, oral transmission is primarily from spiritual mentors to large groups or to individuals. Its purpose is to inspire disciples not merely by confidence in the accuracy of the words, but by confidence also in the authenticity of the mentors' realization of their meaning. When His Holiness the Fourteenth Dalai Lama, for example, transmits a text by reciting it at top speed, pausing at only one or two places to question the masters around him about how to interpret the most difficult passages, he inspires everybody. As he lacks any pretense, his occasional pauses convince us that everything else in the text is completely clear. This inspires us to take the view that the text is perfectly understandable. The deep impression this makes fortifies the potentials of our Buddha-natures so that, with sufficient study and effort, we too may gain similar realization.

~6

The Special Need for a Spiritual Mentor in Highest Tantra

The Special Role of Oral Transmission in Tantra

ORAL TRANSMISSION and inspiration from spiritual mentors play an even larger role in tantra than they do in sutra practice. This is evident from the structure of the tantric texts themselves and from the indispensable role of requesting inspiration from the lineage masters, one by one, in almost every practice.

In *An Illuminating Lamp*, the Indian master Chandrakirti explained the six alternative meanings and four levels of textual interpretation outlined in *An Anthology of Vajra Deep Awareness*. The latter work is one of the Guhyasamaja explanatory tantras for understanding the "vajra-expressions" of the highest class of root tantric texts. Except for *The Kalachakra Tantra*, the "clear tantra," the language of these texts is purposely obscure and conceals many meanings in each of its words. A vajra-expression may have meanings that are (1) explicit and suggestive of something else, (2) suggested and implicit, (3) metaphorical, and (4) nonmetaphorical. Moreover, the language of the expression may be (5) conventional or (6) nonsensical and unconventional. Further, the expression may have (1) literal, (2) shared, (3) hidden, and (4) ultimate levels of interpretation.

In *An Extensive Explanation of "An Illuminating Lamp,"* Sherab-senggey, Gelug founder of the Lower Tantric College, explained why the "hidden tantras" encrypt their meanings in this complex fashion. Although many contributing factors need to be present, success on the tantric path hinges on the inspiration and positive energy gained from a healthy relationship with a tantric master. To ensure that disciples build up that relationship, the language of the tantras is purposely obscure. Without relying on their tantric masters for oral transmission, instruction, and inspiration, disciples cannot connect the explanatory tantras with the root texts to derive the inner significance of the tantric practices.

Diverse Methods for Inspiring Disciples

Disciples on the tantra path may gain inspiration from their mentors to activate their Buddha-natures not merely by hearing the words of oral transmissions, but through all their senses. Tantric masters consecrate tiny herbal pills, *chinlab*, the same word as for inspiration, and give them to disciples to taste and swallow. They do the same with toasted barley dough balls during ceremonies for inspiring them to live long lives dedicated to self-development and to helping others. The disciples' positive attitudes when eating them undoubtedly strengthen their immune systems.

Tantric masters further inspire disciples by touching them on the head either with statues containing relics of lineage figures or with their hands, giving them a "hand-empowerment" (hand-blessing). They also consecrate specially knotted red strings and amulets for disciples to wear around their necks for protection. Touching their heads or giving them talismans is not for the purpose of feeding superstitions or hopes for magic. The intention is to inspire disciples with confidence so that they do not hesitate to use the potentials of their Buddha-natures.

The Nyingma and Kagyü traditions speak of "liberation through hearing, seeing, and being touched." Liberation, here, means gaining inspiration through these sensory experiences to activate one's Buddha-nature. Consequently, spiritual practice becomes especially potent for bringing liberation as quickly as is possible. The Tibetan title of the famous *Tibetan Book of the Dead* translates literally as *Liberation through Hearing [the Words of the Text Recited while] in the Bardo*. For disciples to gain liberation through seeing, Nyingma lamas show them special statues of the founder of their lineage, Guru Rinpochey Padmasambhava. The Karmapas, the highest masters of the Karma Kagyü tradition, perform the black hat ceremony. Disciples gain inspiration for their practices not only by seeing the Karmapa wearing his black hat, which is symbolic of the attainments of the entire lineage, but also by being in the presence of a realized master who is in total meditative absorption.

Tantric masters also give consecrated herbal pills, long-life dough balls, hand-empowerments, protection cords, and amulets to the general public. They also let the public view the special statues of the lineage founders and attend hat ceremonies. However, because members of the general public lack close relationships with these tantric masters, they do not gain the same depth of inspiration as tantric disciples of these masters receive.

The Deepest Need for a Tantric Master

Although all forms of Tibetan Buddhism teach a combined path of sutra and tantra, they all agree that ultimately only the methods of the highest class of tantra can remove the final obstacles preventing enlightenment. Highest tantra includes practices for working with the subtle energy-systems of the body and ways to access the mind's subtlest level, known as clear light. The Nyingma system calls the equivalent level of mind *pure awareness* (*rigpa, rig- pa*). For the sake of simplicity, we shall use *clear light mind* as a general term that also refers to pure awareness.

The salient feature of highest tantra that enables enlightenment is its focus on accessing the individual clear light mind within each person and using it to comprehend voidness. Only this subtlest level of mind can function with the full abilities of a Buddha. Only this level of mind continues into enlightenment and becomes a Buddha's enlightening, fully wise, all-loving mind. Thus, the immediate condition that we need to attain just prior to enlightenment is an activated clear light mind that uninterruptedly sees the void nature of reality or that, in dzogchen terminology, "recognizes its own face."

Although each person's clear light mind naturally exposes itself fully at the time of death, it normally understands nothing at that time. Moreover, clear light mind is extremely difficult to access while we are alive. Although it underlies and accompanies each moment of our experience, it does not function actively while grosser levels of mind are operating. Moments of involuntary violent sucking in of energy, such as the instant before sexual climax, sneezing, or yawning, come close to revealing this subtlest level of mind. However, the explosion of energy the very next instant destroys any possibility of capturing the moment and proceeding in this direction. Like smashing an atom within a mass of matter to release its potentials, accessing and harnessing clear light mind for the realization of voidness requires intense controlled energy.

The experiences during highest tantra empowerments reinforce the potentials of our clear light minds and activate them for making progress. Tantric ceremonies, however, cannot inspire energy on their own. Neither can the complex visualizations or internal yogas of advanced tantra practice. We need qualified tantric masters and healthy, deep relationships with them to bring our potentials fully to life. Only the combination of all these factors can inspire the enormous energy required for accessing, sustaining, and applying our clear light minds.

The Drigung Kagyü fivefold path of *mahamudra* (great seal) practice indicates this point clearly. The Drigung founder, Drigungpa, explained that the first two features necessary for disciples to realize their clear light minds are generating bodhichitta, and, within that state of mind, imagining themselves as Buddha-figures. Without the third feature, however, a healthy relationship with a spiritual mentor, disciples lack the inspiration needed to break through the massive clouds of conceptual thought to uncover their clear light minds.

Clear Light Mind as a Type of Buddha-Nature

Because the clear light mind continues from one life to the next and on through enlightenment, its continuum is the actual basis for the various aspects of Buddha-nature. For this reason, the Nyingma, Kagyü, and Sakya traditions consider clear light mind the deepest Buddha-nature. Clear light mind, however, does not merely carry the other aspects of Buddha-nature with its flow like a river carrying barges. Networks of good qualities, positive potentials, and deep awareness, for example, constitute innate features of clear light mind itself. Thus, we may apply to this context Gampopa's explanation that a healthy relationship with a spiritual mentor is the condition that activates Buddha-nature as the actual cause for reaching enlightenment. A healthy relationship with a tantric master is the condition for activating and harnessing the clear light mind, with all its qualities, potentials, and types of awareness.

The Inner Guru

Often, we hear about outer and inner gurus. An outer guru is a human being who serves as a spiritual mentor. An inner guru, on the other hand, is neither a mysterious voice in a disciple's head giving guidance, nor some mystic in a Himalayan cave sending telepathic messages. In *A Golden Garland of Excellent Explanation*, Tsongkapa explained that on the sutra level, an inner guru is the compassion that grows while traversing the spiritual path. Inspired by compassion, disciples develop bodhichitta which, like a guru, is replete with good qualities and inspires them to attain these capabilities themselves.

In *The Complete Fulfillment of Disciples' Hopes*, Tsongkapa indicated that on the highest tantra level, an inner guru is a disciple's deepest bodhichitta. The First Panchen Lama clarified this point in his Gelug classic, *A Ceremony for Honoring the Gurus* (*Lama Chöpa*; *The Guru Puja*). There, he called deepest bodhichitta *Samantabhadra* (the Totally Excellent One), a Nyingma term for pure awareness. In so doing, he revealed that, in the context of serving as an inner guru, a disciple's deepest bodhichitta is his or her clear light mind when it realizes voidness.

Moreover, since clear light mind, as a type of Buddha-nature, has the potential to recognize its own face and thus to realize voidness, a disciple's clear light mind may also serve as an inner guru, even before gaining self-realization. This extended sense of the term *inner guru* follows from the Buddhist analytical tool known as "giving the name of the result to the cause."

Tantric empowerment, then, requires both an outer and an inner guru. Inspiration from an outer guru, together with a disciple's realizations during the ceremony, provides "causal empowerment" that ripens into actual attainments. The Nyingma tradition explains the mechanism. The ripening process occurs only because an inner guru, as the deepest Buddha-nature, provides "foundational empowerment." As the foundation for all attainments, clear light mind encompasses all the excellent qualities that ripen into Buddhahood.

As an inner guru, clear light mind is also the ultimate source of inspiration. We may understand this in two ways. The Gelug tradition, combining its unique presentation of the Indian *Prasangika-Madhyamaka* school with the Guhyasamaja teachings, analyzes inspiration as a subtle form of energy (*lung, rlung*; Skt. *prana*). The deepest source of inspiring energy is subtlest life- supporting energy, which is the physical support of clear light mind. Since this subtlest energy flows inseparably with clear light mind, access to it comes only through accessing the subtlest level of mind.

The Nyingma, Kagyü, and Sakya traditions follow the Indian *mahasiddha* (greatly accomplished yogi) style and employ a more poetic description. They call clear light mind the "foundation for everything" (Skt. *alaya*). In dzogchen terminology, waves of inspiration are its "effulgent play." In the same way that the brilliance of the sun is a quality that is inseparable from the sun itself, inspiration is an inseparable quality of clear light mind.

The Need for a Root Guru

Dzogchen and mahamudra practices focus the mind on its own nature in order to realize voidness. For mind to focus on mind nondualistically and to realize its void nature requires an exceptionally clear and energized mind that does the focusing and a similarly clear and energized mind upon which to focus. Otherwise, the focusing mind is too weak and the object of its focus is too obscure for there to be any hope of success.

The Kagyü and Gelug/Kagyü mahamudra traditions present both a sutra and a tantra form of this practice. Sakya mahamudra and Nyingma dzogchen treat only its tantra level. Mahamudra practiced on the sutra level focuses the grosser levels of mind on their own natures. This entails using the level of mental consciousness upon which conceptual thought operates to focus both on sensory consciousness and on itself. Tantra-level mahamudra and dzogchen focus clear light mind on its own nature. Success in doing this requires an even clearer and more energized mind than the sutra level demands.

In general, accessing a clear light mind requires more inspiration than any form of the sutra path requires. A healthy relationship with a tantric master provides the extra energy needed. Since a root guru is the spiritual mentor who most strongly inspires a disciple, highest tantra practice proceeds more easily when one's tantric master is also one's root guru. For tantra mahamudra or dzogchen practice, however, a strong and deep relationship with a root tantric guru is indispensable. Therefore, Sakya Pandita asserted, in *The Profound Path of Guru-Yoga*, that requesting inspiration can bring disciples enlightenment only if directed at their empowering root tantric masters. If directed at any of their other mentors from whom they have not received empowerment, their requests can bring, at best, happiness only in this lifetime and just a small amount of inspiration.

The Ultimate Aim of Progressive Relationships with Spiritual Teachers

In *Clear Verses*, Chandrakirti distinguished between interpretable and definitive phenomena. Interpretable phenomena do not exist in the way that they appear to exist. They require interpretation. Their correct interpretation leads to definitive phenomena, which do exist in the way in which they appear to exist. In *A Lamp for Clearly Revealing the Other-Voidness Madhyamaka Tradition*, the Eighth Karmapa explained clear light mind as a definitive phenomenon. Grosser levels of mind and appearance are interpretable in that they do not exist in the way that they appear, yet lead one deeper to the clear light mind.

Let us extend the Eighth Karmapa's discussion of interpretable and definitive phenomena to our present topic. The relationships with a Buddhism professor, a Dharma instructor, a meditation or ritual trainer, a refuge or vow preceptor, and a Mahayana master do not exist in the way that they appear. They seem to form a full sequence of student-teacher relationships that is sufficient for enabling a spiritual seeker to reach enlightenment. The sequence, however, leads to deeper relationships.

The interpretable sequence points first to building a relationship with a root guru as a tantric master. A healthy relationship with a tantric master then brings access to an inner guru, a disciple's clear light mind. Correctly relating to an inner guru leads to a clear light realization of voidness. This realization is the definitive relationship between a spiritual seeker and a spiritual teacher. Gaining this realization, Dragpa-gyeltsen confirmed in *Three Rounds of Inspiration*, is the ultimate aim of progressive relationships with spiritual teachers. By making a disciple's networks of good qualities, positive potentials, and deep awareness fully operational, the realization eliminates the obstacles preventing liberation and enlightenment, either in stages or all at once. Thus, a disciple becomes a Buddha, to the benefit of everyone.

Summary and Conclusion

Relating to progressively more advanced levels of spiritual teachers forms in itself a graded path to enlightenment. The appropriate relationships with a Buddhism professor, a Dharma instructor, and a meditation or ritual trainer lead the way to building a healthy relationship with a spiritual mentor. A wholehearted commitment to a Mahayana master as a spiritual mentor leads deeper to the establishment of a close bond (*damtsig, dam-tshig*; Skt. *samaya*) with a tantric master. Maintaining a close bond with a tantric master energizes the highest tantra methods to bring access to the clear light mind—the inner guru, the definitive level spiritual teacher. Keeping additional close bonds with the inner guru brings the clear light realization of voidness. Thus, proper reliance on the inner guru brings enlightenment.

All four Tibetan Buddhist traditions accept that the deepest aim of the disciple-mentor relationship is to bring about the benefits it grants in highest tantra practice. Thus, although each level of relationship suits a corresponding stage in a disciple's development, graded levels imply a hidden intention of preparing us for progressively deeper relationships. Any Tibetan presentation of the disciple-mentor relationship, then, needs interpretation within this context. A description of what may seem on the surface to be a relationship for a beginner student or for a sutra-level disciple may not necessarily be meant for literal interpretation at that stage. As with the vajra-expressions of a root tantric text, the description may cloak a suggested deeper level of relationship and be meant nonmetaphorically only at that level.

A final important point needs mention. Tsongkapa stated in *A Grand Presentation of the Graded Stages of the Path* that although tantra teaches the most efficient methods for attaining enlightenment, the tantra path may not suit everyone. We may conclude from this point that study with a spiritual teacher leads to building a relationship with a tantric master only if we wish to attain enlightenment through tantric means. If our spiritual goals are more modest or if other methods of practice suit us better, relating to a teacher as a tantric master is not only irrelevant but may potentially be disastrous because of mutual misunderstanding.

PART II:

The Dynamics of a Healthy Student-Teacher Relationship

~7

Establishing a Relationship with
a Spiritual Teacher

Evaluating Tantric Sources
concerning the Disciple-Mentor Relationship

THE SANSKRIT and Tibetan classical Buddhist literature provides the
source material for how to relate to a spiritual mentor. Most of the
texts, however, explicitly refer only to the relationship with a tantric
master. The main examples include Ashvaghosha's *Fifty Stanzas*, its
commentaries, and all texts regarding the procedures of mahamudra,
dzogchen, the path and its results (*lamdray, lam-'bras*), and actualizing
through the guru.

Although many points in these texts have a general level of meaning
shared with sutra, we need carefully to distinguish which have com-
monality with sutra and which are exclusive to highest tantra. Sherab-
senggey explained the criteria. Teachings of shared meaning need to
accord with the main assertions found in the sutras and with the common experience of sutra practitioners. If they are out of harmony and
would easily be misunderstood, they are inappropriate materials for
teaching to practitioners exclusively of sutra.

In the traditional explanation, *sutra practitioners* refers to Mahayana
disciples, as we have defined them. Let us extend the scope of discussion beyond sutra practitioners to include earlier levels of spiritual seekers, starting with beginners who come to Dharma centers as
students of Buddhism. Any teaching from a tantric text with a shared
meaning that applies to all levels of relationship between a spiritual
seeker and a spiritual teacher needs to accord with the beliefs and
common experience of newcomers from the general public who are

interested in Buddhism. If a specific instruction fails to meet this criterion, it does not apply to such newcomers and is inappropriate material to teach them.

For example, the Guhyasamaja and Kalachakra literatures emphasize the need for thoroughly evaluating a tantric master before receiving an empowerment from the person. The literature also holds an injunction to stop looking for faults in a teacher; this, however, is to be followed only after becoming the teacher's tantric disciple, not before taking this step. Moreover, a tantric master also needs to scrutinize a potential disciple before agreeing to confer empowerment. Ashvaghosha explained the reason. The tantric vows that a disciple takes at an empowerment seal a close bond with the tantric master. Each side needs to be sure that he or she can trust the other and him or herself to uphold the bond and all it entails. A loss of trust and belief easily brings spiritual despair.

Mutual examination before two people voluntarily enter a committed relationship accords with commonplace customs and practice. A potential employer and employee interview each other before signing a contract. A couple gets to know each other well before deciding to marry. For a spiritual seeker and teacher to examine each other before committing themselves to a serious course of instruction only makes sense. On the other hand, seeing one's spiritual teacher as a Buddha would seem rather cultish and fanatical to the average person. Clearly, it cannot be a general instruction that applies to people totally new to Buddhism.

The Intended Audience for Graded-Path Texts

All Tibetan Buddhism lineages agree that enlightenment requires a combination of sutra and tantra practice. Thus, before receiving an empowerment—especially into the highest class of tantra—potential tantric disciples need to review the graded stages of the sutra path. They need to understand the graded-path literature within this context. The authors of this literature never intended their texts for newcomers at Western Dharma centers who know nothing about Buddhism. The intended audience for most of the major graded-path texts consisted of the people gathered to receive a highest tantra empowerment. To help prepare the audience, the tantric master taught the sutra portion of one of these texts during the days immediately preceding the ritual. The assumption was that the initiates were already familiar with the material and merely needed a refresher course.

Today as well, Tibetan lamas normally follow their public teachings on the sutra portion of the graded-path texts with tantric empowerments. The lamas may not explicitly state that the teachings form part of the preparation, and the audience may consider the empowerment merely a bonus added at the end of the discourse. Still, the graded-path teachings serve as the preliminary for the empowerment.

Further, the majority of the audience for the graded-path teachings traditionally consisted of monks and nuns. Not only had they already studied the sutra path to a certain extent, they were committed by vows to Buddhist practice as the primary activity for the rest of their lives. Even when the intended audience for a graded-path text was mostly laypeople, as in the case of Peltrül's Nyingma version, the purpose was clear. The outline divided the material of the text into outer and inner preliminaries—preliminaries for highest tantra empowerment and practice.

Evaluating Material from the Graded-Path Texts

The graded-path texts taught before an empowerment fall into one of two categories. Either they cover the stages of the sutra and tantra path together in one volume or they treat only the sutra portion, hint at the tantra stages that follow, and leave the presentation of tantra for a separate text. Explanations of the disciple-mentor relationship that appear in the tantra section of graded-path texts require the same evaluation as explanations from specifically tantric sources. One needs to investigate which of their points have a shared meaning applicable to all levels of relationship.

Aside from some notable exceptions in the Sakya and Drugpa Kagyü literature, the sutra portions of most graded-path texts also explain the disciple-mentor relationship. Although the material is not explicitly tantric, the instructions aim at preparing disciples for the upcoming relationship with a tantric master. This material also requires evaluation to determine its general applicability.

Different Levels of Guru-Meditation Taught in Graded-Path Texts

Starting as early as Longchenpa's *Rest and Restoration in the Nature of the Mind*, the graded-path presentations of the disciple-mentor relationship nearly always include explicit instructions on appropriate thoughts and actions for disciples in relationship to their mentors. The procedures form a common basis of practice shared by all committed disciples of spiritual mentors, whether on the sutra or the tantra level. Some procedures, such as being polite and respectful, comfortably suit any spiritual seeker-teacher relationship. Other instructions, such as to regard one's mentor as a Buddha, require graded explanations depending on the level of disciple-mentor relationship. They fail to qualify, however, as shared teachings that also pertain to relationships with Buddhism professors, Dharma instructors, or meditation or ritual trainers before one is ready to become a disciple committed with vows.

Many of the graded-path texts that cover the sutra and tantra stages in one volume include instructions for meditating on the spiritual mentor. The guru-yoga most frequently taught in them asks disciples to imagine that their bodies, speech, and minds merge with the corresponding three faculties of their spiritual mentors, seen as Buddhas. The meditation normally includes imagining their mentors in the physical forms of Buddha-figures, such as Vajradhara, or imagining Vajradhara in the mentors' hearts. Vajradhara is the embodiment of the fully enlightened clear-light mind of a Buddha. Some guru-yogas ask disciples to imagine their mentors in the forms of lineage masters particularly associated with highest tantra, such as Padmasambhava, taken as a Buddha-figure.

Buddhist seekers frequently focus on visualized images of Buddha Shakyamuni in order to gain concentration, even before entering a disciple-mentor relationship. Focus on a figure specifically associated with highest tantra, however, does not accord with the customs or common experiences of spiritual seekers unconcerned about highest tantra. Therefore, guru-yoga entailing the visualization of such figures is not a general meditation shared with spiritual seekers at stages of the path that precede their conscious preparation for highest tantra practice. Such guru-yoga belongs strictly to highest tantra.

From among the graded-path texts that focus only on the sutra teachings, Atisha's *Stages of Practice with a Guru* began the tradition of outlining a sutra level of guru-yoga. It comprised offering a seven-part invocation and requesting inspiration. A seven-part invocation, as Shantideva outlined, starts with invoking the Three Jewels of Refuge or an appropriate representation of them. The seven parts directed toward them comprise prostrating, making offerings, admitting mistakes, rejoicing in the virtues of others, requesting teaching, beseeching the gurus not to pass away, and dedicating the positive potential built up by the practice.

Later Kadam masters, such as Sangwayjin, extended the meditation to include disciples gaining inspiration from their spiritual mentors by remembering their good qualities and kindness. Tsongkapa and subsequent Gelug masters up to the Fifth Dalai Lama elaborated upon Sangwayjin's model in their graded-path texts. Since every level of spiritual teacher, starting with Buddhism professors, possesses some good qualities and at least the kindness to give instruction, any level of spiritual seeker may gain inspiration by focusing on these aspects. Such practice accords with general experience. Listening to speeches during commemorative ceremonies for national heroes, for example, inspires many.

In *A Blissful Path*, the First Panchen Lama shifted the emphasis in the guru-yoga that Tsongkapa outlined. As part of his presentation of the sutra portion of the graded path, he stressed that disciples need to see their spiritual mentors as Buddhas. By including the visualization of Vajradhara in the mentor's heart, he clearly indicated the highest tantra intent of this step. Subsequent Gelug graded-path texts, up to Pabongka's *Liberation in the Palm of Your Hand*, have followed this highest tantra orientation and expanded on the First Panchen Lama's model. As with the strictly highest tantra forms of guru-yoga, the meditation on seeing the mentor as a Buddha found in later Gelug graded-path texts is not a general practice for spiritual seekers unconcerned with highest tantra.

Many Westerners are confused about this point. Some meet Tibetan Buddhism initially at a highest tantra empowerment, for example Kalachakra, or attend an initiation early in their spiritual paths. They may not understand anything that is happening during the ritual, or they may sit through the procedures merely as observers. Without consciously taking and intending to keep the vows, however, they do not establish a disciple-mentor relationship with the tantric master. Moreover, Wönpo Sherab-jungnay added that members of the audience do not actually receive an empowerment unless they also have some level of conscious experience and insight during the ceremony that purifies mental blocks and plants seeds for realizations. At best, observers at an empowerment receive inspiration, from witnessing the ritual, which builds up potentials for more serious involvement with highest tantra in the future.

The Qualities of a Spiritual Teacher

Since the sutra-level guru-meditation formulated by the Kadam tradition focuses on the good qualities and kindness of a spiritual teacher, it requires knowledge of these qualities and examination of the teacher to determine whether the person has them. The classical texts list the qualifications only for spiritual mentors. The analysis of the words *guru*, *lama*, and *spiritual friend* has revealed some of the more important points. Refuge and vow preceptors, Mahayana masters, and tantric masters each require progressively more talents, capabilities, and positive personality traits. Moreover, higher level teachers share the qualities of lower level ones.

For example, vow preceptors need to have kept their liberation vows purely, whether as laypeople or as monastics. Mahayana masters need, in addition, advanced concentration, stable realization of bodhichitta and voidness, and an advanced level of freedom from disturbing emotions such as greed, attachment, anger, and naivety. Tantric masters, in addition, require mastery of an enormous scope of tantric rituals. This does not mean merely having technical expertise in their procedures. Tantric masters need the ability to bring actual enlightening forces into the rituals.

Newcomers to Buddhism, however, often begin their studies with teachers of less competence than that possessed by spiritual mentors. Nevertheless, earlier level spiritual teachers need to share certain features of mentors. Buddhism professors need substantial learning; Dharma instructors need learning plus insight from personal experience; and meditation or ritual trainers need learning, experience, and expertise in the training methods. Moreover, all levels of spiritual teacher need to be ethical, kindhearted, concerned about others, patient, unpretentious, and emotionally mature. Most of all, in addition to all the above qualities, spiritual teachers need to be inspiring, specifically for us. A teacher may be fully qualified as a spiritual mentor and may even inspire many other disciples. Yet, if he or she fails to move our hearts with inspiration, we will be unable to benefit fully from the relationship.

Fully qualified teachers, however, are extremely rare, not only today but in the past as well. In *Approximating the Deepest Level*, Pundarika, the royal Shambala commentator on Kalachakra, declared, "In this age of conflicts, spiritual mentors have mixed faults and qualities. No one is without shortcomings. Therefore, scrutinize well and rely on those with mostly good qualities."

Thorough Examination

Evaluating a potential spiritual teacher is never a simple process. The Guhyasamaja literature has explained that potential disciples and mentors may need to examine each other's qualities for up to twelve years. The advice refers specifically to scrutinizing one another before receiving or conferring a highest tantra empowerment. It does not imply that the examination be conducted from a distance. As potential tantric disciples, we might check possible tantric masters during the course of studying with them for several years first as our Mahayana masters. Similarly, before deciding to take refuge vows with possible mentors or to become their Mahayana disciples, we might examine their qualities while studying with them first as one of our Buddhism professors, Dharma instructors, or meditation or ritual trainers.

Tsarchen explained extrasensory perception as the most reliable tool for spiritual seekers and teachers to use for examining each other. A person's true qualities may lie hidden, inaccessible to ordinary observation. If seekers or teachers lack special powers, Tsarchen continued, they may try to surmise each other's character and talents through careful scrutiny. For confirmation, they also need to ask questions about each other from people who are valid sources of information. One must never rely merely on someone's fame, charm, or personal charisma. Sakya Pandita put it nicely in *A Precious Treasury of Elegant Sayings*: "The wise know by discerning themselves, while the foolish follow popular trends. When an old dog barks with a clamor, the others come running for no reason at all."

Since few people possess extrasensory perception, most spiritual seekers need to rely on careful scrutiny. Although the classical texts stress that appearances may be deceptive, we need to evaluate them as best as we can. Buddha gave an analogy regarding the dilemma in one of his sutras: "You may be unable to see a fish swimming in the depths of the sea, but you can sense its presence from ripples on the water's surface." Similarly, we may be unable to see the hidden qualities that a teacher has, but we can surmise their presence through indications from the person's behavior.

To acquaint ourselves with a potential teacher's behavior when we are total newcomers to Buddhism, we first ask others whose opinion we respect what they think of the person. If they report that he or she is a charlatan or a scoundrel, there is no need to waste further time. Similarly, we need to check the reliability of a Buddhist author before reading one of his or her books. For newcomers still unable to discriminate between what is and is not authentically Buddhist, attending the lecture of a disreputable teacher or reading a book by a questionable author may easily lead to following an unreliable spiritual path. It is better for newcomers to avoid such danger, if possible. Firsthand acquaintance with questionable teachers or authors is only helpful once we are securely on the Buddhist path, so that we will not be misled, and when newcomers seeking advice about spiritual teachers look to us as trustworthy sources of information.

If, as newcomers, we receive a favorable report about a teacher or an author, we may attend a class that the person gives, or read a book that he or she has written, without the danger of becoming confused or misled. Merely going to someone's lecture, however, or reading his or her book, does not make the person one of our spiritual teachers. Establishing a relationship, even with a Buddhism professor, requires a conscious intention to study with the person.

Many standard texts on relating to spiritual teachers, such as Kong-trül's *Lamp for the Definitive Meaning*, state that seekers need to regard anyone who has taught them even one verse of Dharma as one of their spiritual teachers. This does not refer to casually listening to a discourse on Dharma when merely attending a public talk or when merely sitting in on a university lecture. The point of the statement is that once we have confirmed and accepted a teacher or author as an authentic source, then hearing or reading even one verse of Dharma from the person is utterly precious.

We may further scrutinize a potential teacher by checking our intuitive feelings and other subtle indications. For example, Tibetans normally look at the following signs to determine if they have a karmic relation with a spiritual teacher. When you first meet the person or hear his or her name, do you feel anything special? When you first go to see or try to contact the teacher, do you find the person at home? Are there any favorable omens when you first meet, such as the sun coming out from behind the clouds? What type of dreams do you have after your meeting?

Not all these signs, however, appear in each case. Moreover, their presence or absence may be inconclusive. For example, the presence of a strong intuitive feeling may come from anticipation and an overactive imagination. The absence of an intuitive feeling may be due to a lack of sensitivity. To rely on intuitive feelings and subtle signs requires self-knowledge and a sober mind.

An additional point that we need to investigate is the potential teacher's relationship with the spiritual mentors we already have. Since most teachers lack expertise in everything that we may need to learn, study with a wide diversity of spiritual teachers may benefit us greatly. However, if we accept as an additional teacher someone antagonistic to one of our mentors, we inevitably experience a loyalty conflict, which endangers our progress. Even reading a book written by someone hostile to one of our mentors may cause us confusion. His Holiness the Fourteenth Dalai Lama has summed up the situation with an image. One's spiritual teachers need to fit harmoniously together to form an integrated working unit, as the multiple faces of a Buddha-figure do.

The Qualities of a Spiritual Seeker

To recognize a teacher's positive qualities, spiritual seekers need certain features. Kongtrül stated that without the qualities described by the Indian master Aryadeva in *Four Hundred Stanzas*, disciples would see only shortcomings even in the most talented master. Although Aryadeva's text belongs to the sutra literature, the qualities listed there pertain to all levels of spiritual seekers, from newcomers to tantric disciples. Common sense and experience confirm that anyone who wishes to learn something for someone needs these qualities.

First, seekers need to be open, which means being without attachment to personal opinions and without hostility toward other points of view. Otherwise, preconception and prejudice will blind them to recognizing a teacher's qualities. Second, spiritual seekers need common sense. They need to be able to distinguish between correct explanations and faulty ones. Third, seekers need a strong interest in the Dharma. Unless finding a qualified teacher is vitally important to them, they will skip the effort to examine a candidate properly. Chandrakirti added in his commentary to Aryadeva's text that spiritual seekers also need appreciation and respect for the Dharma and for qualified teachers, and an attentive mind.

Thus, before searching for any level of spiritual teacher, we need to examine ourselves honestly. Most important is to scrutinize our motivation, aim, and openness to studying Buddhism with a teacher. Do we simply wish information from the person, or do we want to learn how to apply the Dharma to our lives or how to meditate? Are we seeking emotional well-being in this lifetime, or a fortunate rebirth, or liberation, or enlightenment? Pretending to be at more advanced levels than we actually are will benefit no one.

Further, we need to evaluate honestly our level of emotional maturity. For example, one of the tantric vows is not to disparage one's tantric master. Thus, as potential tantric disciples, we need the strength of character and emotional stability to remain sober-headed despite anything our tantric masters may say or do. If we find something disagreeable, we need the ability to remain calm and, without anger or recrimination, to see what we can learn from the situation. Thus, the Kadam Geshey Potowa stressed that, more than intelligence, a potential disciple needs good character and a kind heart. His advice is pertinent to forming a healthy relationship with any level of spiritual teacher.

Formalizing a Disciple-Mentor Relationship

Once we have thoroughly examined a potential spiritual teacher and ourselves and have decided that he or she is the proper person for us and that we are receptive and emotionally prepared, we are ready to establish a seeker-teacher relationship. In the case of studying with a spiritual teacher as a Buddhism professor, Dharma instructor, or meditation or ritual trainer, we formalize the relationship simply by enrolling in the class. The procedure is more complex when establishing a disciple-mentor relationship.

A spiritual teacher formally becomes one of our spiritual mentors through our taking refuge, liberation, bodhisattva, or tantric vows in his or her presence. Nothing further explicitly needs to be said or done. Taking vows with someone, however, requires seeking and requesting permission. When a great lama conducts a bodhisattva vow ceremony or confers a tantric empowerment to a large crowd, most people who attend do not have the opportunity beforehand to request permission in a private interview. The request and acceptance occur en masse as part of the ritual. If, however, a spiritual mentor confers vows in a more private setting, either separately from or as part of a tantric empowerment, we need to request and gain permission beforehand to attend.

Once we have committed ourselves with vows to the Buddhist path, we may study various sutra and tantra topics with other teachers whom we have also appropriately checked. Although we might not immediately take vows in their presence, these teachers also become our mentors by virtue simply of our study with them. If, however, we wish to formalize the relationship, we would ask to take bodhisattva and/or tantric vows in their presence at the earliest opportunity—either publicly as part of a mass ceremony or privately if this is possible.

Expectations in a Disciple-Mentor Relationship

Establishing a disciple-mentor relationship with a teacher, with or without taking vows in his or her presence, does not necessarily mean that we go to the person privately for personal advice. Except for occasionally visiting to offer a ceremonial scarf of respect (*kata*, *kha-btags*) or to make some other small offering, many Tibetan disciples have never spoken privately with any of their mentors other than those in whose houses they might live. From a Tibetan point of view, asking about personal meditation practice, even from a lama with whom we live, implies a pretentious, self-important attitude. It gives the impression that we consider ourselves great practitioners. Tibetans highly value humility, especially concerning spiritual matters.

Of course, if a Tibetan actually were a serious practitioner, he or she would seek meditation advice from a mentor. Tibetans, however, have a much higher standard of who qualifies as a serious practitioner than do most Westerners. The mentor consulted would normally be one of the meditator's root gurus. There is no need for all one's mentors to play the same role in one's spiritual life. Primarily, a Tibetan meditator would ask which intensive practice to do next after having completed a retreat. Similarly, he or she might ask which texts to read or which other lamas to consult to supplement his or her meditation. Unless specifically asked by their mentors, most Tibetans would be too humble to disclose their meditation experiences before a great master.

Tibetans are also far shyer to discuss their personal affairs, especially concerning relationships or emotional problems, than are most Westerners. Generally, they avoid discussing such matters with their spiritual mentors. The only situation in which Tibetans would normally consult a mentor about a private matter would be to request a divination with dice (*mo, mo*). Typically, they would ask for a prognostication to determine which rituals to commission and sponsor for eliminating obstacles for a journey or for a business or medical problem.

When a Western spiritual seeker establishes a disciple-mentor relationship with a teacher, he or she often expects a more personal relationship than would a Tibetan. This is in keeping with the emphasis on individuality that is a defining characteristic of Western culture. Asian civilizations, by contrast, place more accent on family, group, or cultural identity. On a more enlightened level, Asians stress the importance of the "here and now." For example, I spent nine years with my root guru, Serkong Rinpochey, as his disciple, interpreter, and English secretary. Although our relationship was extremely close, Rinpochey never once asked me a personal question about my background, family, or private life. I often describe the relationship as "personal impersonal." We dealt only with what was relevant to the moment.

In establishing a disciple relationship with a traditional Tibetan mentor, then, a Westerner needs to be sensitive to the culture. Especially inappropriate is to ask a monk or a nun about marital or sexual problems. In establishing a disciple relationship with a Western spiritual mentor, on the other hand, a Westerner might appropriately ask for personal advice about private emotional problems or initial meditation practice. A mentor, however, is not the equivalent of a confessor or a cheap psychiatrist to whom we reveal each week every detail of our lives. Nor is a mentor a fortune-teller to whom we turn for divination concerning all personal decisions. The Buddhist custom is to seek guidance primarily from the teachings themselves.

A spiritual mentor helps to lead a disciple in the right direction. If a mentor were to solve all our problems for us, we would never grow. The point of entering a disciple-mentor relationship, after all, is to gain spiritual and emotional maturity through developing our discriminating abilities and the warmth of our hearts.

~8

Sutra-Level Guru-Meditation

The Applicability of the Meditation

BY STUDYING the Buddhist path with spiritual teachers, we learn the teachings and the various methods for applying them to our lives. We train in these methods to bring about positive self-transformations. The process of change is never linear. Emotional and spiritual growth comes only slowly, in a seemingly chaotic pattern. For a time, we may see some improvement, but then a crisis or just a passing dark mood may cause a temporary decline. Although short periods inevitably contain their ups and downs due to the enormous diversity of our karmic potentials and the fleeting circumstances that we meet, patterns of growth slowly emerge if we persevere.

Inspiration from our spiritual teachers helps to sustain and energize our practices as we pass through the vicissitudes of daily life. Sutra-level guru-meditation from the Kadam tradition provides an accessible method for gaining inspiration from all levels of teachers, from Buddhism professors to tantric masters. Just as the Kadam lojong teachings serve as common material for all four schools of Tibetan Buddhism, similarly the Kadam style of guru-meditation suits practitioners from any tradition and at all levels of practice. For ease of expression, let us outline the practice in terms of the relationship with a spiritual mentor.

Focusing on Good Qualities While Not Denying Shortcomings

The main body of the Kadam guru-meditation begins with reminding oneself of the benefits of focusing on the good qualities of one's mentor and the drawbacks of dwelling on his or her faults. The assumption is that any spiritual teacher we meet inevitably has a mixture of strong and weak points. Pundarika's voice was not alone in stating this point. Buddha himself acknowledged the fact in *A Cloud of Jewels Sutra*. In quoting these sources in their discussions of spiritual mentors, Tsongkapa, Kongtrül, and other great Tibetan masters have clearly shown their agreement.

Although everyone has strong and weak points, inspiration comes from focusing only on someone's positive qualities. Dwelling on a person's faults and complaining about them merely angers, saddens, or disillusions us. It is not an uplifting activity, nor does it bring any joy. Therefore, to gain inspiration from spiritual teachers, Sangwayjin taught that we need to focus solely on their good qualities, regardless of how many faults they might have.

Tsongkapa clarified the process. Focusing only on a mentor's good qualities does not mean that the person has only good qualities. The meditation does not ask disciples to deny the shortcomings that their mentors actually have, but simply to stop dwelling on them. For example, Serlingpa, Atisha's Sumatran mentor, accepted as the supreme view of voidness the explanation given by the *Chittamatra* (mind-only) school of Buddhist tenets. Atisha, on the other hand, took the Prasangika-Madhyamaka explication to be the most accurate. The Kadam founder never denied this difference in their understandings of reality. Nevertheless, because Serlingpa was the main teacher responsible for his development of bodhichitta, Atisha repeatedly praised his mentor's compassion and kindness as continuing sources of inspiration.

The Analogy with Looking Out a Window at a Passerby

The process of focusing exclusively on a mentor's good qualities while not denying his or her faults resembles the process of looking out the ground-floor window of a house at someone walking past. The viewer sees only the upper part of a body passing by. This does not mean that the passerby lacks the lower half of a torso and legs. The incompleteness of the viewer's vision arises from a restriction in his or her point of view. Similarly, when we focus in meditation on our mentors' good qualities, it is as if we went into a house and looked out a window: we no longer perceive our teachers' shortcomings. The faults still exist, but the restricted viewpoints of our minds in meditation prevent us from seeing the two simultaneously.

Moreover, the restrictions imposed by the window make what the viewer sees seem to exist in an impossible way. The passerby seems to exist as a person with only an upper part of a body, although of course the viewer knows this is absurd. Similarly, because of being restricted, our minds give rise to deceptive appearances. For example, if we were to focus on our mentors' shortcomings, they would deceptively appear at that moment to be the only qualities that they have. We know this is true from ordinary life. When we are annoyed with a friend's behavior and dwell on the person's mistakes, we lose all sight of our friend's good qualities. Therefore, to avoid dwelling on our mentors' shortcomings, we focus in meditation only on their good qualities. Although the restricted scopes of our minds in meditation make the good qualities appear as if they were the only qualities that our mentors have, nevertheless we know the deceptive appearance comes from focusing singularly on good qualities.

Further, although looking at a passerby out a window requires missing the sight of the lower part of the person's body, the situation is temporary. After stepping outside, a viewer again sees the entire body of any passerby. Similarly, although focusing in meditation on only our mentors' good qualities requires temporarily ignoring shortcomings, their faults appear again after we arise from meditation. Now, however, we see our mentors as whole people, with both strong and weak points. Seeing both sides of our mentors prevents us from exaggerating either of the two.

How to Meditate on a Mentor's Good Qualities

Kadam guru-meditation asks disciples to focus on cultivating and making a habit of two mental actions: feeling deeply convinced of the good qualities of their mentors and appreciating their kindness. Consciously feeling this way about the qualities and kindness of their mentors creates states of mind conducive for gaining inspiration. The process works, however, only if disciples meditate properly.

In *A Grand Presentation of the Graded Stages of the Path*, Tsongkapa explained that correct meditation requires clarity about two points: what specifically to focus on and how to regard the object of focus. Otherwise, to use a Western example, if someone wished to paint a picture of an orange, the person might mistakenly focus on an apple rather than on an orange. Moreover, he or she might regard the orange as a snack to eat rather than as an object to paint.

Therefore, after reminding ourselves of the benefits of focusing on our mentors' good qualities and the drawbacks of dwelling on their faults, we continue our guru-meditation by imagining our mentors or looking at photos of them, and distinguishing their strong points, as we understand them. *Distinguishing* (*dushey*, *'du-shes*; Skt. *samjna*), usually translated as *recognition*, is one of the five aggregate factors (Skt. *skandha*) that comprise each moment of our experience. It refers to the mental action of differentiating within a field of awareness certain elements from the rest so that we may focus specifically on them. To focus visually on an orange, for example, we need to distinguish within our fields of vision the shape and color of the fruit from everything else that appears. Consequently, anything other than the orange fades into the background and the fruit appears to be prominent. Similarly, here we distinguish our mentors' good qualities from everything else about them. In doing so, the qualities stand out and our mentors' shortcomings drop to the background.

The focal object of the meditation, then, is the mentors' good qualities. The way in which we focus on them is through believing that these qualities are there and that the person actually has them. *Believing* (*daypa*, *dad-pa*), usually translated as *faith*, means varying things to different people in diverse cultures. Let us examine the classical Buddhist definition in the hope of bringing about a rectification of terms. We shall use as our basis Vasubandhu and Asanga's discussions, as presented by Yeshey-gyeltsen, the tutor of the Seventh Dalai Lama, in *Indicating Clearly the Primary Minds and Mental Factors*.

The Definition of Believing

The Buddhist discussion of *believing* refers neither to beliefs as mental objects that someone passively holds, nor to belief or faith as a general state of mind that characterizes a "believer." Rather, as Asanga explained, *believing* is the constructive mental action of focusing on something existent and knowable, and considering it either existent or true, or considering a fact about it true. Thus, it does not include believing that an unknowable God or Santa Claus exists or that the moon is made of green cheese. Further, believing a fact occurs only while validly cognizing it and implies certitude. Therefore, *believing* also excludes presumption and blind faith, such as believing that the stock market will rise.

There are three ways of believing a fact to be true. (1) Clearheadedly believing a fact about something is a mental action that is clear about a fact and which, like a water purifier, constructively clears the mind. Vasubandhu specified that it clears the mind of disturbing emotions and attitudes toward its object. (2) Believing a fact based on reason is the mental action of considering a fact about something to be true on the basis of thinking about reasons that prove it. (3) Believing a fact with an aspiration concerning it is the mental action of considering true both a fact about something and an aspiration one consequently holds about the object.

Asanga further explained that believing a fact to be true acts as the basis for inciting intention. Intention, in turn, serves as the basis for positive enthusiasm to accomplish a goal.

The Three Ways of Believing
That a Mentor Has Good Qualities

In explaining sutra-level guru-meditation, Tsongkapa specified that disciples need to focus on the good qualities that their mentors actually have, while believing clearheadedly that the mentors truly have them. In delineating only one way of believing these qualities to be a fact, he followed Vasubandhu's presentation of the constructive mental action of believing. Sangwayjin, however, mentioned all three ways of believing as part of his general discussion of the spiritual path. Therefore, applying all three ways of believing in a mentor's qualities to guru-meditation seems an appropriate elaboration for gaining more inspiration, a stronger intention, and greater enthusiasm. We shall follow the order that Yeshey-gyeltsen used for the three, since they form a logical progression:

(1) After distinguishing our mentors' good qualities, we focus on them first while believing clearheadedly that the mentors actually have them. In other words, these qualities are clear to us from having examined our mentors' behavior and character. The more we focus on the qualities and clearheadedly believe them to be a fact, the more we cleanse our minds of disturbing emotions and attitudes toward our mentors, such as arrogance or doubts about the person.

(2) Once we are able to focus clearheadedly on our mentors' actual good qualities and are clear that they have them, we recall what "having good qualities" means. The Sanskrit term for good qualities, *guna*, also appears in the non-Buddhist *Samkhya* school of philosophy as the name for the three universal constituents—intelligence, energy, and mass (Skt. *sattva, rajas,* and *tamas*)—that form an intrinsic part of every phenomenon. In Buddhism, however, the term refers to the good qualities that, as aspects of Buddha-nature, are the intrinsic potentials or properties of the clear light mind. The Tibetan translation *yönten (yon-tan)* means literally the correction of a deficiency. The implication is that, although everyone has the same potentials, realization of them comes through strengthening one's natural abilities in order to overcome shortcomings.

Reminding ourselves of the connotation of the Tibetan term *yönten* enables us to think next about how our mentors gained their qualities through following a process of behavioral cause and effect. Our mentors have become qualified spiritual teachers as the result of intensively training in Dharma. Moreover, we know that our mentors definitely have good qualities, based on irrefutable evidence—our personal experience of the positive effects that our teachers have had on others and on us. Thus, we focus on our mentors' good qualities while believing even more strongly, based on sound reason, that their possession of these qualities is a fact. Our minds are totally free of arrogance or doubts.

(3) Clearheaded about our mentors' good qualities and knowing that they have gained them through a process of behavioral cause and effect, we focus next on these features while believing something about them involving our aspirations. We believe that these qualities are something that we too are able to attain, based on our Buddha-natures and appropriate effort. Moreover, by seeing how much our mentors have helped others and us by having these qualities, we believe them to be something that we need to attain and that we shall strive to attain to help others too. The constructive mental action of believing this about our mentors' good qualities strengthens our development of bodhi-chitta—the mental action of focusing on enlightenment with the strong intention to attain it for the benefit of all. This intention, in turn, serves as the basis for positive enthusiasm to attain the same good qualities as our mentors have.

The Constructive State of Mind That Results
from Believing a Fact

As a constructive mental action, believing a fact is free of disturbing emotions such as naivety, doubt, attachment, resentment, pride, and jealousy. Thus, in clearheadedly believing, based on good reason, that our mentors have good qualities as the result of their efforts, with an aspiration that we can and shall attain them ourselves, our minds are free of naivety (Skt. *moha*) about our potentials and about what we need to do in order to realize them. Our minds are also free of indecision about the matter. While focusing on our mentors' qualities, we neither desperately long to possess our teachers as exclusively ours, nor obsessively long to be part of their inner circles. We do not resent the fact that they have these qualities, nor do we hate ourselves for being inadequate in comparison. We do not arrogantly feel that we lack deficiencies that need correcting, nor do we depressingly feel that our shortcomings are so numerous that we have no chance of success. Further, the mental action of believing that our mentors have good qualities and that we shall attain them ourselves lacks any jealousy toward our teachers or toward our fellow-disciples. Our minds are sober and clear, free of emotional obstacles that would prevent our attaining our mentors' positive features.

Vasubandhu further added that having a sense of values (*ngotsa sheypa, ngo-tsha shes-pa*) and scruples (*trelyö, 'khrel-yod*) always accompanies constructive mental activity. Thus, in believing as fact our mentors' good qualities and our ability to attain these features ourselves, we have a sense of values that includes appreciation and esteem for positive qualities and for persons possessing them. Our sense of values also implies that we stand in healthy awe (*jigpa, 'jigs-pa*) of our mentors. This does not mean that we are terrified of our teachers or that we are stiff, awkward, and humorless when with them. Rather, our respect and awe make us naturally tame and reserved in their presence.

Moreover, we have a sense of scruples that causes us to be horrified at the idea of behaving in a manner that spiritual persons would decry. The horror we feel, however, is not disturbing. It differs greatly from being terrified that we might act improperly and be rejected as a "bad person," which would only make us self-conscious and anxious. Rather, our horror at the idea of acting improperly spurs us on to constructive behavior.

Asanga explained *ngotsa sheypa* as a sense of honor and *trelyö* as a sense of shame. Clearheadedly believing our mentors' good qualities to be a fact contains a sense of honor or self-pride that prevents us from denigrating or making fools of ourselves. It further contains a sense of shame that keeps us from acting in negative or ridiculous ways that would disgrace, embarrass, or disappoint those whom we most respect—our families, our teachers, our friends. We refrain from acting in these shameful ways both in general and specifically in our relationships with our mentors.

The Relation between Believing a Fact to Be True and Liking It

Vasubandhu explained that believing a fact to be true does not imply necessarily being happy about it. For example, believing that life is difficult does not mean that we like the fact. On the other hand, in believing the fact that our mentors have good qualities, we may delight in this fact and like them. Liking someone and delighting in his or her qualities, however, may occur together with a disturbing emotion or a disturbing attitude, or they may be free of both. For example, we may delight in our newborns' being cute, but because of attachment, we cannot restrain ourselves from showing baby pictures to everyone we meet. The type of pleasure that we take in our mentors' good qualities, however, needs to be free of any disturbing emotion or attitude, just as our believing their possession of these qualities to be a fact needs to be free of both.

Asanga indicated another reason why liking someone and clearheadedly believing the facts about the person do not necessarily coincide. For example, we may meet charlatans who claim to be spiritual teachers. We may think that they are highly qualified, when in fact they are pretentious frauds. Although we may like the charlatans greatly, trust them as our teachers, and even find them inspiring, our beliefs about their qualities are false. This is not unusual. In the business world, people often are swindled by frauds whom they find likeable and trustworthy. Liking someone does not guarantee that we regard the person's qualities correctly.

Guru-meditation, then, does not ask us to believe that something false about a teacher is true. The meditation is free of both naivety and incorrect consideration. Even if we like a teacher, we need to regard his or her qualities correctly, without interpolating features or abilities that the person lacks, or exaggerating, underestimating, or denying those that he or she in fact possesses. For example, we would not imagine that our mentors have the omnipotent power to liberate us from all our problems. Although considering our mentors truly to have this ability may give us comfort and may make us feel happy, the happiness that we feel is disturbing because naivety and false hope underlie it. Disappointment and disillusionment inevitably destroy it.

Being Firmly Convinced of a Fact

Believing the fact that one's mentor has good qualities—clearheadedly, based on reason, and with aspiration—naturally leads to the principal mental activity intended for this phase of guru-meditation. The activity is to focus on the qualities of one's mentor with a firm conviction (*möpa*, *mos-pa*) that they are a fact. Let us look more deeply at this technical term. It appears as the first component of the Tibetan compound *mögü* (*mos-gus*), the main attitude or feeling needed for relating to a spiritual mentor in a healthy manner with one's thoughts.

Vasubandhu defined *möpa* as the mental action of apprehending an object of focus as having a good quality. The good quality he meant was the object being interesting enough that one would want to stay focused on it. As a general mental action, it accompanies focusing on anything and its strength may vary from strong to weak. Thus, the mental action corresponds to taking interest in an object while focusing on it.

Asanga, on the other hand, interpreted *good qualities* in the definition as meaning *to be true*. Thus, he restricted the scope of *möpa* and explained it as a mental action that occurs while believing a fact about its object of focus. Thus, Asanga explained being firmly convinced of something as a mental action that focuses on a fact that one has validly ascertained to be like this and not like that. Its function is to make one's belief so firm that others' arguments or opinions will not dissuade one. Shantideva added that firm conviction in a fact grows from long-term familiarity with the consequences that consistently follow from it.

Being firmly convinced of a fact, then, does not arise from blind faith. It requires valid cognition. In *A Supplement to the Middle Way*, Chandrakirti gave three criteria for validating the cognition of a fact.

(1) Appropriate convention must accept the fact to be what one considers it to be. Here, the mentors' features on which we focus must

be those that the Buddhist literature agrees to be requisite qualities of spiritual mentors. If businesspeople consider these features as assets for teachers to possess in order to attract large audiences—for instance, that they be entertaining and adept at telling good jokes—their convention does not validate our considering the features to be positive qualities. The convention of people interested in fame and profit is inappropriate for the situation.

(2) A mind that validly cognizes the conventional phenomenon on which one focuses must not contradict what one considers true about it. Suppose that objective people who know us well correctly see that a certain quality of one of our teachers, such as an authoritarian, feudal manner, is having a negative effect on us. Their valid perception would invalidate our considering this feature to be self-assuredness and our believing it to be a positive quality.

(3) A mind that validly cognizes the deepest way in which things exist also must not contradict what one considers true. Regarding our mentors' abilities as inherently existent in them, as if our teachers were almighty Gods, is an invalid cognition. A mind that correctly sees how things exist knows that good qualities do not exist in that way. Good qualities arise through behavioral cause and effect, by correcting deficiencies.

Appreciating the Kindness of a Mentor

After focusing on the actual good qualities of one's mentor with firm conviction that they are a fact, sutra-level guru-meditation continues with the mental action of "appreciating" (güpa, gus-pa). As the second part of the compound mögü, appreciating requires focusing with continual mindfulness on our mentors' kindness, for instance their kindness in teaching us methods for overcoming our suffering. Appreciating this kindness, according to Vasubandhu, means regarding it with a sense of values—in other words, valuing it with a sense of awe. Yeshey-gyeltsen amplified the meaning: the mental action also entails cherishing and esteeming the kindness. As in the case of believing a fact, appreciating someone's kindness is free of disturbing emotions and attitudes such as pride, attachment, or the guilt of feeling that we do not deserve the kindness.

Appreciating the kindness of one's mentor, then, contains a positive emotional aspect to it. Appreciation entails feeling from the depths of our hearts profound respect and intense love for our mentors because of their kindness. *Love*, here, does not carry its usual Buddhist meaning of wishing someone to be happy. Nor does it imply feeling affection. Rather, love for one's mentor is the heartwarming, uplifting, serenely joyous feeling one has for the person, based on admiration and respect. It neither inflates the mentor's qualities or kindness, nor perturbs the disciple's mind.

For example, in guru-meditation we may think of our mentors' good qualities of selfless generosity in helping us, purely for the sake of our becoming happier people. Firmly convinced of this fact, we focus on their selfless kindness in teaching us with this pure motivation. Gratitude, respect, and love imbue the appreciation we feel. The Tibetan texts describe the feeling as so intense that it causes the hairs to stand erect on our bodies.

Vasubandhu pointed out that appreciating someone for being kind does not mean necessarily liking or delighting in the person. We may appreciate the kindness of someone else's spiritual mentor, but not particularly like this teacher or delight in his or her company. In the case of our own mentors, however, we would both appreciate and delight in them. To like someone as a spiritual mentor implies not only believing that the person has the good qualities that he or she in fact possesses, but also believing that the person is the right mentor for us, based on reason.

Requesting Inspiration

In *Ocean of Quotations Explaining Well [Drigungpa's] "The Essence of the Mahayana Teachings,"* Ngojey- raypa, the Drigung Kagyü founder's disciple, explained the necessity of requesting inspiration. If disciples are firmly convinced of the good qualities of their mentors and appreciate deeply their kindness, they may develop these qualities to a limited extent. However, without consciously requesting inspiration always to have these qualities without decline, they lack the inspiring energy to enhance them further. Thus, as the final step in sutra-style guru-meditation, disciples need to request inspiration and try to feel that they receive it.

The mental action of making a request (*sölwadeb, gsol-ba 'debs*) involves not only fervently wishing for something from someone, but also offering the person one's total openness to receive and to hold what one wishes to obtain. Thus, many factors contribute to gaining inspiration from our spiritual mentors. First, we clearheadedly believe, based on reason, that the good qualities that we see in our mentors are a fact. Moreover, we believe, with aspiration, that we can and shall achieve these qualities ourselves, and we focus with firm conviction on this as an indisputable fact. We value, esteem, and appreciate our mentors for their kindness, and feel gratitude, love, and joy when focusing on them and on their qualities and kindness. These mental actions, plus our strong wish to be uplifted, make us open and receptive to receiving inspiration. The fact that, as a facet of our Buddha-natures, various objects can move our minds completes the complex of causes and circumstances that allow the process of inspiration to occur.

In *Actualizing through One's Guru: The Expansive Sun of Compassion*, Tsangpa-gyaray, the founder of the Drugpa Kagyü lineage, explained as a prerequisite for requesting inspiration the importance of disciples' identifying their faults and shortcomings and disparaging themselves for possessing them. Proud people never think about developing good qualities or enhancing the ones that they have. This instruction suits traditional Tibetans who, as typical mountain people, tend to be rough, independent, stubborn, and proud. They need to look at their own faults. Westerners, on the other hand, come from completely different cultural backgrounds. Most of us suffer from low self-esteem. Focusing on our shortcomings contrasted to our mentors' good qualities may simply make us feel worse about ourselves. Therefore, perhaps a prerequisite more appropriate for Westerners before requesting the inspiration to develop and enhance good qualities might be reaffirming our strong points and potentials for growth.

The Seven-Part Invocation

In *The Profound Path of Guru-Yoga*, Sakya Pandita explained that strong, extensive networks of positive potentials and deep awareness facilitate developing firm conviction in and appreciation of a spiritual mentor. Thus, to strengthen the two networks, all forms of guru-yoga take as their preliminary step the offering of a seven-part invocation. The practice becomes most effective when we invoke and take as focal objects our spiritual mentors as representing the Triple Gem.

As mentioned earlier, the seven parts of the practice are: prostrating, making offerings, admitting mistakes, rejoicing in the virtues of others, requesting teaching, beseeching the gurus not to pass away, and dedicating the positive potential built up by the practice. Prostration is a sign of respect, not a self-demeaning act of worship. Because of firm conviction in our mentors' good qualities and deep appreciation of their kindness, prostrating to our teachers is heartfelt. The respect and homage that we pay through prostration come from personal experience of a living individual. Consequently, they are more sincere than what we might feel regarding Buddhas and bodhisattvas, even if we know their enlightening biographies (*namtar, rnam-thar*). Similarly, when we make offerings to our mentors, we do so because of total love and respect for them. We may be stingy with others, but never with our own children or beloved partners. The same is true with offering generously to our spiritual mentors.

Admitting our mistakes and promising to try to avoid repeating them become more meaningful when done to our spiritual mentors rather than to anyone else. The promise makes a deeper impression on us because we are working with our mentors on our self-development. Further, when we rejoice in the virtues of others, if we focus specifically on our mentors' qualities and deeds, the happiness we feel is greater than when focusing on the virtues of someone with whom we have had no personal contact. We know of our mentors' qualities from personal experience and, because of our close relationships, we naturally take pride and rejoice.

Requesting the gurus to teach and beseeching them not to pass away take on personal relevance and become more poignant when directed toward our own mentors. Lastly, when we dedicate the positive potential built up by the practice toward gaining the good qualities that we see in our mentors, we naturally aim to become Buddhas to help others as effectively as our mentors do. Thus, our practices enhance our development of bodhichitta.

The seven-part invocation also helps us to strengthen our networks of deep awareness. When we admit our mistakes, regret them, promise to try to avoid repeating them, reaffirm the positive direction we are taking in life, and direct the positive potential we build toward counteracting our shortcomings, we start to overcome our feelings of guilt. Guilt comes from identifying oneself as inherently bad for having made mistakes and from believing that one is permanently flawed. We also reaffirm our deep awareness of the absence of impossible ways of existing and our conviction in behavioral cause and effect when we rejoice in our mentors' good qualities. We see that they have resulted from the correction of inadequacies and that with sufficient effort we may attain these qualities as well.

The more we focus on our deep conviction in our mentors' qualities and on our appreciation of their kindness, the more effective our seven-part invocation practices directed toward our mentors become. The more heartfelt our seven-part practices, the more effectively they enhance our conviction in and appreciation of our mentors. Thus, practicing the preliminary seven-part invocation and training in the main body of guru-meditation form a feedback loop. They mutually reinforce and strengthen each other.

Practicing Guru-Meditation Before Finding a Spiritual Mentor

Many spiritual seekers are not yet ready to become the disciples of spiritual mentors. Their present levels of commitment may suit working only with Buddhism professors, Dharma instructors, or meditation or ritual trainers. Even if they are ready to commit themselves to the Buddhist path and to spiritual mentors, they may not yet have found properly qualified mentors. Alternatively, the spiritual teachers available to them may be properly qualified and may even have shown them great kindness. Yet, none seem right to be their mentors. They feel they can relate to them only as their Buddhism professors. Nevertheless, the Kadam style of guru-meditation may still help such seekers to gain inspiration from these teachers at the present stages of their spiritual paths.

Unless our spiritual teachers are total charlatans or complete scoundrels, all of them have at least some good qualities and exhibit at least some level of kindness. Our Buddhism professors, Dharma instructors, or meditation or ritual trainers may lack the qualities of great spiritual mentors. Still, they have some knowledge of the Dharma, some insight from applying the Dharma to life, or some technical expertise in the practice. Our teachers are kind to instruct us, even if their motivations contain the wish to earn a living. If we correctly discern and acknowledge whatever qualities and levels of kindness that our professors, instructors, or trainers in fact possess, we may derive inspiration, through guru-meditation, by focusing on them with conviction and appreciation.

Similarly, we may gain inspiration by reading the enlightening biographies of previous great masters and then taking these figures as focal objects for guru-meditation. Even when we have mentors, focusing on them in the form of the founding figures of their lineage helps us to gain even more inspiration. Practitioners of Karma Kagyü or Gelug guru-yoga, for example, regularly use the form of Gampopa or Tsongkapa. Through such methods, we understand better the causal chain that has accounted for successive mentors gaining their qualities over the generations. With appropriate effort, we may forge the next link in the chain.

Meditating in these ways is far more constructive than bemoaning the fact that we have not yet found a spiritual mentor. In fact, the inspiration we gain may help us to find and to recognize appropriate mentors who suit our disposition and needs. In Buddhist terminology, guru-meditation practiced before finding a mentor "builds up merit." By making us more positive-minded, it strengthens our positive potentials for gaining happiness and constructive growth.

~9
Relating to a Spiritual Mentor with Actions

Translating Trust and Respect for a Mentor into Actions

THE MORE CONVINCED we are of our mentors' good qualities, the more confidently we trust them and their ability to guide us correctly. Similarly, the more deeply we appreciate our mentors' kindness, the more respect we develop for them. A healthy relationship with a spiritual mentor grows from the bedrock of trust and respect.

As the relationship grows, trust and respect naturally translate into actions. Asanga enumerated the most common forms in *Filigree of Mahayana Sutras*. Because disciples firmly believe in the good qualities of their mentors and sincerely appreciate their beneficial work, they are delighted to support it and to give whatever help they can. They automatically wish to show their respect in ways that feel appropriate. The most meaningful way, however, for disciples to demonstrate trust and respect is to follow the advice of their mentors, especially concerning their spiritual practices.

Supporting the Work of a Mentor

According to the classical presentation, the first way of relating to a spiritual mentor through actions is to offer material support. Many texts explicitly say that disciples need to give their mentors their wealth, their families, and even their lives. Without proper explanation, the instruction seems to imply that we need to give our mentors all our money and possessions and to subjugate our families and ourselves as slaves, as members of cults are often pressured to do. Even taking this point to mean that we need to give our mentors lavish gifts leaves a bad taste in most Westerners' mouths.

The intention here is that supporting a mentor's work financially and materially is a natural outgrowth and practical expression of appreciation, respect, confidence, and trust in the person and in his or her efforts. A show of support, then, is sincere and healthy only when made on a voluntary basis. Ngojey-raypa confirmed this fact when he stressed that supporting a mentor's work needs to be free of pretense and hypocrisy. A pretentious offering to win a mentor's favor or to impress other people is not a sincere show of appreciation or respect. Neither is a hypocritical offering made out of guilt or group pressure, but lacking sincere feelings behind it.

Moreover, offering a mentor our families and loved ones does not mean to sell them into bondage. Rather, it may mean, for example, to welcome our mentors into our homes to share the warmth, humor, and hospitality of the family, provided our mentors are interested and our families are so inclined. Inviting a teacher at fitting times, such as holiday seasons, and in appropriate measure is a meaningful way to offer a mentor basic support as a human being. We open the doors to our homes and our families based on appreciation and trust of the teachers and on recognition that they may enjoy relaxing in a warm, human atmosphere.

The Fifth Dalai Lama explained these points clearly. He wrote that although standard Buddhist sources explain that supporting their mentors with their wealth and loved ones strengthens disciples' network of positive potentials, such practices require sensitive, honest thought. Because of family and other responsibilities, the disciples' most valued possessions may be difficult to give or inappropriate to share. Offering them as a way to further their spiritual paths is not something to do without hesitation. Nor is it advice that they may totally discard. If circumstances do not allow them to offer their mentors these types of support, they need to explain this to their teachers and excuse themselves. More important at such times is sincerely aspiring to be able to support their mentors and their work.

The Fifth Dalai Lama continued that if disciples are able to offer some support, they need to consider the appropriate place, time, and measure. In other words, there is no need to apply to present circumstances the examples of the inconceivable acts of selfless giving practiced by extraordinary disciples of the past to exceptional mentors. The classical texts have cited extreme examples to give inspiration, and not to give impossible tasks beyond people's present capacities.

Offering material and financial support to talented, qualified persons whose efforts we appreciate accords with common custom. Universities, for example, offer scholarships to deserving students and people donate to worthy charities. Offering our mentors support, then, has a shared meaning that applies to all levels of teachers. Especially if our spiritual teachers live by donations alone, we need to provide adequate financial and material support if we wish them to continue teaching. Voluntarily supporting their efforts is a healthy expression of appreciation and trust.

Helping a Mentor

The second way to relate in a healthy manner to a spiritual mentor with actions is to offer help and to show respect. We may help our mentors, for example, by making travel arrangements, driving them to appointments, writing letters, or transcribing and editing their teachings. We may show respect by coming on time and by completing as quickly as possible any work for them that we have said that we would do. Moreover, we may show respect by teaching our mentors about our cultures, if they are from different lands, and by explaining any problems we may be having at our Dharma centers. In this way, we help our mentors to understand and to help us further.

Nyenkur (*bsnyen-bkur*), the Tibetan compound translated here as *helping and showing respect* is often rendered into English as *serving and honoring*. The latter choice of terms implies a hierarchical feudal relationship. Consequently, many Western seekers feel that the relation with a spiritual mentor requires them to be servile, which some people may find appealing, perhaps due to low self-esteem. Others find the idea of servitude and subservience repugnant. Let us explore the issue.

Granted that traditional Tibetan society was hierarchical and feudal, many people lacking firsthand experience of such a societal structure judge all examples of it as repressive and exploitative. Their judgments come from preconceptions and, although in some cases their evaluations may be correct, they are often unfair. When people live in harsh and difficult environments without modern conveniences, a division of labor within an extended household is the only realistic way to cope. In an optimal situation, the head of a household provides protection, security, and a wise strategy for dealing with problems and danger, while attendants take care of everyone's physical needs. All contribute to the overall welfare of the household and all sides treat each other with love and respect. As a social system, this can work harmoniously. I personally have witnessed this possibility in my twenty-nine years of living with traditional Tibetans in India.

Traditional Tibetan teachers, particularly tantric masters, have both attendants and apprentices. Although not all attendants are also apprentices, one person may play both roles. Rigid feudal societies may be rightly faulted when they do not allow for social mobility. Nevertheless, when the feudal relationship is between a master and an apprentice, then service and mobility are both implicit. An apprentice eventually becomes a master. In the case of the household of a monastic tulku, when one incarnation passes away, the lama's senior attendant becomes the head of the household and takes charge of finding and raising the next incarnation. Most Tibetan monastic societies, then, allow a certain amount of social mobility. They are not ideal by modern Western standards, but they are also not dens of oppression.

In Western egalitarian societies, we call an attendant an assistant, a secretary, or a housekeeper and we pay the person a salary. Instead of apprentices, we have volunteer interns and persons doing on-the-job training. One major difference, however, between these roles and those in traditional Tibetan societies is that Tibetan attendants and apprentices usually join a teacher's household when they are children. In most cases, the youngsters do not take these positions voluntarily; nevertheless, no one forces them into these roles against their wills. Living with a teacher, after all, is not only an honor, but also one of the best ways to receive an education. In addition, the new household provides a substitute family and material support. Moreover, Tibetan children do far more housework and chores in their own families than any modern Western child does. They do no more work in their teachers' homes than they would do in their parents' houses.

The dwindling number of elders left who grew up in traditional Tibet, as well as the influence of modern education and social norms, is leading to the rapid breakdown of the system of attendants among Tibetans in exile. Although some children who join the monasteries and nunneries still live with and serve their teachers, most live in dormitories, much like at boarding schools. No one has to fetch water from a stream or to forage for fuel. Consequently, most of the younger generation of teachers, especially when living outside their monastic institutions or lay homes, prefer to take care of themselves without attendants.

If the situation is changing among modern Tibetans with one another, it certainly needs to change between Western seekers and Tibetan or Western teachers. This does not mean that modern students need not help their teachers with menial tasks or invite them to a meal. Of course they need to do these things. Especially if the teacher is extremely busy with teaching, advising students, writing, performing ceremonies, and so on, it is totally appropriate for some of the students to cook and to help with the housework to save the teacher's valuable time. If, on the other hand, the teacher has ample free time, catering to the person when modern conveniences are readily available spoils the teacher and may lead to misuse of the students' free time. A "middle path" is needed, taking into consideration, of course, the teacher's age and health, and the students' conditions.

Helping our spiritual teachers, when done according to a middle path, is a healthy way to express belief in their qualities and appreciation of their kindness. It accords with the common customs of society. People naturally help those whom they respect and whose kindness they appreciate. Therefore, helping a spiritual teacher qualifies as a piece of advice with a shared meaning that applies to all levels of teachers, from Buddhism professors to tantric masters.

Showing Respect

The second half of the compound *nyenkur* means to show respect with words and behavior. In traditional Buddhist cultures, disciples showed respect for their spiritual mentors by prostrating before them and circumambulating their houses. Such ways of showing respect are either unnatural or uncomfortable for most Western spiritual seekers. Because they do not accord with common customs, prostration and circumambulating do not qualify as shared practices applicable to all societies.

The essential point here is not the form in which we show respect, but rather the fact that we show it in some form or another. For example, we may stand when our mentors enter the room to teach: we do not need to prostrate, bow, or curtsy to them. Depending upon the individuals involved and the situation and company in which we find ourselves, formal obeisance may be absurd, inappropriate, or awkward.

Certain forms of courtesy, however, are universal. Examples include dressing properly and washing before going to see someone, opening the door for a person, showing someone to his or her seat, offering something appropriate to drink, serving it in a clean glass or cup, keeping quiet and paying attention when someone speaks to us, not interrupting, answering politely, and so on. Courteous behavior and polite words are appropriate with all levels of spiritual teachers and at all stages of the path.

Showing respect, however, needs to be sincere. According to *Difficult Points Concerning Helping and Showing Respect to a Guru*, a pretentious student with a coarse worldly mind may physically help a spiritual mentor in many ways. The person may even show outward forms of politeness. However, unless someone deeply and sincerely respects a mentor, his or her polite actions do not actually show respect.

Taking the Advice of a Mentor

All the classical texts agree that taking the advice of one's mentor is the most meaningful demonstration of one's trust and respect. It constitutes the most significant way of relating in a healthy manner to a spiritual mentor. Many disciples, however, misunderstand the intention of the teaching.

In a healthy relationship, we seek our mentors' advice only concerning important matters that would affect our spiritual development and practice. Asking our mentors to make all our decisions, especially concerning trivial matters, indicates a lack of maturity. Thus, Serkong Rinpochey admonished against asking our mentors open questions, such as "What should I do with my life?" Except for seeking open advice about which practices to focus on next, mature disciples simply inform their mentors of personal plans and inquire if the teachers foresee any problems with them.

A healthy relationship with a spiritual mentor, then, does not include an abrogation of responsibility for one's life. It does not engender psychological dependency, nor does it entail following a mentor's advice unquestioningly like a soldier obeying a command. Buddhism never calls for submissive obedience, even of a monk to his abbot or a nun to her abbess. After all, one of the major qualifications of a disciple that Aryadeva specified is common sense. This means having both the ability to discriminate and freedom of choice.

Gampopa corroborated Aryadeva's point in *A Precious Garland for the Supreme Path*. There, as one of the ten necessities for disciples to be able to follow the path, the Kagyü master listed enacting the advice of their mentors ardently, with discriminating awareness and belief. Discriminating awareness includes not only using common sense concerning how to apply the advice. It also encompasses discriminating between what they are capable of doing and what is beyond their present means, and differentiating between counsel that accords with Buddha's teachings and advice that contradicts the Dharma.

Ashvaghosha made this point perfectly clear, specifically regarding tantric masters. If tantric masters ask their disciples to do something unreasonable that they are incapable of doing, the disciples need to explain politely why they cannot comply. This shared teaching applies to all levels of spiritual teachers. The Indian and Tibetan commentaries on this point provide the scriptural basis and fill out the meaning. If mentors ask their disciples to do something that accords with Buddha's teachings, but which is too much for them to bear, or which they cannot do despite trying their best, the disciples need to excuse themselves politely. If, on the other hand, their mentors press them to do something that contradicts the Dharma—specifically, anything that requires breaking one of their vows—disciples must keep their equanimity and not comply. As Gampopa put it, one needs to hold one's moral ground and not lose one's footing. However, in such cases as well, disciples need to remain polite and explain to their mentors their reasons for turning down the request. Their mentors, after all, may merely be testing their moral resolve, as was the case in one of Buddha's previous lives when his mentor asked him to steal.

Recently, several cases surfaced in which seemingly reputable spiritual teachers coerced their students into having sexual relations with them. Many Westerners became deeply confused. They read in texts, such as Kongtrül's *Lamp for the Definitive Meaning*, that proper disciples must obey whatever their tantric masters tell them to do, as Naropa did when Tilopa told him to jump off a cliff. Tilopa, however, had the power to eat a live fish, snap his fingers over the bones, and bring it back to life. Moreover, Naropa was an ex-abbot of Nalanda Monastery and one of the most learned practitioners of his day. If our teachers and we are at these levels, that is one matter. When we are not, however, then Buddha was very clear that advice for higher level bodhisattvas does not pertain to practitioners of lower levels of attainment.

Honoring the Authority of a Mentor

When Buddhism speaks of a mentor as having authority, this does not mean that a mentor has the authoritarian power and right to command disciples and demand obedience. Instead, here authority implies that a mentor possesses recognized knowledge, expertise, and other good qualities. A mentor's authority derives from authenticity rather than from power, coercion, self-righteousness, or God's will.

Because disciples clearheadedly believe, based on reason, that their mentors' qualifications are authentic, they trust and respect their mentors as authoritative sources of advice concerning spiritual matters. Free of naivety about the limits of their mentors' competence, they do not inflate them into omniscient gods to be obeyed without question. Such naivety is not the intention of the advanced instruction to regard one's mentors as one would a Buddha.

Further, if disciples have close relationships with more than one spiritual mentor, they do not ask each mentor advice concerning the same matter. Asking more than one mentor implies a lack of confidence in the authority of any of them, as if the disciples are waiting until they receive the advice that they want to hear. With discriminating awareness, disciples need to choose the appropriate mentor for asking about a specific matter. Only a fool would ask a lawyer for medical advice.

Asking advice about our spiritual practices refers to the time after we have become disciples of spiritual mentors. Before we have reached that level of commitment, when we are simply students of Buddhism, Dharma pupils, or meditation or ritual trainees, we would not seek such advice. More appropriately, we might ask our Buddhism professors questions about the teachings, our Dharma instructors queries about how a teaching pertains to life, or our meditation or ritual trainers technical questions regarding posture. Such cases also require discriminating awareness. We would only accept their answers if they accord with the Dharma.

Serkong Rinpochey warned that even the most learned masters sometimes make a slip of the tongue, translators frequently make mistakes, and students often mishear what is said. If anything one hears seems odd, one needs to check it with the standard Buddhist texts. As when receiving advice that does not accord with the teachings, one needs to explain the discrepancy politely to one's teacher and ask for clarification.

Often people wish to practice Buddhism as part of a committed spiritual path to self-transformation, but have not yet found spiritual mentors. In such cases, they have no choice but to seek advice from their Dharma instructors or meditation trainers concerning how to begin practicing on more serious levels. Any advice they receive, however, is only provisional until they find and establish a relation with a qualified spiritual mentor.

Emulating a Mentor

Peltrül explained that before committing themselves to a spiritual mentor, potential disciples need to examine the person thoroughly. Once they have become convinced of the person's qualifications and authority and they have become disciples, they need scrupulously to follow the teacher's advice regarding their practices. In the end, they need to emulate the mentor's realizations and behavior.

Some people take this instruction literally to mean that they need to do everything exactly as their mentors do. The instruction, however, does not pertain to personal matters or to political or cultural opinions. If our mentors are Tibetan and we are Western, we do not need to adopt Tibetan customs and drink butter tea. Nor do we need to regard women in a traditional patriarchal fashion. Also, we do not need to receive every empowerment and study every text that our mentors have, nor train in every meditation that they practice. The instruction to emulate one's mentor means to gain authentic realizations and then to behave accordingly. One needs great care in this matter. As Peltrül's disciple Ngawang Pelzang explained in *Lecture Notes on "Personal Instructions from My Totally Excellent Guru,"* without first acquiring the level of realization of one's mentor, to try to emulate his or her behavior is both pretentious and dangerous.

Rectifying the Term Devotion

The Tibetan term *tenpa* (*bsten-pa*) sums up a healthy relationship with a spiritual mentor. The usual English translation is *devotion*, hence the term *guru-devotion*. Devotion, however, carries a misleading connotation. It conjures the picture of a devoted servant or a devotee of a god or a cult. It also implies a combination of emotional fervor and mindless obedience.

Tenpa, however, is a verb that means to come close to someone in one's thoughts and actions, and to rely on the person with confidence. It does not imply, however, coming close to a charlatan or a scoundrel, or relying neurotically on someone, even if the person is competent to help us. Thus, I have translated it here as *building a healthy relationship*. One builds such a relationship not only with a spiritual teacher, but also with a doctor.

According to *Difficult Points Concerning Helping and Showing Respect to a Guru, tenpa* also connotes pleasing one's guru in the proper manner. The proper or healthy way for disciples to please their mentors is to come close in the sense of modeling themselves after their mentors and following their advice to transform their minds and help all beings. It does not mean trying to ingratiate themselves with lavish gifts or practicing the Dharma only to please their teachers. As Buddha explained in *Special Verses Grouped by Topic*: "One may be close to a spiritual mentor for one's entire life. Yet, if one does not learn the Dharma taught by him or her, [one's experience of the teachings] is [as meager] as the taste of stew on a ladle."

~10

Overcoming Emotional Blocks in Developing Trust, Appreciation, or Respect

Applying Sutra-Level Guru-Meditation
to a Faulty or Abusive Teacher

HIS HOLINESS the Fourteenth Dalai Lama had two regents during his minority. They taught him extensively and conferred upon him numerous tantric empowerments. They also engaged in a power struggle and had their followers take up arms against each other. His Holiness has explained that on his meditation seat, he had no problem in focusing with conviction on the good qualities that each regent in fact had. He also had no problem in appreciating the kindness that each had shown him. Yet, when he arose from his meditation seat, he publicly denounced his regents' political intrigues. His Holiness has described that he felt no contradiction in doing this and did not find it emotionally upsetting.

Some Westerners face similar situations with several of their spiritual teachers. For example, some famous masters disagree strongly about the status of a controversial Dharma-protector and the consequences of propitiating it. They abuse their positions as spiritual mentors and, with threats of hell, forbid their disciples to have anything to do with teachers on the opposite side of the dispute. Other famous masters disagree violently over the identification of the incarnation of the highest lamas of their lineage. A few have even taken police action against each other's claims over inherited property. Sutra-level guru-meditation, as His Holiness the Dalai Lama has experienced, may help traumatized Western Dharma students to deal with these difficult, perplexing circumstances. It may also help those who have been sexually abused by their spiritual teachers or exploited by them for power or money. It may apply as well to disciples of abusive teachers, who have not been personally maligned, but have been devastated by learning of the actions of their teachers.

Many disciples find such situations too difficult to handle, especially if they have already built disciple-mentor relationships with both parties in a dispute. *The Abbreviated Kalachakra Tantra* advised that if disciples find too many objective faults in their spiritual mentors and they can no longer support close relationships with them, they need not continue studying with these teachers. They may keep a respectful distance, even if they have received highest tantra empowerments from them.

Whether or not we keep a distance from disturbing or abusive teachers, it is important to try to stop dwelling on their perplexing behavior or faults. Obsession with such matters only deepens confusion and spiritual despair. We must begin a healing process. Eventually, without denying the mentors' problematic sides, we may still be able to benefit from thinking about their good qualities and kindness.

Reviewing a Teacher's Faults and Mistakes

Hurt and confused disciples frequently experience emotional blocks in focusing on the good qualities of contentious or abusive mentors. With the passage of time and the help of support groups, they may overcome the manifest emotional fallout from their traumatic experiences. The spiritual damage, however, is often quite deep. Denial or repression of the problem solves very little. For thorough healing, spiritually wounded disciples need eventually to be able to view their mentors' faults and mistakes clearheadedly, free of naivety, anger, or recrimination.

The Fifth Dalai Lama added a preliminary step to the Kadam style of guru-meditation that addresses the problem. Before discerning and focusing on the good qualities and kindness of their mentors, disciples need to bring to conscious awareness the teachers' shortcomings and work on their view of them. The process resembles a surgical procedure. Cleaning an infected wound requires cutting it open, even though lancing the abscess and exposing the infection temporarily increases the pain. In the case of a festering spiritual wound, the hidden infection may be denial or suppressed rage. To purge the infection requires reopening the wound and bringing to the surface what festers beneath, even though the procedure temporarily may bring more emotional pain. The operation must wait, of course, until the injured person has sufficiently recovered from the initial trauma and has regained the emotional strength to attack the problem.

Creating a Protected Mental Space for Addressing Spiritual Wounds

To lance and heal a spiritual wound requires not only that the injured person has sufficient emotional strength. The operation also requires the support of a conducive, protected space; otherwise, the procedure itself may be too traumatic. In guru-meditation, the preliminary practices provide the appropriate mental space to contain and support the sometimes-painful meditation procedure of reexamining our mentors' faults and the way in which we have been viewing them. The preliminaries create the space through reaffirming our safe direction in life, renewing our bodhichitta motivation, and practicing the seven-part invocation directed toward the Buddhas and past and present great masters.

Focusing on the ability of the Triple Gem to provide a safe direction in life—and especially focusing on the Buddhist approach of working on ourselves to overcome the emotional problems we face—helps to reestablish a spiritual anchor. We need such an anchor when we have lost belief in the spiritual path and are drifting in life with no clear direction. Reaffirming the necessity to heal our emotional wounds in order to focus our attention more fully on others in need of assistance helps to revitalize our efforts along the path.

Focusing objectively on the good qualities of the Buddhas and of past and present great masters and showing respect through prostrating and making offerings help to reaffirm our sense of values. Without a sense of values, we will be unable to discern any good points in an abusive teacher. Openly admitting the disappointment and pain that we feel over our mentors' mistakes or failures helps to relieve some of the emotional tightness that may be preventing our further progress. Our mentors may not have lived up to the measure of the Buddhas. However, rejoicing in the good qualities and deeds of past and present great masters helps us to overcome the despondent thought that qualified mentors do not exist.

Requesting other great masters to teach and not to pass away helps to open our hearts and minds to continuing on the spiritual path. Dedicating to the healing process the positive frame of mind and potential built up by the preliminary practice helps us to complete our construction of a protected, conducive mental space. When practiced with sincere feeling, the preliminaries for guru-meditation help to produce the emotional stability needed to reexamine objectively our mentors' faults.

Examining the Appearances That the Mind Creates

The surgical procedure of the meditation begins with bringing to conscious awareness the flaws of our mentors. Once these are exposed, we need to examine clearheadedly whether our teachers presently continue to have these shortcomings or to make these mistakes. We may be dwelling on past history. To heal, for example, the wounds of abuse, we need to acknowledge whether or not an abusive teacher has admitted and repented previous mistakes and reformed his or her behavior. Such acknowledgement does not excuse the teacher's previous misconduct, but an honest appraisal of the situation requires dealing with all the facts.

Moreover, examining the faults of our mentors requires focusing on shortcomings that they actually have. We need to sort out defects that we may be projecting because of our disturbing emotions or attitudes. Such projection often happens with problems less severe than spiritual abuse. For example, jealousy of other disciples may cause us to imagine that our mentors are ignoring us because of lack of concern for our welfare. In fact, however, our teachers may simply be attending to the needs of all the disciples, without any favorites.

Moreover, we need to discriminate between actual faults, such as unethical behavior, and seeming faults that merely reflect a different way of doing things than we would prefer. People often confuse the two and think that anything they dislike about a teacher is an objective fault with negative consequences. A mentor's style may be inconvenient or inefficient; this may annoy us at times and cause us to lose sight of his or her good qualities. Yet, insistence that a teacher's manner totally match our own dispositions reveals an unrealistic expectation.

Further, the faults that we focus on need to be relevant to our mentors' ability to guide us on the spiritual path. The fact that our mentors may lack the competence to teach us everything required for becoming a Buddha does not negate their abilities to benefit us at our present stages. Confirming the accuracy, currentness, and importance of the faults that we discern in our mentors enables us to sort out and dismiss distortions and outdated or irrelevant aspects.

Next, we need to examine the process whereby our minds produce and project deceptive appearances. Karmic obstacles from our previous experiences and our psychological profile may cause our minds to make flaws appear in our teachers that accord with our karma, such as that they care nothing for us. Our lack of awareness of behavioral cause and effect and of reality causes us to believe that these appearances are accurate. Moreover, whether or not the appearances are accurate, the deeply engrained habit of viewing things without awareness of reality causes our minds to make the faults we discern appear to exist in ways that do not accord with reality. Our minds make them appear to exist as permanent flaws, inherent and ultimately findable within our spiritual mentors and making them exist as deficient or terrible people, independently of causes, circumstances, and a conceptual framework. Lack of awareness then causes us to believe that our mentors truly exist in these impossible ways.

Guru-meditation does not ask us to deny the accurate conventional appearances of what our mentors' faults or mistakes may be. Our mentors may in fact be too busy to see us whenever we want, or may in fact be abusive. What the meditation asks us to do instead is to refute and dismiss our confused belief in the deeply deceptive appearances of how our mentors have come to exist with the particular faults that they actually have. We need to understand the logical absurdity and thus the impossibility that our mentors have particular flaws by virtue of some permanent, findable, internal defects that by their own powers, independently of anything else, make them inherently tainted people.

Such an understanding allows us to see how our mentors' faults and mistakes have arisen dependently on an enormous number of complex factors. This understanding allows the healing process to occur. It also enables us to ignore, for the moment, the faults that our mentors in fact may have, to focus instead in guru-meditation on their good qualities, and even to derive inspiration from them. We may do this whether we continue to study with them or we decide to keep a distance. If we keep a distance from our mentors, our understanding of how their faults and mistakes have arisen enables us to make that distance a respectful one, and one with which we are at peace.

The Analogy with Contextual Therapy for Victims of Abuse

In *Invisible Loyalties*, Boszormenyi-Nagy, the Hungarian founder of contextual therapy, suggested sensitive ways to heal the psychological injuries of victims of physical or sexual abuse. The methods he outlined parallel in many ways the approach taken in sutra-level guru-meditation. His analysis may augment our understanding of how the meditation may help to heal the wounds of students deeply hurt by abusive spiritual teachers.

Boszormenyi-Nagy explained that the first step in the healing process is for abuse victims to acknowledge their pain and that they are entitled to feel bad. They have in fact been violated, and for them to deny the truth will only add fuel to suppressed anger or feelings of guilt. Similarly, if we personally have been abused by our spiritual mentors or have learned from reliable sources that our teachers have maligned other students, we too need first to acknowledge our pain and our "entitlement" to feel bad. We were in fact wronged or let down. Guru-meditation may include this acknowledgement as part of its preliminary practice of openly admitting one's difficulties.

Contextual therapy calls next for trying to understand the context in which the abuse arose from both the perpetrators' and the victims' sides. This does not mean that one should rationalize the faulty behavior or the mistakes in judgment on the perpetrators' parts, nor that the victims should take on the entire blame and feel guilty. Rather, abuse victims need to see clearly how the situations arose dependently on causes and conditions. The process parallels the conclusion reached in guru-meditation by deconstructing the deceptive appearances that one's mind projects concerning how one's mentor exists with his or her faults.

Victims of abuse also need to acknowledge that they are entitled to a better deal in life. In Buddhist terms, entitlement to happiness comes by virtue of having an innate network of positive potentials as part of Buddha-nature. Nevertheless, abuse victims need to earn that happiness by acting decently. For example, war refugees are entitled, simply as human beings, to homes and a livelihood in host countries. Yet, they need to earn good treatment by following the law and leading upright lives. Similarly, abused spiritual seekers need to reaffirm the necessity of following the guidelines of the Dharma.

Many victims of abuse have negative self-images. Either consciously or unconsciously, they blame themselves for what happened and may feel that they do not deserve better treatment. Even if they feel entitled to better treatment, they may resign themselves to further abuse. A similar pattern often emerges with victims who are told and feel that they are special. During the abusive relationship, an inflated sense of self-worth make them unaware of being victims of abuse. They often deny the abuse and defend the perpetrators, even if confronted with the facts. Then, when their abusers find other "chosen ones," they feel humiliated, experience sudden deflation of their self-images, and become deeply hurt or completely outraged.

In all such cases, the victims need to dispel their identification with negative self-images in order to gain or regain emotional stability. The same guideline applies to similar types of abused seekers for gaining or regaining healthy relationships with spiritual teachers. So long as they identify with being unworthy, they continue to open themselves to possible manipulation and abuse.

The next step in the healing process in contextual therapy is determining clearheadedly the legacy that the abuse victims may take from their relationships with the perpetrators. Is it just outrage, bitterness, and an inability to trust anyone else in the future, or can the victims take something more positive from them? The therapy encourages focusing on the positive factors gained from the relationship and discourages dwelling on the negative ones. Such constructive focus enables the victims to be loyal to the positive aspects and to incorporate them into their lives. In the case of incest, the process enables the victims to take the best from past generations and to pass it on to their offspring.

The process also helps the victims to avoid acting with misplaced unconscious loyalty to the abusers' negative aspects. Such loyalties may result in the victims' being inconsiderate of themselves and, due to feelings of guilt, denying their rights to have healthy relationships—conforming to the subtle message conveyed by abuse. Consequently, victims of abuse frequently experience mental blocks about emotional and physical intimacy, and may not feel entitled to get married or to become parents.

In guru-meditation, abused disciples can likewise focus on their abusive mentors' good qualities and stop dwelling on the teachers' improper behavior. Acknowledging the positive things that they in fact have gained in the disciple-mentor relationships with these teachers enables the disciples to repay the teachers as best as they can, in conscious, positive manners, by carrying on their spiritual traditions and trying to pass them on to others. In doing so, they "earn entitlement" to get on with their spiritual lives and to build healthy relationships with other teachers. If they only feel bitter or outraged, whether or not such feelings are accompanied with unconscious guilt due to a belief that the abuse occurred because of their personal shortcomings and faults—"I was not a good enough disciple"—they deprive themselves of feeling entitled to another trusting relationship. Dharma students traumatized by abusive teachers often become so disillusioned that they are unable to continue on the spiritual path.

Teachers Involved in Controversy

The approach used in Kadam guru-meditation, supplemented with the insights of contextual therapy, may also be helpful in dealing with confusion over teachers involved with spiritual controversy, but free of abusive behavior about it. Suppose, for example, our spiritual mentors do not command us, upon threat of hell, to uphold or to abandon a specific Dharma-protector or a specific candidate as the incarnation of a great master, and thus do not abuse us in this way. Still, our mentors may privately practice or shun the protector, or may simply point out the advantages and disadvantages of doing or not doing the practice, while leaving the choice up to us. The same may be the case with respect to supporting one or another tulku candidate. We may have a different opinion from our mentors and agree with the other side, yet feel that in so doing, we are being disloyal. A healthy approach to the relationship would be to focus on and be loyal to the positive qualities of our mentors by adopting them in our behavior, while not accepting and not dwelling on the aspects with which we disagree.

The same advice holds true if we have already become disciples of teachers from both sides of a controversy. Both teachers may be on power trips and insist that we denounce and abandon the other side, or both may leave the decision up to us, or one may be one way and the other may be the other. It hardly matters. As His Holiness the Fourteenth Dalai Lama advised, people need to make up their own minds

based on their limited powers of logic and reason and on their understanding of the scriptural sources. If spiritual seekers base their decisions on seeing both teachers as Buddhas or on reasoning merely from
the ultimate viewpoint of voidness or the clear light mind, they will be
unable to decide anything. Alternatively, they may need to decide that
the issue is unimportant or irrelevant to their levels of spiritual practice
and, with equanimity, maintain a distance from the controversy.

Whether we decide to keep a distance from one or both teachers, or
to keep a relationship with each, we still may benefit from the Kadam
style of sutra-level guru-meditation. We need to focus on the good
qualities of each of our teachers and avoid dwelling on their destructive or enigmatic actions.

Overcoming Emotional Blocks in Appreciating Kindness

In *A Lamp for the Definitive Meaning,* Kongtrül correlated an essential
element of bodhichitta meditation with guru-meditation. One method
for disciples to develop bodhichitta entails recognizing all beings as
having been their mothers in some previous life and focusing on their
mothers' kindness. Similarly, guru-meditation requires focusing on
their mentors' kindness.

Many Westerners, however, have difficulty focusing on the kindness of their mothers. Unable to find the goodness and kindness in
their mothers, most cannot find any goodness in themselves either.
Although they may be desperate for love and kindness, their mental blocks often prevent them from recognizing and appreciating the
kindness of others, for instance their spiritual mentors. No matter how
much kindness they receive, it is never enough.

One of the reasons for being unable to acknowledge our mothers'
kindness may be that they fail to live up to our models of ideal parents.
Similarly, when our spiritual mentors have shortcomings and do not
live up to our models of ideal teachers, we may also have difficulty
recognizing their kindness. Like children yearning for ideal love, we
feel cheated if our mentors fail to meet our expectations.

Our emotional blocks in appreciating the kindness of our less-than-
perfect mentors may derive from faults in mental labeling. Madhyamaka philosophy explains that words and concepts of knowable
general phenomena, such as kindness, are mental labels that refer to
a broad set of specific examples. If, however, we have fixed ideas of

what kindness is, then we grasp at *kindness* to refer to only one specific form of kindness. Our fixed ideas make us unable to include other forms of considerate behavior in our concepts of kindness. Thus, we are unable to recognize and label those forms of behavior as kind and, consequently, we do not appreciate them.

For example, we may feel that being kind means to show warmth and physical affection. Our mothers may not be particularly warm, for a variety of reasons. They rarely cuddled us when we were children. Perhaps they showed affection in other ways, such as by taking meticulous care of our physical needs. Our mothers' behavior, however, did not match our fixed ideas of kindness. Because we hold only our limited ideas of kindness as the defining characteristics of an ideally kind mother, we are unable to label our mothers' physical care of us as kind.

A similar fault in mental labeling may be blocking us from recognizing and appreciating our mentors' kindness. We may have mental pictures of an ideal spiritual mentor—one who spends all his or her time exclusively on us, with loving warmth and affection like our ideal mothers or fathers would. Our spiritual mentors, however, may have many other disciples besides us and may not be particularly demonstrative of physical warmth. Moreover, in a society that is particularly hypersensitive to possible sexual harassment, our mentors may feel it better to be reserved in showing affection. They show kindness in taking meticulous care of our spiritual needs, teaching us with consistent dedication and enthusiasm despite our being less-than-perfect students. To recognize and appreciate our mentors' kindness and to gain inspiration from it in guru-meditation, we need to loosen and expand our restricted concepts of kindness. Correct mental labeling is another requirement for a proper rectification of terms.

Overcoming Emotional Blocks in Showing Respect

Many Westerners, particularly from the younger generations, have difficulty showing respect. They do not respect anything or anyone, perhaps because they feel that nothing or no one is trustworthy. Consistently, others have let them down or betrayed their trust, often starting with working parents who were forced by the pressures of modern life to leave them in childcare with strangers when they were toddlers. They see promises and treaties frequently broken, and political and spiritual leaders often involved in scandals. They feel that anyone who trusts someone in a position of leadership, or who trusts the words of such a person, is hopelessly idealistic and naive. Often, they lack respect even for themselves. Their unconscious feelings manifest in the attitude of: "Anything is OK; it doesn't matter."

Consider the example of victims of child abuse. People whose parents have abused them as children usually lack any confidence in behavioral cause and effect. No matter how they acted, their parents got drunk and abused them. The treatment they received did not follow from their behavior. Even if they behaved well, they were violated or beaten. Such victims need to have their confidence restored in the proper workings of behavioral cause and effect.

Behavioral cause and effect, or karma, works in an extremely complex, nonlinear manner. It is not like kicking a ball and the ball goes flying. The ways in which parents respond to situations or events are not determined simply by those events, but by their personality profiles and personal histories, other happenings of the day, economic pressures, and so on. Thus, children's own behavior is not the sole determining cause of their receiving abuse from parents. Often, their conduct simply provides circumstances that trigger deeper psychological mechanisms in their parents. To gain self-respect, abused children need to gain a broader understanding of the manifold factors that have contributed to their parents' abusive treatment.

Guru-meditation similarly asks us to understand the wide scope of causes and circumstances that have brought about not only our mentors' achievements, but also their failures. The more we understand behavioral cause and effect, the more clearheaded we become about our mentors. Clearheaded belief and trust in a mentor are free of naivety.

To expect an abusive parent to act as would an ideal parent is simply naive. An abused child is correct in not trusting the person to be perfect. Similarly, if we idealize our mentors, we may blind ourselves to the workings of behavioral cause and effect that contribute to their actual conduct. When our mentors fail to live up to our ideals, we no longer trust them and find great difficulty in showing respect. If, however, we understand at least the principles of behavioral cause and effect, we trust that our mentors will behave according to them. We will not be disappointed.

For example, we may be practicing the Dharma sincerely, but our mentors may be too tired or busy to see us. If we expect that our mentors will always be available when we want advice, our trust in this happening is naive. If we expect the impossible, our mentors will inevitably let us down. If, on the other hand, we understand behavioral cause and effect, we trust in something more reasonable happening. We trust that our mentors will give us equitable amounts of time and attention if and when circumstances permit.

Reasonable trust derives from rational thinking, not from naivety or idealistic dreams. With such trust, we do not disparage our teachers as being bad mentors because they have no time for us now. Similarly, we do not put ourselves down by imagining that our mentors' unavailability now is due to our being bad disciples. Thus, reasonable trust allows clearheaded respect for one's mentor and for oneself.

~11
Seeing a Mentor as a Buddha

The Relation between a Mentor's Functioning
as a Buddha and Being a Buddha

BEYOND THE SUGGESTION to focus with firm conviction and appreciation on the good qualities and kindness that their mentors actually have, the sutras and tantras instruct disciples to regard these qualities and kindness as those of a Buddha. As disciples advance in their practice, they gain progressively deeper understanding of the relation between their mentors and Buddhas. Eventually, as practitioners of highest tantra, they need to see that their tantric masters are Buddhas.

The later Gelug graded-path texts added seeing that one's mentor is a Buddha to their presentations of guru-meditation. The meditation focuses on understanding why a mentor must be a Buddha. The first reason is scriptural authority: Buddha stated in several sutras and tantras that in later times he shall appear in the form of spiritual mentors and that disciples then need to respect their mentors as they would respect him.

The next four reasons are inferences from logic. (1) Because the enlightening influence of the Buddha operates without any break in continuity, it must still be operating at present. (2) For that influence to reach disciples, it needs to pass through a medium, namely the medium of properly qualified mentors, as with the analogy of the need for a magnifying glass to focus the rays of the sun on kindling. (3) The way in which the confused minds of disciples makes things appear is unreliable. Therefore, although mentors may appear to have inherent flaws, this appearance of their mode of existence does not correspond to how they actually exist. (4) Because disciples' minds are limited, they would only be able to see and relate to a manifestation of Buddha that appeared with conventional limitations. Therefore, to help disciples, mentors necessarily appear to have conventional shortcomings.

Most Westerners find this presentation lacking. Either it fails to convince them that their mentors are Buddhas or it leads them to accept the proposition with inadequate understanding. Thus, they misunderstand the instruction to see their mentors as Buddhas.

In *A Commentary on [Dignaga's "Compendium of] Validly Cognizing Minds,"* Dharmakirti stated that the defining characteristic of a phenomenon that arises from causes and conditions is its ability to perform a function for a specific audience. Because of this ability, the phenomenon is what it is. Thus, for instance, a watch that performs the function of a toy for a baby is not simply a watch *functioning as* a toy: it *is* a toy, for the baby.

The Madhyamaka explanation clarifies this point: the object is only *contingently* a toy, not *ultimately* a toy. It is not the case that the watch contains a concrete, findable defining characteristic, like a genetic code, that by its own power makes it ultimately a watch. Nor is it the case that the item here is an object that has two such characteristics in it, which by their own powers make it ultimately both a watch and a toy, either simultaneously or alternatively. Nor is it the case that the object itself is ultimately something undefined, which is neither of the two. It is a watch or a toy contingent on its ability to function validly as a watch for an adult or a toy for a baby, without ultimately being a watch, a toy, both, or neither.

The confusion here is that the four logical inferences cited in the graded-path texts demonstrate that spiritual mentors *function as* Buddhas for their disciples, while the scriptural quotations state that they *are* Buddhas. By the above explanation, the two statements are equivalent, but only in the sense that mentors are contingently Buddhas, not ultimately Buddhas. Westerners who are unaware of the Madhyamaka distinction between contingent and ultimate existence find the entire presentation totally baffling. Their confusion becomes even more perplexing because a magnifying glass does not need to be the sun in order to act as a medium for the sun. Therefore, when the texts recommend seeing that a mentor is a Buddha, we need to understand this to mean seeing the person only contingently as a Buddha, inasmuch as he or she validly functions as a Buddha for disciples.

Mentally Labeling a Mentor as a Physician
or as a Buddha

In *A Sutra Spread Out Like a Tree-Trunk*, Buddha recommended that disciples discern their spiritual mentors as physicians, themselves as patients, the Dharma as a medicine, and its diligent practice as the way to be cured. A spiritual mentor, after all, teaches methods to heal disciples of shortcomings and difficulties. Let us supplement the above explanation of contingent and ultimate identities with the Prasangika-Madhyamaka analysis of mental labeling to understand the validity of this vision.

Spiritual mentors are only contingently doctors inasmuch as they can validly function as doctors for disciples. More precisely, they are only *conventionally* doctors inasmuch as they can be validly labeled as doctors by disciples. Valid mental labeling requires a valid basis for the labeling. Here, the basis is the ability of mentors to function validly as doctors for healing their disciples of shortcomings and difficulties. This does not imply, however, that spiritual mentors are doctors in all senses of the word, either ultimately or even conventionally. No one would expect his or her mentor to be able to perform brain surgery. Labeling mentors as doctors is merely a convention, drawn in order to affect disciples' attitudes so that they may derive the most benefit from their relationships with their teachers. After all, as mentioned previously, the term *tenpa*, rendered as "building a healthy relationship," refers equally to the relationships of patients to doctors and of disciples to spiritual mentors.

Further, the great Indian monastic university of Nalanda, which specialized exclusively in sutra studies, followed a custom that all Tibetan monastic centers of learning subsequently have adopted. During classes, the monk students are to regard their teachers as Buddhas, themselves as bodhisattvas, their classrooms as pure Buddha-fields, the subject matter as the purest Dharma, and the occasion as timeless. These five features characterize the situation of a Buddha teaching in a *sambhogakaya* form. *Sambhogakaya* is a network of subtle forms, made of transparent light, which can teach the full scope of the Mahayana teachings to the most advanced disciples.

Discerning a mentor's activity of teaching the Dharma and using it as a basis for ascribing him or her a name allows a valid labeling of the person as a sambhogakaya Buddha. As in the case of labeling a mentor a doctor, labeling a mentor a Buddha does not mean that he or she is ultimately, or even conventionally, a Buddha in the full sense of the word. Disciples would hardly expect that their mentors could multiply into billions of forms or walk through walls. Following this convention of labeling merely affects disciples' attitudes so that they have greater respect for the seriousness of their studies. Moreover, as Sakya Pandita wrote in *The Profound Path of Guru-Yoga*, depending on whether disciples view their mentors as ordinary beings, bodhisattvas, or Buddhas, they gain the inspiration of one or the other.

Therefore, when regarding our mentors conventionally as Buddhas, we discern only certain features about them and on that basis we label them Buddhas. We do not label our mentors as Buddhas based on everything about them, but rather based only on their good qualities. The strength of these qualities does not affect the validity of the labeling. Whether eyes are strong or weak, we validly label them eyes if they enable us to see. Similarly, whether our mentors' skills in communicating the Dharma are great or small, we validly label the skills as Buddha-qualities if they enable us to learn Buddha's teachings.

Moreover, the mental labeling of our mentors as Buddhas is valid by Chandrakirti's three criteria. (1) Nalanda had the established convention of labeling a spiritual mentor a Buddha and our mentors follow the Nalanda tradition of teaching the Dharma. (2) A mind that can validly apprehend what is conventionally true does not contradict the labeling. Our mentors perform the functions of a Buddha in leading us to enlightenment through explaining Buddha's teachings. We experience the beneficial effects of their teachings the more we put them into practice. (3) A mind that can validly apprehend the deepest truth about how things exist also does not contradict the labeling. Labeling our mentors as Buddhas does not imply that their actions of teaching the Dharma, by their own powers, independently of anything else, make our mentors ultimately, or even conventionally, omniscient Buddhas. Our mentors exist and function as Buddhas for us only inasmuch as we can validly label them as Buddhas and Buddhas are what our mental labels refer to.

The Nonliteral Use of the Label Buddha

Regarding a spiritual mentor as a Buddha has a shared meaning common to sutra and tantra. The sutras and their commentaries instruct disciples to see their mentors as Buddhas when they receive teachings or when they take refuge or bodhisattva vows. The highest tantras instruct disciples to do the same at all times. Chandrakirti taught that highest tantra teachings with a general meaning shared with sutra are to be taken literally only if they accord with common experience. Because regarding one's teacher as a Buddha does not accord with common experience, it is not to be taken literally. Sakya Pandita explicitly made this point in *The Divisions of the Three Sets of Vows*. There he wrote, "The Prajnaparamita texts state that disciples need to regard their mentors as if the teachers were Buddhas. They do not claim that the mentors actually are Buddhas."

A shared teaching that is not to be taken literally has different levels of meaning depending on the context. Each level needs interpretation to clarify the intended meaning. Moreover, the levels of interpretation common to sutra and the early stages of tantra practice are all intended to lead us deeper. They lead to the definitive, ultimate level of meaning concerning the clear light mind and the realization of voidness with it.

Progressive Levels of Interpretation

In *A Last Testament Letter Cast to the Wind*, the Gelug master Gyelrong Tsültrim-nyima explained three progressive levels on which disciples need to see their spiritual mentors as amalgams of the Buddha-figures Avalokiteshvara, Manjushri, and Vajrapani. On the first level, their mentors are like them in their good qualities; on the second, they have their qualities; and on the third, their mentors are the three figures.

In an oral commentary, Serkong Rinpoche correlated Gyelrong's three levels with the three progressive ways in which disciples need to view their mentors as Buddhas found in the *shravaka* (listener) sutra, bodhisattva sutra, and highest tantra explanations. The shravaka sutras, often called the *Hinayana* (modest vehicle) sutras, include the Pali canon of the Theravada tradition and the Sanskrit canons of seventeen other early Indian Buddhist schools. From a shravaka point of view, their mentors are similar to Buddhas in having developed a Buddha's good qualities. From a bodhisattva standpoint, their mentors are emanations of Buddhas and thus contain these qualities; while from the viewpoint of highest tantra, they are Buddhas. These three interpretations derive from a difference in the description of Shakyamuni

Buddha found in the shravaka sutras, the bodhisattva sutras, and the highest tantras.

The shravaka sutras explain that Shakyamuni was born as an ordinary being, Prince Siddhartha, and that he developed his good qualities during his lifetime to become a Buddha. Thus, on a shravaka level, we focus on our mentors as similar to Shakyamuni in that they started life as ordinary people and developed good qualities through strenuous effort. Focusing on this aspect of our mentors helps us to realize that we also have started the spiritual path as ordinary beings. With appropriate hard work, we too may correct our deficiencies and gain the qualities of a Buddha. This realization helps us to develop the shravaka motivation, the determination to be free of our shortcomings.

According to the bodhisattva sutras, Shakyamuni Buddha reached enlightenment eons ago. Out of compassion, he consciously took birth as Prince Siddhartha in the form of a supreme emanation (nirmanakaya, tulku) to demonstrate to others the manner of becoming a Buddha. Understanding Shakyamuni in this way helps us to realize that enlightenment does not end with death. Buddhas continue to help others until everyone has become enlightened. Thus, seeing our mentors as further emanations of Buddha supports our understanding that Shakyamuni is continuing to manifest for everyone's sake. This helps us to gain the courage to keep our bodhisattva motivation, bodhichitta, to strive to become Buddhas as our mentors have done and to help others for as long as is needed.

The Tibetan tulku system encourages the bodhisattva sutra view of spiritual mentors. Although objectively one does not need to be a Buddha to start a line of tulkus, Tibetan disciples regard their mentors as enlightened tulkus, whether or not spiritual authorities recognize them as rinpocheys. Because Shakyamuni manifests in an extensive network of tulkus, disciples see their mentors as Shakyamuni tulkus, if not also as tulkus of other traditionally recognized lines.

According to the highest tantra explanation, while Shakyamuni Buddha taught *The Prajnaparamita Sutras* on Vultures' Peak, he simultaneously appeared as Vajradhara and taught the tantras. Thus, Shakya-muni is both Prince Siddhartha and Vajradhara. Similarly, on the highest tantra level we need to see that from one point of view our tantric masters are the spiritual teachers we see before us, but on another level they are simultaneously Vajradharas. Therefore, tantra guru-yoga often entails imagining Vajradhara in a mentor's heart. Visualizing this helps us to realize that, on one level, our tantric masters and we have ordinary minds and bodies, but simultaneously, on the deepest level, we both have clear light minds, subtlest communicative vibrations, and subtlest energy-wind. In other words, on the deepest level, we all have the materials for an enlightening mind, speech, and body of a Buddha.

In tantra guru-yoga, disciples need to see their mentors as Buddhas on all three levels—shravaka sutra, bodhisattva sutra, and highest tantra. Thus, in *A Ceremony to Honor the Gurus*, the First Panchen Lama taught disciples to visualize their tantric masters externally in the forms of Tsongkapa as a monk with shravaka vows. In Tsongkapa's heart sits Shakyamuni, the teacher of the bodhisattva sutras. In Shakyamuni's heart sits Vajradhara, the source of the highest tantras. In Vajradhara's heart is a syllable *hum*, symbolizing clear light mind.

Moreover, as the First Panchen Lama explained in *The Essence of [Kaydrubjey's] "Ocean of Actual Attainments,"* the stacked figures also represent the gross, subtle, and subtlest levels of body, speech, and mind. Regarding one's tantric master as a Buddha on all three levels of each leads to the ultimate, definite source of Buddhahood—clear light subtlest mind and the subtlest communicative vibration and subtlest energy-wind inseparable from it.

The Meaning of a Tantric Master's Being a Buddha

The statement in highest tantra that one's tantric master is a Buddha is extremely perplexing. It has a level of meaning shared with sutra and tantra, namely, as explained before, that for their disciples, mentors are both contingently and conventionally Buddhas inasmuch as they can validly function for them as Buddhas and, on that basis, can be validly labeled by them as Buddhas. Mentors, however, are never inherently and ultimately Buddhas, since inherent, ultimate existence as this or that, by the power of findable defining characteristics, is impossible. Here, however, the statement that one's tantric master is a Buddha has additional deeper meanings specific to highest tantra practice.

Some spiritual seekers take the highest tantra statement to have a literal meaning. Consequently, they view all their tantric masters' actions, words, and emotional states as perfect. This frequently happens with dzogchen masters, since dzogchen supposedly means that everything is perfect. In *Ascertaining the Three Vows*, the Nyingma master Ngari Panchen, however, made the situation clear. He explained that, in private, dzogchen masters may occasionally need to act in contradiction to the norms of generally accepted behavior. However, when in the public eye or in the company of beginners who may lose faith, dzogchen masters need to uphold strictly the liberation and bodhisattva vows. Thus, if popular spiritual teachers act improperly with students at Dharma centers, they are violating the basic Buddhist principles. Naivety over this point may open spiritual seekers to possible abuse.

Some disciples are skeptical. They feel that the statement concerning tantric masters' being Buddhas cannot possibly mean what it says. Their mentors may be like Buddhas in having gained good qualities through hard work. Their mentors may even be similar to Buddha-emanations, serving as containers for the Buddha-qualities that they see in them. Regarding their mentors actually as Buddhas may be a helpful ploy of mental labeling for gaining the most inspiration from the person, but they think that surely it is just a mental trick. Their skeptical attitudes deprive them of realizing the deepest insights to be gained from the teaching. The Sakya master Ngorchen clearly stated in *A Beautiful Ornament for the Three Continua* that in the context of highest tantra, the tantric master is not merely *like* a Buddha; he or she *is* a Buddha.

In *The Heart of the Tantras: The Fivefold Practice [of Mahamudra]*, the Drigung Kagyü master Rigdzin Chökyi-dragpa explained the deeper meaning of a tantric master's being a Buddha. The meaning derives from the characteristically tantric practice of working toward Buddhahood through methods that resemble the resultant state one is striving to attain. The usual human appearance of the body of a tantric master and its simultaneous appearance as the enlightening body of a Buddha, particularly during an empowerment, are two facts about the same attribute of one phenomenon (*ngowochig, ngo-bo gcig*; "they are one by nature"). The phenomenon here is a tantric master; the attribute is the appearance of his or her physical body; the two facts about that attribute are that the appearance can validly be as a usual human and as the enlightening body of a Buddha.

The usual human appearance of a tantric master's body is that it is thin or fat, gets tired, sometimes becomes sick, and grows old. The enlightening body of a Buddha, however, is made of transparent light and energy, appears in a wide array of Buddha-forms, can multiply, can pass through solid objects, and never tires, gets sick, or grows old. The two appearances are two facts about the physical body of a tantric master and, in this sense, our tantric masters are Buddhas—although, of course, not inherently and ultimately Buddhas.

Moreover, our tantric masters are Buddhas also in the sense that their speech and minds have both usual human appearances and appearances as a Buddha's enlightening speech and mind. The human appearance of their speech is that it sometimes falters, is unclear, or fails to speak our languages. A Buddha's enlightening speech, on the other hand, communicates perfectly in every language, without faltering or ever being unclear. The human appearance of their minds is that they sometimes become angry, lack warmth, or fail to understand what we mean. A Buddha's enlightening mind, by contrast, is totally free of disturbing emotions, has equal love for all beings, and understands everything perfectly.

Yet, if we look at our tantric masters, how can their bodies be both flesh and blood and transparent light and energy? How can they be both old and eternally youthful? How can two seemingly incompatible facts about the appearance of our tantric masters' bodies both be true? We need to explore the matter more deeply.

Viewing One Phenomenon Validly from Different Viewpoints

In *A Supplement to the Middle Way*, Chandrakirti gave a relevant example. Suppose that three groups—ghosts, humans, and divine beings (gods)—all looked at the liquid in a specific cup. Because of different karmic propensities, ghosts would see it as pus, humans as water, and divine beings as nectar. Since the liquid does not exist with an inherent, ultimate identity as any of the three substances, the perception of each group would be valid from its own point of view. Moreover, each group would experience the taste of the liquid according to the appearance it perceived. Yet, pus, water, and nectar are not the same.

Chandrakirti's analysis also applies to our previous example of an adult and a baby looking at the same object. The adult would see it as a watch and would know the hour by looking at it; the baby would see it as a toy and play with it. Because the object does not exist with an inherent, ultimate identity as a watch or a toy, the perception and experience of each would be valid. Yet, a watch and a toy are not the same.

The situation is equivalent regarding a newcomer and a tantric disciple looking at a Buddhist teacher. The newcomer would see the teacher's body as human; the teacher's tantric disciple would perceive it as the body of a Buddha-figure. Because a body does not exist with an inherent, ultimate identity as flesh and blood or as light and energy, both perceptions would be valid. Yet, a solid flesh-and-blood body is not identical to a transparent body made of light and energy.

Even one person may validly see the same object as two different things and validly make use of it in both ways. Someone may both play with a watch as a toy and still accurately tell the time with it. One does not preclude the other. Similarly, we may see our tantric masters' bodies as human when our mentors are ill. During empowerments, however, we may see the same bodies as those of Buddha-figures, which can never fall sick. Both perceptions are correct from their own points of view. The tantric vision, however, does not negate the necessity to take our mentors to the doctor when they have come down with flu.

The Meaning of Inseparable

Another way of saying that the perceptions of our tantric masters as ordinary humans and as Buddha-figures are equally valid is to say that the two perceptions, or the two perceived appearances, are inseparable (*yermey, dbyer-med*). *Inseparable*, here, means that if one validly occurs from one point of view, the other validly occurs from another viewpoint. Only in this sense are our tantric masters inseparably ordinary humans and Buddhas. *Inseparable*, then, in this context, does not mean that the two appearances need to occur simultaneously. When one perceives one appearance, one does not need simultaneously to perceive the other.

Inseparable Impure and Pure Appearances

The teachings on "inseparable samsara and nirvana" from the Sakya system of the path and its results indicate several levels of meaning of the assertion that our tantric masters are inseparably ordinary humans and Buddhas. These teachings may help us to understand better this difficult point. From among the many meanings of *samsara* and *nirvana*, let us focus here on samsara as signifying "impure" or "ordinary appearances" and nirvana as meaning "pure appearances." Further, let us focus on the two inseparable appearances in reference to our tantric masters' bodies.

Inseparable impure and pure appearances have three levels of significance relevant here. (1) The impure appearances of our tantric masters' bodies may refer to their appearances as ordinary humans. Their pure appearances may refer to their appearances as Buddha-figures. The two appearances are inseparable, somewhat as are two quantum levels of energy at which subatomic particles may vibrate. Thus, our tantric masters' having bodies with inseparable ordinary human and Buddha forms means that their bodies may validly appear as one or the other depending on the point of view, like a liquid may appear as pus, water, or nectar. Their bodies, however, do not ultimately exist with inherent human or Buddha appearances, or with both or with neither.

Moreover, there are no concrete, findable characteristic marks within our tantric masters' bodies that by their own powers make them appear in human or Buddha forms. As in the case of quantum levels of energy within an atom, different levels of appearance exist as mere possibilities, totally dependent on other factors, and not as independently existent, concrete entities.

(2) The impure appearances of our tantric masters' bodies may refer to their appearances as having conventional faults, such as improper behavior. Their impure appearances may also refer to their appearances as having a mixture of conventional faults and good qualities. Their pure appearances are ones having only conventional good qualities, such as compassion. All three appearances occur, although not necessarily at the same moment, and are inseparably valid, each from a different viewpoint. Inherent, concrete flaws or assets, however, do not exist within our tantric masters, making them ultimately impure, pure, or a mixture of both.

(3) The impure appearances of our tantric masters' bodies may refer to their deceptive appearances as if existing in impossible manners. Their pure appearances may refer to their nondeceptive appearances as existing in the ways in which they actually exist. For ease of discussion, let us call the former type of impure appearances "appearances of independent existence" and the latter type of pure appearances "appearances of dependent existence." Our tantric masters' bodies appear inseparably as dependently and independently existent depending on the minds that perceive them. There are no concrete, findable features

within them—not even voidness itself—which by their own powers make them exist either dependently or independently.

Further, the three meanings of impure and pure appearances may overlap in several ways. The appearances of our tantric masters' bodies as humans may be as humans with or without conventional faults. Whether appearing as human bodies with conventional faults or as human bodies with only good qualities, our tantric masters' bodies may appear independently existent or dependently existent. The appearances of our tantric masters' bodies as the enlightening bodies of Buddha-figures, however, would only appear exclusively with good qualities. The bodies of Buddha-figures do not have conventional faults. Nevertheless, the appearances of our tantric masters' bodies as those of Buddha-figures may appear independently existent or dependently existent.

The Basis for Labeling as a Buddha the Pure Appearance of a Mentor

Disciples may label their tantric masters as Buddhas based on the pure appearances of them as humans or as Buddha-figures, both with good qualities, whether the qualities appear to exist dependently or independently. Because good qualities are functions of Buddha-nature, deeper bases for validly labeling their tantric masters as Buddhas are their mentors' Buddha-natures. However, people may not yet realize the potential qualities of their Buddha-natures, may only partially realize them, or may fully realize them. The question, then, naturally arises concerning the validity of labeling people as Buddhas based on unrealized or only partially realized Buddha-natures. The question pertains equally to disciples' seeing their tantric masters as Buddhas and, in tantra practice, to disciples' seeing themselves and all others as Buddha-figures. For an answer, we need to turn to the highest tantra teachings.

In the context of highest tantra, as explained previously, Buddha-nature may refer to the clear-light mind. Although each Tibetan tradition explains this differently, they all agree that one aspect of the nature of the clear light mind is that it is the source of all Buddha-qualities. Another aspect of its nature is that it is devoid of existing in impossible ways. Whether the clear light mind is totally obscured, partially obscured, or completely free of fleeting stains, these factual aspects of its nature remain the same. Moreover, whether the Buddha-qualities of the clear light mind are only in potential form, are partially operational, or are fully functional, still the nature of the clear light mind remains the same.

In short, the deepest basis for mentally labeling a tantric master as a Buddha is the master's clear light mind. The basis for labeling is not the fleeting stains that may or may not be obscuring that mind. Nor is the basis the strength of the manifest qualities of that mind. Thus, the mental labeling of a tantric master as a Buddha based on clear light mind is always valid.

Mentally labeling our tantric masters as Buddhas based on clear light mind leads to the definitive, ultimate meaning of the instruction to see that one's tantric master is a Buddha. Seeing that the flaws that appear in our external gurus are dependently arising fleeting stains enables us to see that the flaws that appear in our internal gurus—our clear light minds—are also dependently arising and fleeting. This insight is essential for actualizing the Buddha-qualities of our own clear light minds.

According to *Difficult Points Concerning Helping and Showing Respect to a Guru*, although everyone has a clear light mind, devoid by nature, viewing one's dog as a Buddha does not have the same benefit as viewing one's tantric master as a Buddha. Therefore, although the clear light minds of our tantric masters are valid bases for labeling them as Buddhas, their other good qualities, plus the inspiration we gain from them, make the labeling more effective in bringing us insight. The main qualities that may serve as further bases for labeling our tantric masters as Buddhas are their compassion, bodhichitta, and far-reaching attitudes (perfections), and the fact of their conferring upon us highest tantra empowerments.

~12

Advanced Points Concerning Seeing That a Tantric Master Is a Buddha

Basis, Pathway, and Resultant Viewpoints

MOST TIBETAN TEXTS that discuss tantric masters' being Buddhas explain the topic of impure and pure appearances from a specific viewpoint. Often, however, the texts neglect to state their point of view. This may cause confusion.

In *The Sublime Continuum*, Maitreya explained three viewpoints of looking at inseparable impure and pure appearances. One may look at these appearances from the viewpoints of a Buddha-nature not yet realized, partially realized, or fully realized. In other words, inseparable impure and pure appearances appear differently when fleeting stains overlay one's Buddha-nature, when the stains are partially gone, and when the stains are completely absent.

Since *purification* is another name for the process of ridding oneself of fleeting stains, Maitreya called the three viewpoints "impure," "impure and pure," and "completely pure"—yet another usage of the terms *impure* and *pure*. Later commentators have named the three viewpoints "basis," "pathway," and "resultant" levels. The appearances from each of the three points of view are valid from their own cognitive perspectives, just as is the case with the appearances of a certain object as a watch or a toy.

The Viewpoints Typical of the Four Tibetan Lineages

The texts from each of the four Tibetan lineages of Buddhism tend to discuss the topic of impure and pure appearances primarily from one or another of the three points of view. The great Rimey master Jamyangkyentzey-wangpo explained that Gelug mentors tend to speak from a basis point of view, Sakya mentors from a pathway viewpoint, and Nyingma and Kagyü mentors from the standpoint of the resultant level of a Buddha. The basis level looks from the side of impure appearances; the pathway level looks from the side of appearances as both impure and pure; and the resultant level looks from the pure side. The analysis is complicated because most authors mix the various meanings of *impure* and *pure* in their presentations.

Kadam and early Gelug texts on the disciple-mentor relationship tend to discuss the topic from the point of view of spiritual mentors in general and their impure appearances. They fully acknowledge that our mentors have impure human forms with conventional faults that appear independently existent. On a basis level, however, we cannot focus on both impure and pure appearances simultaneously. Therefore, without denying our mentors' impure human appearances, we may focus in guru-meditation on their pure human appearances as having only good qualities, but dependently existent. After all, we take safe direction from good qualities, not from faults, and, with renunciation, we determine to rid ourselves of shortcomings, not of good qualities. Moreover, we may develop good qualities and eliminate faults only if they are dependently existent.

Later Gelug graded-path texts also present the topic of the disciple-mentor relationship from the basis point of view. The texts explain that through the influence of our karma, our minds may make our mentors appear in a variety of forms, either with flaws or with exclusively good qualities. We are capable of focusing merely on someone's good qualities and ignoring the person's faults, as in the case of a conceited person regarding him or herself as perfect. Personal opinion is unreliable. Therefore, since focusing only on our mentors' good qualities has many benefits, as supported by scriptural authority and logic, we focus in guru-meditation on our mentors' pure appearances.

Sakya texts discuss the disciple-mentor relationship almost exclusively within the highest tantra context. Thus, they discuss it from the pathway viewpoint of the inseparability of impure and pure appearances. The human and Buddha-figure forms of our tantric masters are inseparable facts about the appearances of their bodies, speech, and minds. If one is the case from one point of view, the other is also the case from another viewpoint. Likewise inseparable are the impure appearances of our tantric masters with conventional faults and their pure appearances with only good qualities. Each occurs and is valid from a specific point of view.

Nyingma and Kagyü texts, on the other hand, tend to present the disciple-mentor relationship from the resultant viewpoint of pure appearances of Buddhas. From this point of view, our tantric masters are Buddha-figures, with only good qualities. On the deepest level, our tantric masters are, in fact, the inner guru—the fully realized clear light mind free of stains and complete with all Buddha-qualities. The enlightening minds of Buddhas give rise only to pure appearances of dependent existence, both on the sambhogakaya level of subtle appearances and on the nirmanakaya level of grosser appearances. Subtle appearances include the forms of Buddha-figures having only good qualities, while grosser appearances include human forms seemingly having faults.

Undefined Usage of the Terms Impure and Pure

Since impure and pure appearances have several meanings, an appearance may be pure in one sense of the word, and impure in another. Many texts, however, use the two terms without specifying the precise meaning intended. Their lack of specificity often serves as a further source of confusion or misunderstanding.

For example, highest tantra texts instruct disciples to see their tantric masters in pure forms. Any faults perceived in the master are figments of the imagination. Without differentiating the various meanings of pure, disciples may easily mistake the statement to mean that even if mentors sexually abuse students, their actions are the perfect conduct of enlightened beings. After all, any perception of a teacher's abusive behavior as a fault is a projection of the imagination and therefore false.

The intended meaning of the statement, however, is quite different. The impure appearance of a tantric master's abusive behavior as independently existent is a fabrication of a confused mind. The abusive behavior has arisen dependently on many causes and circumstances. Although the deceptive appearance of how the behavior exists is false, the fact that the behavior is abusive is true.

Beyond Good or Bad

Many Nyingma and Kagyü texts discuss a tantric master's behavior as beyond good or bad. They are not speaking, however, about the basis level of what an action, such as abuse, conventionally is, or what effects such an action produces. Buddhism does not relativize everything to the point that all phenomena lose their conventional identities. Abusive behavior damages both the perpetrator and the victim. *Beyond good or bad* means beyond the dualistic categories of independently good or bad. It is not a denial of behavioral cause and effect. Because pure actions are unassociated with confusion from a resultant point of view, they are beyond merely karmic cause and effect. However, pure actions still produce effects. Otherwise, a Buddha's enlightening actions could not benefit anyone.

The question remains how a pure action can produce suffering. Although an action may be pure from a resultant point of view, it may be both pure and impure from a pathway viewpoint, and impure from a basis stance. All three points of view are valid and lead to valid experience. Thus, tantric masters may view their own abusive behavior from a resultant level of a fully realized clear light mind and thereby experience no suffering from the action, although their reputations may fall. The victims, however, validly view and experience the abuse from a basis level of an unrealized Buddha-nature and consequently suffer greatly. Therefore, out of compassion, properly qualified tantric masters always refrain from abusive behavior.

Pure behavior, however, sometimes requires causing short-term suffering to bring about long-term benefit, as when performing surgery. Nevertheless, the Nyingma master Ngari Panchen's point still stands. Tantric or dzogchen masters, especially those in the public eye, refrain from acting in conventionally destructive ways when others knowing of it would lose their admiration and faith in Buddhists and Buddhism. Tantric masters, in fact, promise to uphold this guideline as one of their secondary bodhisattva vows.

Thus, the practice of seeing that one's tantric mentor is a Buddha in no way negates the conventional validity of impure appearances. An impure appearance of an abusive spiritual mentor as having inherent flaws is ultimately invalid because inherent existence, independent of anything, is impossible. Nevertheless, the impure appearance may be conventionally valid concerning the fact that the behavior of the abusive teacher is faulty and has caused suffering. All Tibetan traditions accept a valid distinction between accurate and distorted conventional truths. All Tibetan traditions equally reject the so-called Hoshang position that constructive and destructive actions lack any distinction.

Transforming Negative Circumstances into Positive Ones

Another aspect of seeing that one's mentor is a Buddha is to take all his or her actions as teachings, even if some actions are, in fact, faulty or destructive. The instruction derives from the Kadam tradition. In *Seven Points for Cleansing Attitudes*, the Kadam Geshey Chaykawa taught that disciples may transform negative circumstances into positive ones by focusing on the lessons that they may learn from them. The Kadam Geshey Langri-tangpa gave similar advice in *Eight Stanzas on Cleansing Attitudes*. Even if others harm them completely unfairly, disciples need to look upon these people as their spiritual mentors.

One of the tantric vows for establishing a close bond with a tantric master is to refrain from becoming angry at or disrespectful of the teacher, regardless of what he or she may say or do. If we apply the Kadam instruction to this vow, then even if our tantric masters act unethically or cause harm, we try to learn a lesson from the situation. The lesson may simply be to hold back from acting destructively like this ourselves. This is the general meaning of the instruction, shared by sutra and tantra practitioners. On a highest tantra level, if we are advanced in our practices, we may use the incident to recognize the structure of one of the five types of deep awareness (Buddha-wisdom)—such as mirror-like or individualizing awareness—underlying the faulty action.

The Nyingma and Kagyü traditions correlate the five types of awareness with the five disturbing emotions—such as anger or longing desire—that we may see in our mentors. The Sakya tradition correlates the five with the five aggregate factors—such as consciousness or distinguishing—that comprise their faulty behavior, or with faults that we may see in our tantric masters' bodies, speech, minds, qualities, or actions. Recognizing the deep awareness level underlying our mentors' disturbing emotions, aggregate factors, or faulty actions helps us to recognize this deeper level underlying our own confusion. Focusing on our underlying deep awareness helps us to reach our clear light minds and to understand that our own faults are also merely fleeting stains.

Learning a lesson from the faulty behavior of one's mentor, however, does not mean denying that the behavior was faulty. After confirming the validity of our perception of the behavior, we may correctly conclude that the conventional appearance of it as faulty is accurate. If we find the fault unbearable, we may follow the advice of *The Kalachakra Tantra* and decide to keep a distance from the teacher. This advice applies, with a general meaning, to all levels of teachers. Nevertheless, a healthy stance would be still to maintain respect for the person's good qualities and appreciation for his or her kindness. Without such an attitude, we may damage our spiritual progress by fixating on feelings of bitterness, outrage, recrimination, or guilt. On the other hand, with such an attitude, we may still transform negative circumstances into positive ones and gain inspiration from the good qualities that a faulty teacher nevertheless has.

During an Empowerment, Seeing That a Tantric Master Is a Buddha

Seeing that one's tantric master is a Buddha not only brings about the greatest inspiration for realizing one's clear light mind, it is essential for the empowerment process in highest tantra. All four Tibetan lineages concur on this point, although each explains the mechanism differently. Let us outline briefly their varied explanations. Understanding several valid ways to see that our tantric masters are Buddhas may help us to gain clarity about this difficult point.

The Sakya, Nyingma, and Kagyü traditions explain the empowering process in terms of disciples' gaining conscious experiences of various aspects of their Buddha-natures. The first of the four highest tantra empowerments pertains to the body aspect of Buddha-nature; the second pertains to speech; the third to mind; and the fourth to the integrated network of the three faculties.

From a pathway viewpoint that equally emphasizes impure and pure appearances of tantric masters, disciples need to see during empowerments that the bodies, speech, and minds of the tantric masters have two valid quantum levels. They appear and exist both as ordinary human faculties and as the enlightening faculties of Buddha-figures. They need to realize that these levels appear and exist inseparably because of the tantric masters' Buddha-natures—specifically because of the tantric masters' clear light minds as the foundations for everything that appears about them.

We all have clear light minds as aspects of our Buddha- natures. According to the Sakya explanation, clear light mind contains the "foundational seeds" for the enlightening body, speech, and mind of a Buddha. Understanding that our tantric masters actually have enlightening bodies, speech, and minds from a certain valid point of view reinforces and strengthens the foundational seeds for the three enlightening faculties in our own clear light minds. The understanding accomplishes this by planting "causal seeds" in our clear light minds for realizing our foundational seeds. Through this process, our conscious understanding during an initiation ceremony empowers the foundational seeds to ripen into attainment of a Buddha's body, speech, and mind.

From a resultant point of view, disciples need to see during empowerments that all the enlightening qualities of body, speech, and mind are complete in the tantric masters' "mind-vajras"—their clear light minds. The Nyingma tradition explains that the Buddha-qualities' being complete in our own clear light minds provides "foundational empowerment." Seeing these qualities complete in our tantric masters supplements this foundation with a "causal empowerment" that ripens these qualities. Although the Buddha-qualities are inseparable from the clear light mind, as the rays of sunlight are inseparable from the sun, nevertheless fleeting stains obscure their functioning. Causal empowerment energizes the purification process so that the qualities ripen and thus shine and function free of stains.

The Kagyü lineages also explain from a resultant viewpoint. The Drigung Kagyü tradition of fivefold mahamudra practice, for example, explains that during empowerments disciples need to see that the aggregates, elements, and so forth of the tantric masters abide primordially in the nature of the male and female Buddhas. For something to abide in the nature (rangzhin, rang-bzhin) of something else means for it to exist and to function in the same way. For example, five aggregate factors of body and mind comprise each moment of our ordinary experience, while five types of deep awareness, symbolized by five dhyani Buddhas, comprise each moment of a Buddha's experience. Dhyani Buddhas are representations of various aspects of Buddha-nature. Both the five aggregates and the five types of awareness exist as aspects of "simultaneously arising nondual deep awareness"—in other words, as aspects of the clear light mind. Both sets of five function similarly to comprise experience. Seeing our tantric masters' bodies, speech, and minds as networks (body mandalas) of dhyani Buddhas plants the seeds and empowers us to realize networks of the same natures within ourselves.

Seeing That a Tantric Master Is a Buddha in Gelug Empowerments

Even if one explains, from the viewpoint of the path or the result, that a tantric master is a Buddha, still, on the basis level, the mentor is not literally an omniscient Buddha. Therefore, because of this and other logical inconsistencies, Gelug gesheys advise keeping off the debate grounds the topic of the spiritual mentor's being a Buddha. Instead, the Gelug tradition explains the meaning of a tantric master's aggregates being dhyani Buddhas from the viewpoint of the basis for enlightenment.

Aku Sherab-gyatso indicated this viewpoint in *A Reminder for Not Forgetting the Visualizations Described for the First Stage of the Path of Guhyasamaja.* The five aggregate factors of experience are the transforming (*nyerlen, nyer-len;* material) causes and the five types of deep awareness are the simultaneously acting conditions for attaining the five dhyani Buddhas. Just as seeds transform into sprouts through the actions of water and sunlight occurring simultaneously with their presence, the five aggregates transform into the five dhyani Buddhas through the five types of awareness functioning simultaneously with them. During highest tantra empowerments, disciples need to see their tantric masters' aggregates as dhyani Buddhas in the sense that the masters have transformed their basic aggregates into dhyani Buddhas through cultivating the five types of deep awareness. This inspires the disciples to do the same.

In the Gelug tradition, the empowering process hinges on disciples' gaining a conscious experience of a blissful understanding of voidness at each of the four highest tantra empowerments, rather than a conscious experience of Buddha-nature. At each stage, the conscious experience plants a seed to gain a blissful understanding of voidness with the clear light mind. This understanding is equivalent to realizing one's Buddha-nature on the deepest level, as explained by the other

Tibetan traditions. Consciously experiencing some level of blissful understanding of voidness during a Gelug empowerment, however, does not relate directly to seeing that the tantric master is a Buddha in the context of the procedures.

In *The Path to Enlightenment*, His Holiness the Fourteenth Dalai Lama explained that, in a Gelug context, although disciples need to see the tantric master as a Buddha in all four highest tantra empowerments, the conferring master's being a Buddha is interpretable in the first three empowerments. Only in the fourth empowerment is the tantric master's being a Buddha a definitive fact. As explained earlier, interpretable phenomena do not exist in the way in which they appear, but they help to lead one to definitive phenomena, which do exist in the way they appear. In the first three highest tantra empowerments, the tantric master appears as a Buddha, but does not necessarily exist as one. Nevertheless, seeing the master as a Buddha during these steps leads disciples to seeing, in the fourth empowerment, that the tantric master not only appears as a Buddha, but also definitively is a Buddha.

The first highest tantra empowerment plants seeds for realizing the generation stage; the second for realizing the illusory body—a body made of subtlest energy-wind. The third plants seeds for realizing the clear light mind; and the fourth for realizing the two truths simultaneously—in this context, the clear light mind and the appearance of its emanations. An unenlightened being may realize the generation stage, illusory body, and clear light mind. Only a Buddha, however, can realize the two truths simultaneously. Thus, from the basis viewpoint taken in the explanations of the Gelug tradition, unenlightened beings may confer the first three empowerments based on their personal experiences. Only a Buddha, however, can describe the simultaneous perception of the two truths from personal experience and thereby confer the fourth empowerment by the force of his or her words. Therefore, to receive the fourth empowerment, disciples need to see that the tantric master definitively is a Buddha.

Causal, Pathway, and Resultant Empowerment

The Gelug tradition offers an additional explanation of seeing that the tantric master is a Buddha within the context of receiving a highest tantra empowerment. In *A Grand Presentation of the Graded Stages of the Secret Mantra Path*, Tsongkapa discussed three stages of empowerment:

causal empowerment that ripens, pathway empowerment that liberates, and resultant empowerment of liberation. The Seventh Dalai Lama explained the three in *Illumination Clarifying the Actual Meaning of Empowerment*. The external tantric master, through following a ritual, confers the causal empowerment that ripens. The inspiration and conscious experiences that disciples receive plant the seeds that ripen into their attainments of enlightenment. When they realize voidness nonconceptually with their clear light minds, their realizations empower their actual liberation, in stages, from the fleeting stains. Thus, the inner guru confers the pathway empowerment that liberates. With the conclusion of the spiritual path, the disciples' attainment of enlightenment confers the resultant empowerment of complete liberation from all fleeting stains.

Causal empowerment from an external master leads to pathway empowerment from an inner guru, which leads to resultant empowerment from the enlightened mind of a Buddha. Thus, seeing that the external tantric master is a Buddha leads to the definitive level of the resultant empowerment. The master who confers resultant empowerment actually is a Buddha in all respects: the definitive empowering master is the Buddha that the disciples then become.

A Tantric Master's Being Inseparable from a Buddha versus a Tantric Master's Having Attained Enlightenment

Wönpo Sherab-jungnay explained that without the conscious experience of understanding the inseparability of their tantric masters as ordinary humans and as Buddha-figures, disciples do not actually receive an empowerment. The understanding need not be deep or profound, but must occur at least on an intellectual level during the ritual. The Drigung Kagyü master also stated, however, that tantric masters do not need to have attained enlightenment in order to be qualified to confer an empowerment. None of the lists of qualifications for highest tantra masters includes that they must actually be enlightened. Thus, seeing one's external tantric master as inseparable from a Buddha does not necessarily mean that the mentor has attained enlightenment.

Wönpo Sherab-jungnay explained three levels of qualifications for conferring a highest tantra empowerment. Best, of course, is if the tantric masters have actually reached the enlightened stage of Vajradhara. Second best is if they have attained stability in the generation stage practices and have achieved a nonconceptual level in the complete stage practice. Minimally, the masters need to have a thorough knowledge of the generation and complete stage practices and the ability to perform the ritual procedures without mistakes.

During empowerments, tantric masters do not transfer insight or causal seeds to disciples the way one tosses a ball for a person to catch. The conscious experiences or insights that define the empowerment process arise dependently on the qualifications of both the tantric masters and the disciples, the procedures of the ritual (particularly the taking of vows), the ambiance that the ritual creates, and the inspiration that the disciples feel.

Seeing All Teachers as Buddhas

Both the sutras and tantras say that disciples need to regard equally as a Buddha someone who taught them even one verse of Dharma and someone who taught them the entire spiritual path. Pabongka cited the Gelug meditation master Drubkang Geleg-gyatso, for example, as having been unable to gain any realization until he could see the pure appearance of the disrobed nun who taught him to read. Westerners frequently have difficulty with this example because they interpret it to mean that unless they see their kindergarten teachers as Buddhas, they will not make progress on the spiritual path. Many imagine that the instructions concerning their tantric masters during empowerments pertain to every teacher they have ever had.

The traditional Tibetan and the modern Western educational systems, however, are extremely different. Tibetan children traditionally used prayers and Dharma texts to learn reading, not children's storybooks with sentences like "See Spot run. Run, Spot, run." Although seeing everyone as a Buddha, including one's kindergarten teacher, is helpful for realizing Buddha-nature, the instructions on building a disciple-mentor relationship pertain only to one's spiritual teachers.

In general, once we have built a disciple-mentor relationship with one teacher, we need to regard and treat all our spiritual teachers, even our previous Buddhism professors, with the same respect as we show our mentors. Before that, when we are still relating to teachers as Buddhism professors or Dharma instructors, we of course show the persons respect. Nevertheless, regarding them as we would spiritual mentors is inappropriate.

The same instruction pertains to disciples' seeing pure appearances of the bodies, speech, and minds of all their spiritual teachers. In *The Divisions of the Three Sets of Vows*, Sakya Pandita explained clearly that disciples do this only after having received highest tantra empowerments. If highest tantra practice entails seeing pure appearances of ourselves, our environments, and all beings within them, the practice surely includes seeing the pure Buddha-nature aspects of all our teachers as well. This does not mean however, that we seek instruction on our tantric practices from our Buddhism professors, let alone from our kindergarten teachers.

Actualizing Enlightenment through Seeing That a Tantric Master Is a Buddha

The good qualities of a tantric master and the good qualities of a Buddha both refer to the same attribute of one phenomenon—the clear light mind—whether one looks at the qualities from a basis, pathway, or resultant viewpoint. According to the Sakya presentation of *alaya* (the foundation for everything), from the basis point of view good qualities are the defining characteristics of the clear light mind. From the pathway viewpoint, they are the corrections that come from removing fleeting stains. On the resultant level, they are the fully realized potentials of the clear light mind. These three statements are true whether one looks at good qualities in one's mentor or in a Buddha. By focusing on the qualities of one's mentor as those of a Buddha, one gains inspiration to realize that one's own good qualities are similarly functions of one's clear light mind on the three inseparable levels. This realization is essential for actualizing the resultant level to become a Buddha.

Actualizing the inseparable basis, pathway, and resultant levels of our own good qualities is only possible through the highest tantra methods. This is because only the highest tantra methods enable us to access their foundation and source—our clear light minds. Within the framework of understanding voidness with this subtlest level of mind, we may then arise in the pure forms of Buddha-figures with the good qualities of our clear light minds operational on all levels.

To activate the potentials of our Buddha-natures to reach this supreme attainment, we need to receive highest tantra empowerments. To strengthen these potentials, we then imagine, with generation stage practice, that we now have the pure forms of Buddha-figures with all the Buddha-qualities functional on their resultant levels. To actualize the potentials, we need to access our clear light minds with complete stage practice. However, without a healthy relationship with a tantric master—as Tsangpa-gyaray explained—the tantric process cannot occur.

Specific Explanation Regarding Empowerment and Generation Stage Practice

Causal empowerment cannot occur without a qualified tantric master, a properly conducted ritual, and a qualified disciple with conviction in, appreciation of, and inspiration from the mentor's qualities. The taking of vows requires the presence of a master seen as a Buddha. The planting of causal seeds requires seeing the body, speech, and mind of the tantric master as inseparable from the enlightening faculties of a Buddha. Moreover, the planting of seeds requires inspiration from a tantric master seen as a Buddha to gain a joyful experience of voidness.

Inspiration from a tantric master is likewise indispensable for generation stage practice. Bodhichitta is a heart and mind focused on enlightenment with the aspiration to become a Buddha to benefit everyone. Sutra practice focuses on enlightenment as represented by a Buddha. Focusing, however, on the resultant level of all good qualities may be difficult when it is done in reference to a generic Buddha or, on the generation stage, to oneself visualized as a Buddha-figure. A vivid reference as an object of focus makes the resultant level more accessible for meditation.

Highest tantra practice, therefore, focuses on the tantric master as inseparable from a Buddha. The inspiration felt from the mentor, plus the firm conviction in and appreciation of his or her qualities that come from personal experience of them, makes the object of focus extremely vivid. Thus, focusing on the mentor's good qualities as inseparable from the Buddha-qualities helps to energize, sustain, and enhance bodhichitta.

Moreover, when disciples visualize in tantric guru-yoga that they receive inspiration and the four empowerments from the mentor's Buddha-qualities of body, speech, and mind, they strengthen their networks of positive potentials and deep awareness. The strengthening enables the tantric disciples to actualize the good qualities of their clear light minds. Consequently, the visualization of themselves as Buddha-figures with these qualities becomes more vivid. As Tsangpa-gyaray indicated, no matter how technically correct disciples' tantric visualizations may be, without the uplifting energy of a healthy relationship with a tantric master they will fail to bring self-transformation leading to enlightenment.

Complete Stage Practice

Complete stage practice accesses clear light mind either by dissolving the energy-winds that serve as the basis for the grosser levels of consciousness, or by energizing the mind through increasingly more intense levels of bliss. In tantric guru-yoga, disciples focus on their tantric masters with intense conviction in the masters' qualities as the qualities of a Buddha. Because of the inspiration felt from the relationship, the more the disciples focus on their mentors' qualities, the more joyous they become. Because the entire tantric process occurs within the sphere of the understanding of voidness, the joy, energy, and inspiration experienced from focusing on the tantric master are not disturbing. They do not boil over into unbridled ecstasy or translate into fanatic devotion as often happens in relation to a pop star or a demagogue. On the contrary, the joyous energy felt stabilizes and refines the mind.

Moreover, the tantras explain that the more fuel on a fire, the hotter it burns. Thus, the stronger the emotion, the more energized and intense the mind becomes. If this is the case concerning disturbing emotions such as longing desire, it is especially true regarding a nondisturbing emotion of joyous inspiration.

When tantric disciples with a basic understanding of voidness imagine that all gross appearances collect into their visualized mentor/Buddhas and then that their mentor/Buddhas become tiny and merge into their hearts, the visualization process helps them to dissolve the internal energy-winds that produce deceptive appearances. As the dissolution occurs, their minds become subtler while in a joyous, energized state that understands voidness. The resulting mind, backed with the additional energy of a bodhichitta motivation, has the required intensity and refinement to reveal and to identify its clear light nature.

Introduction by a Tantric Master to the Nature of the Mind

An alternative way for disciples to access their clear light minds is through direct introduction to this subtlest level of mind by their tantric masters. Although the Nyingma tradition specializes in these methods, they also appear in the Sakya and Kagyü teachings. Sakya Pandita gave one of the clearest examples in *The Profound Path of Guru-Yoga*. During an appropriate ceremony, properly prepared disciples focus with quiet, alert minds on the center of their tantric masters' brows. Simultaneously, the mentors focus on the voidness of their clear light minds, recite a certain mantra, hold up a vajra, and ring a bell. If the disciples have sufficient strength of positive potential, deep awareness, firm conviction in the fact that the tantric master is a Buddha, and inspiration, they may gain an experience of clear light mind. The experience occurs through a process of dependent arising from these causes and conditions.

Ultimately, then, seeing that their tantric masters are Buddhas enables disciples to realize, on the basis of clear light mind, their own good qualities as inseparable from both the mentors' qualities and the qualities of a Buddha. Ngojey-raypa explained that, with this realization, when disciples subsequently remove the fleeting stains from their clear light minds, they become one with their mentors. This does not mean, the Drigung Kagyü master continued, that the disciples become the same persons or replicas of their tantric masters, or that they now hold the same opinions about everything as their mentors do. Their minds' becoming one with the inseparable minds of their mentors and the Buddhas means that the disciples have reached the final attainment of an enlightening mind.

In short, seeing our mentors as Buddhas has many levels of meaning. A healthy relationship with a spiritual teacher requires clarity about which level of meaning pertains to us at each stage of the spiritual path. At no stage, however, is the teaching meant for the literal interpretation that our teachers are omniscient or can manifest simultaneously in countless forms. Throughout the spiritual path to enlightenment, we need to maintain common sense and continually enhance our discriminating awareness to discern between what is appropriate and what is not.

Guru-Meditation Relevant for Beginners in the West

Many Westerners begin to study Dharma without any interest in tantra or intention to engage eventually in its practice. Some, however, make their first contact with Tibetan Buddhism at tantric empowerments.

As stated earlier, if they attend the rituals merely as observers without consciously taking and intending to keep the vows, they do not establish disciple-mentor relationships with the tantric masters. Moreover, as Wönpo Sherab-jungnay added, members of the audience do not actually receive the empowerment unless they have also had a conscious experience and insight during the ceremony that has purified mental blocks and has planted seeds for realizations. Without fulfilling these prerequisites during the empowerment, they might later engage in tantric practices, but their progress would be minimal.

The specifically tantric practices of guru-yoga and the manner of relating to a tantric master, then, are not germane to most Western Dharma students during the early stages of their spiritual journeys. One might reasonably argue that the instructions on the disciple-mentor relationship found in the graded-path texts that explicitly or implicitly emphasize tantra are also too advanced for Westerners at these stages. More appropriate for people who are not yet ready to commit themselves to the Buddhist path with lifelong vows would be the sutra-level practices of guru-yoga deriving from the Kadam tradition. This is because the sutra-level meditations to gain inspiration from a teacher's good qualities not only aim to prepare students for a tantric disciple-mentor relationship, they also are suitable for a relationship with a Buddhism professor, Dharma instructor, or meditation or ritual trainer. They are basic exercises comfortably shared by committed Mahayana and tantric disciples and uncommitted students of Buddhism who wish to gain the maximum benefit from the relationship with a spiritual teacher.

PART III:

Unhealthy Relationships with Spiritual Teachers

~13

Overdependence and Rebellion

Avoiding Overdependence on Others for Spiritual Energy

EVEN AFTER COMMITTING oneself to a spiritual path and establishing a disciple-mentor relationship, maintaining energy and motivation in one's spiritual practice may often present a challenge. Thus, seekers need a variety of ways to help lift themselves from the inevitable moments of feeling uninspired and unmotivated. The classical texts recommend staying in close contact with other practitioners and with spiritual teachers when one finds oneself in need of support. Also helpful for raising spiritual energy may be thinking of loved ones or the needy, or perhaps recalling a spiritual journey to Asia.

Although such methods may temporarily lift our spirits to a certain extent, our energy may remain mostly low, especially when we are primarily on our own. The problem may be overdependence on external factors, particularly an unhealthy overdependence on others. Although being in a supportive environment and keeping good company may help to provide circumstances conducive for sustaining a spiritual practice, they are not enough. Ultimately, the motivating emotion and uplifting energy for self-transformation must come from within.

The Connections Sutra clearly indicated this fact: "Buddhas cannot wash away others' negative potentials, nor remove their suffering like one would pull out a thorn from a foot. They cannot transfer their realizations to anyone. They can only indicate the way by teaching about reality." Psychotherapy makes the same point. No matter what a therapist might do, insight and understanding must come from the side of the client.

We may also infer this truth from an explanation that Sakya Pandita gave in *The Profound Path of Guru-Yoga* concerning the previously cited analogy of the sun, a magnifying glass, and kindling. Without a magnifying glass to focus the rays of the sun, the heat of the sun by itself cannot bring kindling to the flame. Nevertheless, the energy of fire ultimately comes from the potential of the kindling to burn. Similarly, without a healthy relationship with a spiritual mentor to focus the waves of the Buddhas' inspiration, the energy of the waves by itself cannot spark a disciple to enlightenment. Nevertheless, the energy of enlightenment ultimately comes from the networks of good qualities, positive potentials, and deep awareness within a disciple. On the deepest level, the energy comes from a disciple's inner guru—his or her clear light mind.

Moreover, Sakya Pandita continued, if kindling is damp or stacked in disorder, it will not catch fire. Similarly, if a disciple's mind is unruly or soggy with irrelevant thoughts, preconceptions, or doubts, it will not come to blaze with inspiration. Effects arise dependently from a combination of causes and factors.

Cultural Factors in Western and Tibetan Overdependence

Many people in the West find life overwhelmingly complex and confusing. Because anxiety, tension, and worry fill their minds, they cannot find inner sources of strength. The kindling is wet and in disarray. Their emotional states are unstable and nothing inspires them. With typical Western low self-esteem, they are unsure of themselves. Afraid of making mistakes, some may want to give the responsibility for decisions to others. They desperately long for someone to know what is happening and to take care of everything, like an ideal father or God.

Some may join the army so that they simply need to follow orders and not think for themselves. Those who are more spiritually inclined may turn to a Dharma center. Although their spiritual longing may be genuine, the emotional and cultural baggage that they bring along may cause them to seek relationships with spiritual teachers as father or authority figures. They may wish to establish such relationships to enable them to give up responsibility for making decisions in their lives. Many hope that this will make life easier and solve their problems.

Westerners who enter this type of overdependency relationship, however, do so only on a voluntary basis. No one likes to be forced to obey someone else. If people have chosen to submit themselves to another person, and they have chosen the individual to whom they submit, they usually feel comfortable with the situation.

"Biblical thinking" may unconsciously contribute to this typically Western pattern of behavior. For example, the concept of original sin may foster a feeling of inherent guilt and low self-opinion. Consequently, someone might feel that taking a wrong decision in life would prove his or her unworthiness and might lead to being further rejected as a bad person, as if being further cast out from paradise. It feels safer to let someone else make one's decisions.

Moreover, modern Western customs of child rearing may reinforce a doctrinally supported feeling of rejection or abandonment because of something being inherently wrong with oneself, or they may foster such feelings by themselves. Many Western mothers no longer breast-feed their babies, carry them on their backs all day, or sleep with them at night as mothers in traditional societies do. Instead, they feed their babies with bottles, keep them in playpens, strollers, or day care while awake, and leave them alone in cribs at night. From the babies' viewpoints, they have been cast out from paradise. Consequently, insufficient body contact as a baby may lead not only to the culturally specific modern Western syndrome of alienation from one's body and feelings, but also to an unconscious longing for acceptance, affection, and even redemption. Western spiritual seekers caught in these syndromes sometimes turn to spiritual teachers in the unconscious hope of satisfying these needs. The urgency of their unconscious drives may lead to overdependence.

Occasionally, overdependent Western seekers encounter Tibetans who are also overly dependent on spiritual masters and they may justify their own behavior on this basis. The cultural influences and psychology behind the traditional Tibetan form of overdependence on a spiritual teacher, however, differ significantly from those behind the typical Western pattern. Many Tibetans, like other Asians, shy away from accepting responsibility for taking decisions because they fear losing face in their communities or disgracing their families if they fail. Thus, mostly social and familial considerations, rather than individual ones, drive them to give responsibility to lamas for their decisions.

Moreover, Tibetans would typically choose not just any lama with whom to have this type of overdependence relationship, but would turn to the lamas or rinpocheys who head the monasteries in their local regions. This happens even among Tibetans in exile, where geographic limitations on the choice of lama do not pertain. Again, social and communal factors affect a Tibetan's decision, and not individual preferences as in the case of Westerners. Moreover, Tibetans do not feel forced to choose the lamas of their local regions: they feel the choice is naturally fitting according to social norms. Group or individual pressure is hardly needed.

Whether an overdependence relationship with a spiritual teacher arises within a Western or a Tibetan sociopsychological context, such a relationship is fundamentally unhealthy. It does not foster the maturity that a spiritual path to liberation and enlightenment seeks to develop. Certainly, a healthy relationship with a spiritual mentor entails consulting a teacher for advice concerning spiritual matters. It also entails deriving inspiration from the person. A spiritual mentor, however, is not God, an all-powerful father or mother, or a feudal lord. He or she cannot solve all our problems for us. Obedient submission or subservient deference to a mentor's will, even when made on a voluntary basis, can neither redeem us nor make up for having been seemingly abandoned by our parents as children because we were bad or had something wrong with us. Nor can it exempt us from responsibility for failure or from losing face. Spiritual seekers, whether Western or Tibetan, who suffer from an overdependence syndrome need to focus on their Buddha-natures and work on clearing their relationships with their spiritual teachers from this unhealthy aspect.

Overdependence Based on a Western Orientation toward Ethics

In *Establishing Method and Discriminating Awareness*, the greatly accomplished Indian yogi Anangavajra explained how to gain inspiration in a healthy manner from a spiritual mentor. One of the most important factors is the strength of character that comes from keeping one's vows and close bonds with ethical practice. The self-rule that comes from maintaining ethical self-discipline provides the maturity and stability needed to gain inspiration from a mentor without becoming overdependent. This is because the basis for Buddhist ethics is discriminating awareness. By discriminating between the benefits and disadvantages of various actions, practitioners restrain from destructive conduct that will cause only harm. Being ethical, then, depends entirely on oneself.

Western cultures, in contrast, derive their ethics from a mixture of Biblical and ancient Greek thought. Consequently, they base their ethics on obedience to authority. In obeying laws either commanded by God or promulgated by legislature, one becomes an ethical person. A Western sense of ethics, then, often promotes psychological dependence on gaining approval and reward from authority and avoiding its censure and punishment. Thus, many Western spiritual seekers experience that their discipline to meditate, for example, comes from the unconscious wish to be good disciples and to gain the approval of their mentors. When the energy for spiritual practice derives from a mentor's inspiring guilt and fear of rejection, rather than inspiring self-confident resolve, the disciple-mentor relationship has become unhealthy.

Overdependence on Guided Meditation

Part of the discipline in Tibetan monastic institutions is maintaining a strict schedule of daily, monthly, and annual assemblies. At set times throughout the day and night, the monks and nuns convene, sometimes all together, sometimes in smaller groups, to recite prayers and to chant and perform tantric rituals. Each monastery and nunnery, and each of its subdivisions, are responsible for the regular periodic performance of a specific set of prayers and rituals from the lineage. The tantric ritual texts describe series of visualizations, as well as desired mental states, such as bodhichitta and the understanding of voidness. While chanting together, the participants try to visualize and enter the states that they are reciting. The abbot or abbess and various lamas may attend, but only as participants sitting in the front row on slightly raised seats; a chant master leads the choral recitation. No one sits facing the group and leading the ritual, either by describing the procedures at the start of the session or by guiding it step by step.

Although participation in group recitation of monastic rituals involves meditation, most Tibetan monks and nuns have additional daily personal practices, which they do on their own. Their private practices usually include chanting and performing further tantric rituals and, for some, sitting in silent meditation. Similarly, Tibetan lay practitioners also meditate on their own. Traditional Tibetan Buddhism does not employ the custom of silent group meditation, either with or without a leader. Consequently, when traditional Tibetan masters first come to the West and are asked to lead group meditations, many have no idea what the Western students are talking about.

Tibetans learn to meditate by having a teacher explain the instructions and then by practicing alone in their rooms. The teacher hardly ever meditates with the students, even at the beginning stages of the training. In contrast, most Westerners need someone to meditate with them at first, to help them overcome the confusion and barriers that may arise from engaging in a practice from a foreign culture. Thus, most Westerners inevitably begin to meditate in a group that is led by a teacher.

Many Westerners, however, lack the discipline to meditate on their own after learning the basics. Therefore, they find that continued group meditation, especially when led by a teacher, helps them to build beneficial habits. Whether the meditation is silent or involves group chanting of a ritual, they find it helpful for a teacher to sit in front each time, to describe the procedure at the beginning, and then to meditate with them throughout the session. Moreover, those bewildered by some of the more complex silent practices find guided meditation particularly useful. Using his or her own words, a teacher describes in stages the visualizations, understandings, and feelings that students are trying to generate. As they listen, the meditators try to imagine and feel these things while suspending any extraneous, independent thoughts. Habitual reliance, however, on any form of group meditation may sometimes lead to overdependence on these styles of practice and on the teachers who lead them.

In most cases, teachers lead meditation for benevolent purposes. However, since led meditation works by the power of suggestion, particularly when silent meditation is guided step by step, a teacher with a tendency toward abusing power may contribute to the overdependence. The abuse may take a gross, devious form if motivated by the self-serving wish for control, such as when a teacher tries to manipulate disciples to worship the guru by including images of him or herself in the visualization. In extreme cases, the leader of a cult may even use led meditation to brainwash followers to commit mass suicide at an impending end of the world. In more subtle and benign cases of exploitation of power, a teacher may sincerely wish to benefit disciples.

Yet, an unconscious drive to gain energy and fulfillment from helping others in an active demonstrable way may underlie the person's over-use of led meditation.

There is no doubt that the directive energy of a charismatic teacher and a group dynamic may contribute to our gaining initial medita-tive experiences as novice practitioners. Most newcomers, in fact, have difficulty in learning meditation without such direction. Spiritual development through meditation, however, needs to be self-sustain-ing. Once we gain a certain level of discipline and experience through group meditation led by a teacher, however, we need to strengthen that discipline and experience through solitary practice. Otherwise, we risk the danger of becoming addicted to led meditation, as if it were a rec-reational drug. By being mindful of these points from the start, we may avoid the pitfalls of becoming overdependent on a teacher, or even on tape cassettes, for meditation practice.

Moreover, we need to examine both our own motivations and those of teachers for participating in led meditation. Even if the teacher is trying to gain power from directing others, we may derive the benefit of led meditation by having sufficient clarity of purpose. If a teacher is trying to brainwash spiritual seekers into negative ways of think-ing, we need to recognize the syndrome and withdraw. If, however, the teacher has an overprotective or manipulative approach to helping seekers gain positive ways of thinking, we may include this shortcom-ing in the section of sutra-level guru-meditation that concerns focusing on the mentor's faults.

Overdependence on Having All Questions Answered for Oneself

Buddha used many methods for leading disciples along the spiritual path. Sometimes when disciples asked questions, Buddha employed the Socratic approach of querying back. The purpose was to help them to gain insight and to answer the questions through their own pow-ers of reasoning. Alternatively, Buddha gave only partial answers and hinted at the rest. This style also encouraged disciples to figure out the answers through reason or personal experience. Occasionally, Buddha used enigmatic means and answered with paradoxes or with seemingly irrelevant statements, which might shock disciples into deeper levels of understanding. In response to other questions, Buddha remained silent. Any answer that he might have given would have confused disciples whose preconceptions were still too thick to understand fully. Certain questions, however, Buddha answered clearly, precisely, and authoritatively, to dispel confusion. Thus, Buddha was a master of "skillful means."

Qualified spiritual mentors employ the same range of methods as Buddha used for leading disciples and for answering questions. Sometimes, however, teachers may give authoritarian rather than authoritative answers. This may discourage free enquiry and thought. Rather than helping disciples to develop the powers of discrimination and reason, such teachers may encourage overdependence by giving categorical answers to all questions. The situation depends on the conscious and unconscious motivations of the teachers and on their levels of proficiency in using skillful means.

Certain spiritual seekers may be prone to dependency on dogmatic teachers. They find life so confusing that they want everything to be clear-cut and certain. They do not wish to think for themselves. Such an attitude, however, is not conducive for spiritual growth. Therefore, if spiritual teachers give only partial or enigmatic answers to questions, we need to understand that this is a teaching method. Appreciating the method helps to avoid frustration and impatience with unsatisfying answers. If, on the other hand, teachers try to stifle our minds, we need to remember Buddha's advice in *A Sutra on [Pure Realms] Spread Out in a Dense Array*: "Do not accept my Dharma merely out of respect for me, but analyze and check it the way a goldsmith analyzes gold, by rubbing, cutting and melting it."

The Issue of Submission

Some Westerners enter relationships with spiritual teachers along the model of Catholic nuns who marry Jesus and vow total unquestioning obedience to higher authority. They feel that if they surrender, open their hearts, and let their mentors act through them, they will be able to serve the world. On a psychological level, this syndrome sometimes derives from low self-esteem and from feelings that self-worth comes from "belonging" to a spiritually superior being. Although the syndrome is more typical of women spiritual seekers in relation to male teachers, it often arises also in men.

Voluntary submission to an idealized person and the wish to belong to someone greater than themselves may easily open spiritual seekers to various forms of abuse. If they are abused, either sexually or in less severe ways, the experience may reinforce their low self-opinions: they may feel that they deserved the bad treatment. Alternatively, the abuse may cause them subsequently to close their hearts to anyone else. On the surface, submission may seem like a loss of ego and therefore a Buddhist virtue. However, if the submission is for unconsciously gaining a sense of self-worth and for self-affirmation through belonging to someone greater, it undermines rather than strengthens a healthy sense of self. A feeling of self-worth comes primarily from acknowledging one's own potentials and from using them to benefit others as much as one can.

Moreover, Western disciples who presume that Buddhism shares the Biblical approach to ethics may mistakenly imagine that Tibetan lamas morally judge them. This may lead to inappropriately introducing the concept of guilt into the dynamics of the relationship. If students fail to do everything their mentors ask, they feel guilty and unworthy. Therefore, fearing rejection because of being "bad disciples," they feel they must submit without question and always obey.

From a Buddhist standpoint, behavioral cause and effect function without a higher authority passing judgment. A person avoids destructive behavior not because of fear of punishment, but because of wishing to avoid the suffering that unhealthy behavior brings. As explained above, obedience to laws created by God or promulgated by an elected legislature is a culturally specific virtue, not a universal one.

A healthy relationship with a spiritual mentor, then, does not entail submission or belonging to the mentor. Nor does it entail guilt-based obedience. One must differentiate clearly between being a mentor's disciple and belonging to a mentor.

Gender Prejudice

The position of women in most traditional Asian societies is inferior to that of men. Prejudice was so rampant in ancient Indian society during Buddha's time, for example, that to avoid disdain by a patriarchal society, Buddha and his followers even codified gender bias in the monastic rules of discipline. Thus, numerous traditional Tibetan mentors, particularly monks, share the legacy of this prejudice, either consciously or unconsciously, despite Buddha's teaching that the mind has no inherent gender. Their overt or subtle denigration of women often humiliates and discourages Western female students. The situation frequently leads to major blocks in the spiritual progress of these women.

Complaining about the prejudice and campaigning for traditional Tibetans to change their values often bring only more frustration, bitterness, and anger. As when dwelling on any conventional fault of a mentor, fixating on a teacher's gender bias is counterproductive. Although making traditional Tibetan teachers aware of the suffering that their attitudes cause women disciples is extremely important, expecting sudden revolutionary change may be unrealistic. On the other hand, denying the prejudice or repressing feelings of humiliation and pain undermines the spiritual and emotional health of the disciple.

Sutra-level guru-meditation suggests an approach that may help during the interim before sexual equality comes to the spiritual sphere. If our mentors suffer from gender prejudice, we need first to admit to ourselves that they have this shortcoming. Even if our mentors cannot or will not acknowledge their biases as faults, our open acknowledgement of them helps to assuage the pain. Next, we need to focus on the fact that this fault in the mentors is devoid of existing as an inherent flaw, but has arisen dependently on various cultural and personal factors. This understanding may allow us then to focus on our mentors' good qualities and kindness and, consequently, to derive the benefits obtainable from the relationship.

The Influence of Ancient Greek Thought on Being an Individual

Another unconscious influence on Western thought is the image of the hero challenging the supremacy of the gods, which comes from ancient Greece. In accord with this image, many Westerners, both male and female, feel inwardly driven to rebel against authority and tradition. This may manifest in several ways.

Westerners may seek to establish their equality by proving their creativity and strength as independent individuals. Thus, some may rebel against the traditions of their parents or society and join Dharma centers as an unconscious way to assert their individualities. They need not be on their own to assert their individuality: often people feel they assert it by following alternative fashions or by joining alternative movements. Unconscious rebellious motives, however, may jeopardize the chances of a healthy relationship with a spiritual teacher.

For example, some disciples may avoid or reject their mentors' continuing guidance once they feel they have spiritually "grown up." Spiritual mentors teach disciples to stand on their own two feet and to make enlightened decisions based on compassion and wisdom. Nevertheless, making spiritually mature decisions does not necessitate inevitably rejecting one's mentor and his or her advice as a threat to one's independence or individuality. Thus, if hubris drives disciples to rebel against restrictions, they inevitably come into conflict with their mentors.

The culturally supported drive to challenge and surpass accepted standards of competence may also manifest as an unconscious drive to achieve enlightenment and become the perfect mentor in order to excel and outdo everyone—as if training to win the Olympics. This may lead to competition with one's mentor, and cultural chauvinism may reinforce the syndrome. For example, some disciples and even some insufficiently qualified spiritual teachers may arrogantly feel that a modern Western approach to Buddhism is obviously superior to outdated, superstitious traditional ways. They believe that, by using this approach, they may, in fact, become greater masters than their mentors are. A healthy disciple-mentor relationship, however, requires humble appreciation of the mentor's kindness and profound respect for his or her qualities, even after becoming a Buddha oneself.

Tension over the Issue of Being Creative

The Tibetan concept of creativity differs greatly from the Western idea. For traditional Tibetans, as for most Asian cultures, creativity comes in harmoniously applying a traditional motif to an individual circumstance. In temple architecture, for example, one seeks to fit classic designs to new landscape settings. The Western concept of creativity, on the other hand, is to invent something new—and not only new, but also frequently something better in some sense than anything previously done. In a Western cultural context, then, being creative is a means to establish one's uniqueness as an individual. There may be a competitive motive behind it. Alternatively, or in combination with this motive, the Western creative drive may be fueled by an obsessive, individual pursuit of ideal beauty, unconsciously equated with truth and goodness. The concepts are distinctly legacies of ancient Greek thought.

Moreover, Indo-Tibetan cosmology sees present history as a gradual degeneration of the times rather than as an evolutionary process of inevitable progress. Therefore, traditional Tibetans view unique new ideas with suspicion rather than with excitement at the prospect of improvement.

Western disciples who lack appreciation of these cultural differences concerning creativity sometimes wish to rebel against traditional Tibetan mentors who discourage inventiveness when applied to the Dharma. Tibetan Buddhism, however, does allow for innovative approaches, in the form of skillful means. After all, Buddha emphasized the need to teach Dharma in manners that effectively suit different personalities and cultures. Teaching or doing something in a new manner, however, is for benefiting others, not for asserting one's unique and superior creativity, or for expressing one's individuality, or for finding the most elegant solution. If we keep this distinction in mind and sort out our motivations for change, we may avoid feeling our individualities threatened when working with traditional Tibetan teachers.

~14
Transference and Regression

Description of the Phenomena in Classical Psychoanalysis

TRANSFERENCE AND REGRESSION are phenomena that occur in most
ordinary human relationships. In classical Freudian psychoanalysis,
as described by Menninger in *Theory of Psychoanalytic Technique*, they
are encouraged and employed as working tools. The client lies on a
couch with the analyst sitting behind unseen, somewhat like a parent
remaining invisible to a baby lying in a carriage. The client opens him
or herself up to the analyst, but the analyst remains for the most part
unresponsive and silent. The client feels frustrated and irrationally
transfers or projects onto the "blank slate" analyst the image of a parent or some other troublesome figure from childhood who did not pay
enough attention to him or her. Wishing for help, but not receiving it,
the client regresses to childish patterns.

The regression typically goes through stages. The client has obediently followed the analyst's instructions to reveal his or her innermost
thoughts and feelings. Yet, the client has seemingly failed to please
the analyst and so has not received any reward for being a "good"
patient. The object that the client feels denied regresses from help, to
attention, to acknowledgement, to approval, to love, to affection. The
feeling regresses from wanting, to craving, to absolutely requiring, to
demanding. The frustration at not receiving the desired object similarly regresses to anger, then rage.

The client's rage may boil over into the equivalent of an infantile
temper tantrum. The analyst obviously does not love him or her. The
client may wish to find the analyst's weaknesses and hurt the person.
He or she may transfer not merely the image of a negligent parent onto

the analyst, but also the image of an unresponsive partner. The client may flirt with the analyst, try to seduce the person, and if rejected, cause a scandal by claiming that the analyst was trying to seduce her or him. Transference and regression may be multifaceted.

Optimally, the client eventually reaches a crisis point and, as with the breaking of a fever, releases the infantile rage. The client sees that expressing his or her pain and anger does not lead to being branded a "bad" child and to being rejected or abandoned. The analyst continues to act with the same stability and calmness that has characterized the entire relationship. Slowly, the client learns to have reasonable expectations and to recognize different ways in which others may feel comfortable to fulfill them. The client becomes a mature adult.

The Phenomena in Disciple-Mentor Relationships

According to post-Freudian usage, regression to a younger stage in life may not only be degenerative; it may also be an improvement. Someone may regress to a juvenile, immature mode of behavior, as Freud described it, or to an open-minded, innocent childlike manner of relating to the world. Restorative regression ideally happens in a healthy disciple-mentor relationship in which the example of the teacher inspires a seeker to drop rigid modes of thinking and behaving that cause only suffering. Transference and degenerative regression, on the other hand, commonly occur in an unhealthy disciple-mentor relationship, especially when a mentor fails to respond in the ways a disciple would like. Let us examine the phenomena.

A disciple may obediently follow his or her mentor's teachings and try to please the person with offerings, service, and practice. Yet, the mentor remains unmoved—in the Kadam Geshey Sharawa's words, like a tiger looking at grass. The mentor may be busy with many other students, may travel frequently, and may have little or no time for personal attention to each disciple. A disciple with tendencies toward overdependence, submission, or rebellion may be psychologically unable to cope with these facts.

If we find ourselves in such situations, we may easily regress in a degenerative manner. We may transfer and project onto the teacher the image of an inattentive parent or unresponsive lover. We want, crave, and may even demand acknowledgement, attention, help, love, praise, and affection. Frustrated, we may feel anger and rage, but may feel guilty about it. Because of low self-esteem, some of us dare not express our anger for fear of being branded and abandoned as "bad" disciples. Worse, we may be terrified that our feelings constitute "a breach of guru-devotion" and will lead to burning in hell, as many Buddhist texts describe. Our struggles to suppress frustration and anger, and our feelings of guilt, in fact create living hells for us. In Buddhist terms, a hell is not a place of punishment for disobedience, but an experience of torment created by one's own confused, destructive thoughts and actions.

Resolution of Problems Arising from Transference and Degenerative Regression

The Fifth Dalai Lama's instructions on guru-meditation may be helpful in resolving problems that arise from transference and degenerative regression with a spiritual mentor. If we are caught in the hellish mental state that the syndrome creates, we need first to realize that not only is it all right to drop our fear and guilt about what we might feel about our teachers, but it is essential—although, of course, not easy to do. Fear and guilt about our feelings do not help anything. Once we are able to relax our emotional barriers by using, for example, some of the Buddhist meditation methods for quieting the mind, we then need to let the disturbing feelings arise and try to identify them. We may then ask ourselves, "Where are these feelings coming from? What am I really trying to say?" The situation affords an excellent opportunity to learn more about ourselves.

If we recognize the phenomena of transference and degenerative regression, we next need to bring to consciousness the faults we see in our mentors. We then need to distinguish between the facts of their actual conduct and the projected images of unsatisfying parents or disappointing lovers. Acknowledging the frustration that we feel, we need to see that our mentors' lack of response comes from causes and conditions, such as having many responsibilities. Moreover, the lack of attention or acknowledgement that we receive is not a rejection and does not mean that we are bad disciples. The guilt we may feel neither confirms nor proves our inherent inadequacy.

Delving to the root of our angry frustration and eliminating the confusion that is causing it—in other words, meditating on voidness and dependent arising—bring longer lasting results than trying to purge ourselves of rage by venting it. Venting suppressed rage may simply reinforce a habit of anger. In most cases, however, voidness meditation on angry frustration requires repetition and deepening before it starts to lessen the intensity and frequency of the problem recurring. Results follow nonlinearly and miracle cures hardly ever happen.

Further Steps in the Resolution Process, Suggested by Contextual Therapy

A further cause contributing to transference and degenerative regression may be culturally specific. From a Western point of view, the universe is just and fair, whether because God is its creator and ruler or because of the rule of legislated law. Thus, if we have followed our mentors' instructions and practiced conscientiously, we feel that we have earned the right to acknowledgement and praise, and the entitlement to receive them. If our mentors do not give what we feel we have rightly earned, we believe they are acting unfairly. This may cause us to feel frustrated, hurt, and even enraged. We may regress to the feelings of children who scream that it is unfair when denied the reward of staying up late after they have finished all their homework.

According to the approach of contextual therapy, we are entitled to feel bad when our mentors seemingly treat us unfairly, although we are not entitled to revenge. To overcome the pain, we need also to acknowledge our entitlement to be happy about the sincere practices that we have done. Even if no one else acknowledges our right to feel happy, self-acknowledgement gives the affirmation and strength that may enable us to understand and to forgive the mentors' limitations. It also allows us to acknowledge the respect and appreciation rightfully due to our mentors because of their good qualities and kindness. Moreover, the reassurance and calmness gained from self-acknowledgement may give us the clarity and openness of mind to see that our mentors may in fact be acknowledging our efforts in previously unrecognized ways.

Pleasing a Spiritual Mentor

The issue of gaining acknowledgement from a spiritual mentor is especially baffling for Westerners because the classical texts on the disciple-mentor relationship repeatedly stress pleasing one's mentor. The ritual texts typically contain such prayers as: "May I please my guru. May all the Buddhas be pleased with me." The problem is how to know that the mentor is pleased. Various cultures condition people to express their pleasure in different ways. When Western disciples lack familiarity with Tibetan customs, they may be unable to recognize how a traditional Tibetan mentor would express pleasure with a disciple.

Low self-esteem is not an issue for most Tibetans, whereas overconfidence and arrogance typically are problems. Therefore, a traditional Tibetan mentor would avoid complimenting a disciple to his or her face since it might increase the person's inordinate feelings of self-worth. A mentor would normally praise a disciple only to others, when the disciple was elsewhere. Moreover, Tibetans lack the Western notion that unless a sentiment is verbalized, it is not actually real. Most Tibetan couples, for example, would neither say "I love you" to each other, nor require an "I love you" to feel secure or loved. Tibetans express their love through taking care of each other. Thus, a Tibetan mentor would acknowledge a disciple's efforts and show pleasure only indirectly, for example by taking the person seriously and giving further teachings.

Moreover, Tibetans do not feel the need to be with another person constantly, or even frequently, in order to sustain a close relationship. In traditional Tibet, people often made long caravan journeys and were away from loved ones for several years at a time. Therefore, spending little time with a disciple is normal and not a sign of displeasure, rejection, or abandonment.

A major way in which Tibetans show that they care about someone is to point out the person's faults and to give a light scolding. They may also warn the person against possible mistakes and, in general, give the person a hard time so that he or she may learn and grow. If someone does not really care about another person, he or she would not go to such bother. This pattern of behavior typifies not only traditional Tibetan mentors, but also traditional Tibetan fathers.

Most Western disciples, however, totally misinterpret the traditional Tibetan manner of taking someone seriously and showing care and concern. Instead of feeling that they have pleased their Tibetan mentors, they feel they have displeased or disappointed them. In many cases, they may project unpleasant experiences with their parents onto situations with their mentors. Consequently, they may regress and respond in adolescent ways. For example, they may see stern Tibetan paternal advice as judgmental Western fatherly disapproval. They may take it as harsh criticism and as a threat to their integrity, individuality, and independence. They may see warnings against mistakes as signs that their mentors neither trust nor respect them. Instead of helping the disciples to mature, the Tibetan manner may simply exacerbate their low self-esteem. Consequently, they may either rebel or feel even worse about themselves. They are convinced that their mentors are unkind.

Thus, developing a firm conviction in a mentor's good qualities and appreciation for his or her kindness sometimes requires an additional step. Disciples may need to recognize ways of acknowledging and showing pleasure with someone that differ from what they know from their cultures and which they expect to be universal. Success in this step enables them, in Bozsormenyi-Nagy's words, "to overcome feeling shortchanged or cheated and to accept payment in a different currency for the acknowledgement to which they are rightly entitled."

Guru-meditation, then, as supplemented with the contextual therapy approach, would proceed through the following steps. First, as with the step of rejoicing during the seven-part invocation, we need to acknowledge and feel good about our practices ourselves. Then, if our mentors have not been showing us the types of attention or signs of pleasure with our practices that we would like, we need to admit this consciously. Complaining about the fact, however, and feeling that our mentors need to adopt our ways will only depress or annoy us, rather than uplift us. After all, our expectations were unrealistic. Therefore, we need next to realize that the cultural or personal limitations our mentors may possess have arisen from a variety of causes, but do not constitute inherent flaws in the mentors' character. Thus, we focus on the voidness of our mentors' shortcomings as existing inherently.

Next, if our mentors are traditional Tibetans, we need to recall typical Tibetan ways of acknowledging a disciple's efforts and showing pleasure. Then, bringing to mind our mentors' conduct toward us, we may be better able to recognize the good qualities and kindness for what they are. When we are able to identify correctly the ways in which our mentors acknowledge disciples and show pleasure—in other words, when we learn to understand our mentors' cultural language—we may then focus with firm conviction on these clear signs that they show. We may then truly appreciate our mentors' qualities and kindness.

Deeper Resolution through Voidness Meditation

The contextual therapy approach may be helpful in dealing with the problem of wishing to please one's mentor and being unable to recognize unfamiliar ways of showing acknowledgement and pleasure. Nevertheless, even if we are able to accept our Tibetan mentors' cultural and personal customs, we may still crave emotional strokes for our good practices. If we cannot gain them in familiar forms from our Tibetan mentors, we may feel that perhaps if we please our Western teachers, we will gain praise and attention from them. Such an attitude inevitably leads to frustration and suffering. We need to see that underlying our wish for acknowledgment and our wish to please may be an unconscious obsession with gaining acceptance and approval. Without delving deeper and applying voidness meditation, this more serious problem may remain unresolved.

As stated earlier, two specifically Western assumptions may contribute to the problem: the assumption that the universe is fair and the unconscious belief that we are guilty of original sin. From the Buddhist viewpoint, these two unquestioned assumptions are based on confusion about how the universe and we exist. Buddhism does not share the Western belief that the universe is just or fair. Nor does it assert that the universe is unfair or that things happen at random. Everything occurs as the result of an extremely complex network of interrelated causes and circumstances, with neither an impartial source of just laws nor an impartial judge to administer them fairly. Moreover, the first noble truth Buddha taught is that life contains suffering. We may follow our mentors' advice and, for a complex of reasons, never receive acknowledgement for it. If we believe that the universe must be fair and so we expect, crave, or demand acknowledgement or signs of pleasure, we only create more suffering.

The wish for acknowledgement often masks a wish for approval and acceptance, which often masks low self-esteem, based on an unconscious belief in being inherently sinful. Painful emotional experiences often confirm and reinforce this belief. Moreover, receiving acknowledgement in the hope that it will establish our worth means establishing our worth as independently existent individuals. This obsession derives from confusion about how we exist. Acknowledgement, whether by others or by ourselves, may make us temporarily feel better. However, the feeling of happiness soon disappears unless accompanied by an understanding of reality.

Ultimately, we need to realize that although we exist as individuals, there is no solid "me" inside who is inherently inadequate and who needs to receive affirmation or to please others to feel worthy or real. Although ultimately acknowledgement is irrelevant, nevertheless it is important that we not feel that we were stupid for needing it. Acknowledgement is necessary while we are still bound within the confines of culturally specific thought and belief. Without that acknowledgement, breaking out of those confines may be too difficult for most people to manage.

If acknowledgement does not come in recognizable forms from our mentors, parents, lovers, or friends, self-acknowledgement is a definite help. However, we need to be careful in its application. As we go beyond cultural limitations, stopping the self-acknowledgement prematurely may still leave us with low self-esteem. Moreover, feeling stupid about what we previously felt merely reinforces a low self-opinion. With a deep understanding of voidness, however, even forgiving ourselves for having acted foolishly becomes superfluous.

In healthy relationships with spiritual mentors, disciples follow a teacher's instructions, practice diligently, and even help the mentor financially and physically without any need or wish for acknowledgement or praise. Disciples do all this to benefit themselves and others, and not simply for pats on the head. Pleasing our mentors, then, is not for receiving self-affirmation through an acknowledgment, a thank-you, or any sign of their pleasure. Pleasing our mentors is for gaining greater ability in helping others.

Countertransference

In psychoanalysis, analysts may unconsciously respond to their clients' transference and degenerative regression with countertransference. For example, suppose a client unconsciously transfers an image of a busy father and regresses to demanding attention. In response, the analyst may unconsciously countertransfer an image of a demanding parent and become defensive or annoyed. Note that both transference and countertransference, as Freud defined them, are unconscious processes. Other common results of countertransference are unconsciously to become protective, manipulative, flattered, disappointed, or romantically interested. Part of the training to become an analyst is to notice any signs of unconscious countertransference and, by bringing them to conscious awareness, to refrain from acting upon them.

If students or disciples transfer images of parents or lovers onto spiritual teachers and regress to juvenile or otherwise inappropriate behavioral patterns, fully qualified mentors would respond without countertransference. Even if the disciples make unreasonable demands or declare romantic love, such mentors let their words pass through them without inflating the situations into concrete and independently existent incidents. Maintaining calmness, equanimity, and warm, caring concern, well-qualified mentors act like gentle mirrors. A mirror allows people to gain true glimpses of themselves, but without actually assuming the features of anyone before it.

Normally, qualified mentors do not confront disciples with their projections, nor scold them for thinking or acting inappropriately. Tibetan mentors, for example, usually scold disciples only for improper actions with others; because of humility, mentors cannot demand proper treatment for themselves. Rather, through consistently impeccable behavior, mentors provide circumstances conducive for disciples to gain awareness and insight into the situation at hand. Eventually, disciples come to see their projected fantasies. Unlike psychoanalysts, then, spiritual mentors do not encourage the transference and degenerative regression process. However, like good analysts, mentors deal with the process wisely and compassionately if it occurs.

Responding Maturely to Countertransference

Most spiritual mentors are not enlightened beings, and consequently they still have at least the remnants of disturbing habits. Thus, spiritual mentors may still experience unconscious countertransference. If this occurs, the mentors would follow the same procedures that analysts follow. They would try to become aware of the feelings of countertransference and refrain from acting upon them. Some spiritual teachers, however, are deficient in certain good qualities and might act out the impulses that arise from unconscious countertransference. For example, in response to idol-worship, flattery, or flirting on the part of students, spiritual teachers might respond in romantically forward ways.

If countertransference is directed at us, we need to check carefully the causes of the problem. During the first phase of sutra-level guru-meditation, we need to examine objectively whether a teacher's fault is partially in response to our own transference and regression or is coming solely from other sources. If we discover that our own behavior is partially responsible, we need to work on curtailing that behavior. If the teacher still does not stop his or her inappropriate or even abusive actions, we may follow Ashvaghosha's advice. We would politely explain to the teacher, in private, that the inappropriate behavior is making us uncomfortable and we would ask the teacher kindly to explain why he or she is acting that way. Alternatively, we may follow the Kalachakra teachings and keep a respectful distance.

Embarrassing a teacher in public, so that he or she loses face, would only be a last resort to stop extremely abusive cases. If we think of resorting to such drastic measures, we need to be especially clear that our motive is purely to spare others and the teacher from further pain. If the action to disgrace a teacher is a personal vendetta undertaken out of revenge, it may cause more harm than good. It may bring great confusion to the mentor's other disciples who have benefited greatly from his or her teachings. It may leave them in states of spiritual despair and leave us in bitter, negative states of mind. Abusive behavior, whether or not fueled by countertransference, requires sensitive, wise, and compassionate means to bring it to an end.

Summary

A healthy relationship with a spiritual teacher requires a safe direction in life, a bodhichitta motivation, and, above all, a good understanding of voidness. Without these prerequisites, any attempt at building a relationship runs the danger of unbridled transference and degenerative regression.

A relationship with a spiritual mentor is not the same as one with a psychoanalyst. A mentor does not hold regular private sessions with the disciple to supervise the transference and regression process and to keep it under control. Therefore, if transference and degenerative regression occur, as they frequently do, sutra-level guru-meditation, supplemented by steps suggested by contextual therapy, may help to eliminate the problem.

Fear in a Disciple-Mentor Relationship

Fear of a "Breach of Guru-Devotion"

ALMOST EVERY classical text on the disciple-mentor relationship includes a section on the hellish suffering that follows from what is usually translated as "a breach of guru-devotion." The material derives mostly from Ashvaghosha's vivid description of the horrors, which in turn summarizes some passages from the tantras. Although the point pertains specifically to relationships with tantric masters, most Tibetan authors take it to have a shared meaning that applies to relationships with sutra masters as well.

Studying this teaching causes many Westerners to inject a devastating element of fear into their relationships with their spiritual teachers. Fear of hell easily leads to a cult mentality and may open them to abuse from unscrupulous teachers. They become afraid to protest against improper behavior or to leave their teachers upon fear of burning in hell. To avoid this type of unhealthy relationship, they need to investigate the teaching carefully.

First, they need to know exactly which types of attitudes and behavior the texts describe as leading to hell. Otherwise, if the translation term *guru-devotion* has already misled them, the dubious phrase "a breach of guru-devotion" may have confused them even further. Then, they need to understand the Buddhist concept of hell. Lastly, they need to appreciate the psychological implication of fear within a Western cultural setting.

Self-Destructive Actions regarding a Spiritual Mentor

Disastrous self-destructive actions regarding a spiritual teacher fall into three categories: (1) building a disciple-mentor relationship with a misleading teacher, (2) disbelieving the good qualities that one's mentor actually has, and thinking with a distorted, antagonistic attitude about them, and (3) relating distortedly to one's properly qualified mentor. Relating distortedly means being in violation of the first root tantric vow: to avoid scorning or deriding one's tantric master. It also includes violating either of the first two tantric vows outlined in *The Kalachakra Tantra*: disturbing the mind of one's tantric master or transgressing an instruction that he or she has given.

In the context of a breach of guru-devotion, both thinking with a distorted, antagonistic attitude and relating distortedly refer to changes in disciples' manners of relating to their qualified mentors after establishing healthy disciple-mentor relationships with them. The two do not refer to disciples' thinking or acting hostilely toward spiritual mentors who are not their mentors. Nor does it refer to other peoples' thinking or acting hostilely towards the disciples' mentors—although hostile thought or behavior directed by any person toward another is, of course, destructive. Both the agent and the object of a breach of guru-devotion are specific.

Further, a misleading teacher is someone who is ruled by disturbing emotions, such as greed, attachment, anger, or naivety; who pretends to have qualities that he or she lacks; or who hides his or her actual shortcomings. Moreover, such a person has a weak sense of ethics, teaches only for personal gain, or gives incorrect information and instruction. Naive spiritual seekers may incorrectly consider some of the person's faults as assets or ascribe good qualities to the person that he or she lacks. Consequently, they build distorted relationships that are based on deception and lies.

Thinking with a distorted, antagonistic attitude is one of the ten fundamentally destructive actions described in Buddhism and constitutes a violation of one of the bodhisattva vows. It means to deny or repudiate what is true about someone or something, and entails planning to spread one's prejudiced opinions to others. Here, it refers to disciples' denying or repudiating the good qualities that their spiritual mentors actually have and planning to spread false information about the persons. The destructive way of thinking goes far beyond merely disbelieving in the good qualities that their mentors have.

Further, according to the Prasangika-Madhyamaka explanation, thinking with a distorted, antagonistic attitude may also include interpolating something false. Here, the destructive thinking would be for disciples to invent and project negative qualities onto their mentors that the teachers objectively lack.

Moreover, according to Tsongkapa's *Grand Exposition of the Graded Stages of the Path*, the motivation behind thinking with a distorted, antagonistic attitude needs to include five further disturbing emotions and attitudes: (1) one needs to be stubbornly blind to the actual qualities of someone; (2) one needs to be contentious, from having a perverse sense of enjoying being negative; (3) one needs to be convinced of the distortion, based on incorrect consideration and analysis; (4) one needs to be mean, unwilling to accept that others have good qualities; and (5) one needs to be headstrong in wishing to bring down the person, without the least bit of shame about it and without thinking it improper.

Distorted, antagonistic thinking about one's spiritual mentor, then, does not include all thought about his or her actual limitations or shortcomings. For disciples to think that their mentors are not fully enlightened beings who can speak every language in the world falls outside the sphere of this destructive way of thinking. So does thinking that the actual faults or mistakes of their mentors are in fact conventional faults and mistakes. Similarly, the destructive action does not include disciples' disagreeing with their traditional mentors' opinions that women lack the spiritual ability of men. Nor does it include deciding to keep a respectful distance from abusive spiritual mentors.

On the other hand, consider the case of disciples who dwell on their mentors' actual faults or mistakes and, with antagonistic attitudes, wish to publicize them. The way of thinking does not repudiate actual good qualities or invent fictitious negative ones. Thus, the mental act does not constitute distorted, antagonistic thinking. However, if any of the five disturbing emotions and attitudes that Tsongkapa described accompany the thought, the act is negative and creates suffering.

Transgressing Tantric Vows concerning Interaction with a Mentor

For disciples to scorn or deride their mentors means for them to reject their previous respectful and appreciative attitudes toward their teachers and to show them contempt. The self-destructive action may include faulting or ridiculing the mentors, intentionally being disrespectful or impolite, or thinking or saying that their teachings are useless. In *An Illuminating Lamp*, Chandrakirti gave the example of a disciple who gained an intellectual understanding of voidness from receiving instruction from his mentor and from carefully thinking over it. Throughout the process, the disciple had conviction in the mentor's qualifications and appreciation for his kindness in teaching the topic. The disciple then came to despise the teacher and to think that the teachings were nothing special. So long as the disciple held these negative attitudes, he had no chance of gaining a deep understanding of voidness in meditation. In *Refined Gold*, the Third Dalai Lama pointed out that disparaging one's mentor usually comes from dwelling on the teacher's faults, whether real or imagined.

For disciples to disturb the minds of their mentors means for them to insult their teachers by acting or speaking destructively, because of disturbing emotions or attitudes, and not even thinking of refraining from doing so at any point during the act. Destructive actions include taking a life, physically causing harm, robbing, or acting sexually inappropriately. Destructive speech includes lying, speaking divisively, speaking harshly or abusively, and interrupting with idle chatter. Whether the disciples direct the destructive actions at their mentors or at other beings, the action would insult and displease their mentors.

The act of transgressing instructions that mentors have given is to commit in a hidden fashion any of the ten destructive actions or to violate any of the vows, after receiving specific instructions to avoid such behavior. The ten destructive actions include the physical and verbal acts just mentioned as well as thinking covetously, with malice, or with a distorted, antagonistic attitude. The motivation needs to be a disturbing emotion or attitude. Moreover, the disciples need to recognize that destructive behavior displeases their mentors and to think nothing of engaging in it anyway.

Unlike the case of disturbing the mentor's mind, here the teacher need not necessarily learn of the misconduct or show displeasure. Transgressing an instruction, then, does not include disciples' politely refusing to act destructively or to transgress their vows if their mentors insist. Nor does it include respectfully excusing themselves from doing something beyond their capacities or means.

The self-destructive thoughts and actions regarding one's mentor, then, are totally specific and require an extremely negative mind to commit in the full sense. Moreover, distortedly and antagonistically thinking about one's mentor, disparaging the person, disturbing his or her mind, or transgressing an instruction that he or she has given requires four additional binding factors before totally disastrous results may follow: (1) the disciples need to regard the negative actions as free of detriment, see only advantages to them, and undertake the actions with no regrets; (2) having been in the negative habit before, they need to lack any intention to refrain now or in the future from repeating the acts; (3) they need to delight in the negative actions and undertake them with a perverse sense of joy; and (4) they need to lack any sense of self-honor or concern about disgracing their families or teachers, and need to lack any intention to repair the self-damage they are causing.

Further, even if disciples have acted in any of the self- defeating ways regarding their mentors—whether with all four factors present or only a few—Ashvaghosha clearly indicated how they can avoid experiencing the disastrous consequences. The disciples need to admit to their mentors their destructive conduct or thought, acknowledge it as a mistake, and apologize. In apologizing, they need to feel regret, not guilt, about the negative action, promise to try to avoid repeating it, and reaffirm their safe direction in life and bodhichitta motivation. To strengthen the positive potential arising from the relationship and to confirm the close bond, they need also to make small offerings to their mentors as tokens of appreciation and respect. Even if their mentors have already passed away, disciples may follow the procedure before pictures of their teachers or while imagining them as present. Western disciples, however, need special care to avoid misconceiving that making offerings to their mentors is a way to buy dispensation from their sins.

Hellish States of Mind

The connotation of the Sanskrit word for a hell, *naraka*, is a joyless state. The Tibetan equivalent, *nyelwa* (*dmyal-ba*), connotes a state that is difficult to get out of. The Buddhist concept of a hell, then, is a tortured, tormented mental and physical state that lacks any joy and in which one feels trapped and unable to escape. Although the classical texts contain vivid descriptions, the important point is the state of mind and accompanying physical feeling they describe.

Following a misleading teacher can bring the disasters of unsound practice or spiritual abuse that can ruin enthusiasm for the spiritual path. It can turn open-minded seekers into bitter cynics, completely closed to further steps toward liberation and enlightenment. The joyless, disillusioned mental state of such people is difficult to break. It is a living hell. We may understand this point by considering the analogy of being hurt in an unhealthy relationship with a seemingly upright partner or friend who has betrayed our trust. We may be so devastated by the disastrous experience that we close up emotionally and are afraid of entering another relationship. We may even repudiate the value of any relationships at all.

Similarly tortured are disciples who first have conviction in their mentors' actual qualities and appreciation for the actual kindness the mentors have shown, but then for some disturbing reason, have changes of heart. When this happens, they become obsessed with denying their mentors' qualities and kindness, with projecting invented faults, or with dwelling morbidly on the actual faults the mentors have. They may feel contempt for their mentors and act destructively or violate their vows out of spite, hoping that doing so will displease or hurt their teachers.

A similar phenomenon may happen with our true friends or loving, kind partners. A change of heart may come from deep psychological factors such as low self-esteem and paranoia. Feeling unworthy of receiving kindness or love, we may deny the attention and affection that we have actually received. Afraid of abandonment, we may reject the partners first, to avoid the pain of later being rejected. We may even try to hurt our partners or to force the abandonment by acting terribly with them or by having an affair. A change of heart may also come from the influence of misleading friends.

Such a mental state is clearly tormented and tortured. It creates a personal hell that lacks any joy and is difficult to escape. It may even weaken the immune system and bring on or aggravate a sickness. According to the Buddhist explanation of karma, most negative actions bring their results in future lives. Nevertheless, when a person directs an extremely destructive action at someone who has outstandingly good qualities and who has been especially kind, the results may ripen within this lifetime. The hellish consequences of thinking or acting distortedly and antagonistically toward our mentors, then, frequently occur shortly after the act.

Fear within a Western Context

Because many Western spiritual seekers lack clarity about which thoughts and actions regarding their mentors bring hellish results, they fear thinking or doing something that in fact does not lead to disaster at all. For example, they may fear accurately seeing as mistakes actual faults in their mentors, such as misjudgment, abusive conduct, or involvement in spiritual power politics. Their mentors' every action, they may think, must be perfect, because the mentors are fully enlightened Buddhas.

Misunderstanding the concept of guru-devotion and of seeing that the mentor is a Buddha may brainwash disciples into feeling that they must deny the truth. The conflict inevitably leads to anxiety and tension. They may fear criticism from fellow Dharma students if they bring up something about the teachers at their centers that disturbs them or does not seem right. They hold themselves back from speaking about the mistakes they see, for fear of being branded bad disciples and heretics who will burn in hell.

Further, some disciples may feel guilty for doubting even for a moment that their mentors are literally enlightened beings. Typically, Western seekers feel that to question their mentors' omniscience indicates that something is wrong with them. Thus, fear of punishment feeds a Western sense of inherent guilt and inadequacy, and low self-esteem. Moreover, a feeling of helplessness compounds the fear because, in Biblical thought, hell is eternal, with no way out.

According to the Buddhist teachings, only specific, extremely negative thoughts and actions toward a mentor result in a hellish state of mind; and, regardless of how terrible, no hellish state lasts forever. Through regret, open admission of their mistakes, and so forth, disciples may avoid or recover from tortured spiritual devastation. Nevertheless, many Western disciples question the benefit of contemplating the hellish consequences of distortedly relating to a mentor, which sutra-level guru-meditation standardly includes as one of its preliminary steps.

The Reason for the Descriptions of the Hells

As explained earlier, Western ethics derives from a belief in divinely or legislatively promulgated laws. Obedience to the law defines someone as a good person or citizen, worthy of reward, while disobedience makes the person bad and deserving of punishment. Therefore, many

Western spiritual seekers unconsciously see the discussion of hells as describing punishment for disobeying the rules of unquestioning guru-devotion.

Buddhist ethics, on the other hand, does not involve obedience or moral judgment. People cause themselves suffering by acting destructively, motivated by greed, attachment, anger, or naivety. If they become aware of the effects of negative behavior and wish to avoid experiencing suffering, they need to try to refrain from acting in these ways. Thus, the description of hells in Buddhist texts is not intended to make people feel guilty or to scare people with low self-esteem into obedience. The description is intended to educate people about the consequences of self-destructive behavior.

Consider the case of traditional Tibetans. Because most do not typically suffer from low self-esteem, learning about hellish suffering does not cause them to feel guilty or terrified of disobeying sacred laws. However, the knowledge may help Tibetans to lessen their arrogant, unbridled behavior. Westerners may learn from this example.

Modern Western spiritual seekers often reject the idea of divine punishment, yet many may still be subject to guilt and low self-esteem. If they do not cower in fear of a breach of guru-devotion, they may compensate for low self-opinion by acting with unbridled arrogance. For example, as part of an unconscious process of transference and degenerative regression, they may impudently accuse a teacher of backward thinking when he or she teaches them something that they do not find pleasing, such as about hellish suffering. Like children feeling superior to their parents, they may haughtily feel that Western scientific beliefs are better than primitive Tibetan superstition that merely adds fuel to feelings of guilt and low self-esteem.

If we think like this, we might do better to look at the psychological truth of the hellish states of mind that distortions of the disciple-mentor relationship create. If we wish to avoid these tortured states, we need to gain a correct understanding of the teachings concerning a healthy relationship with a spiritual mentor.

Fear Related to Issues Concerning Dharma-Protectors and Tulku Candidates

Nowadays, much confusion reigns over Dharma- protectors and tulku candidates. One great master supports one opinion and another asserts the opposite. Many of the problems that Western disciples face in light of the controversies arise from their lack of clarity about the teachings and from the unhealthy relationships with their spiritual mentors that have developed from this unclarity. For example, many disciples feel that they must loyally support their teachers' opinions because they are afraid that if they do not, they will be committing a breach of guru devotion. They will no longer be seeing that their mentors are Buddhas and will therefore burn in hell.

It is necessary to remember, however, that we need to maintain discriminating awareness and common sense throughout our relationships with spiritual mentors. Moreover, disagreeing with our mentors over certain points does not mean a lack of belief in the mentors' basic good qualities. Nor does it mean that we have rejected the teaching that a mentor is both an ordinary human and a Buddha from different valid points of view. Concerning certain disputed issues, however, we must reach a conclusion ourselves. The question, of course, is how to decide.

In cases concerning meditation experience, more than one point of view may be correct. For example, Kaydrubjey, Gyaltsabjey, and Kaydrub Norzang-gyatso, three Gelug masters of equal eminence, differed in their Kalachakra commentaries concerning how many subtle energy-drops one needs to stack in the central energy-channel to attain the path of seeing—the stage at which one gains nonconceptual realization of voidness. Each description is valid, based on the experience of an accomplished practitioner. Disciples can decide which description is valid for them based only on personal meditation experience. Certainly not every disciple of each of the three masters had the same meditation experience as his or her teacher had.

In other cases, one side of a disagreement may be objectively wrong, regardless of point of view or personal meditation experience. Disciples can reach this conclusion, however, only on the basis of deepening their studies and their skills in logic. Nevertheless, whether or not it is valid to assert that a controversial protector is a Buddha or that a specific candidate is the incarnation of a certain lama, there is no need to disparage either side.

Deciding Extremely Obscure Issues

Valid meditation experience and logic may decide certain issues, such as whether a Chittamatra view of voidness can eliminate all obstacles preventing liberation and enlightenment. They are inadequate, however, to decide extremely obscure issues, such as karma and rebirth. In such cases, Dharmakirti recommended in *A Commentary on [Dignaga's "Compendium of] Validly Cognizing Minds,"* one needs to rely on valid sources of information. Experience and logic can validate what Buddha explained about obvious and obscure phenomena, such as concentration and voidness. Moreover, since Buddha's sole motivation for teaching was compassion for others so that they may avoid suffering, and since this motivation was sufficiently sincere and strong to enable him to overcome even the instincts of confusion, Dharmakirti argued that one can be confident that Buddha is a valid source of information. Therefore, what Buddha explained about extremely obscure phenomena is also valid.

If disciples rely solely on valid sources of information, however, to settle controversial issues, they can find passages from the Buddhist scriptures and from the collected works of the great masters to justify almost anything. Moreover, if disciples have received empowerments from tantric masters on both sides of an issue and have been regarding both literally as omniscient Buddhas and therefore both as valid sources of information, the disciples still cannot decide which one is correct.

In *A Lamp for the Definitive Meaning*, Kongtrül stated that if tantric masters have the transmission of their lineage, they require no further examination. Seekers can trust their validity as qualified mentors, because to hold the transmission of a lineage means to realize and embody its authentic teachings. In some cases, however, the lamas on both sides of a controversy may equally be lineage holders. Using Kongtrül's criterion is still insufficient.

Buddha taught four guidelines regarding what to rely on: (1) do not rely on a teacher's fame or reputation, but on what he or she has to say; (2) do not rely on the eloquence of his or her words, but on their meaning; (3) do not rely on words of interpretable meaning intended to lead deeper, but on those of definitive meaning to which they lead; and (4) to fathom the definitive meaning, do not rely on ordinary levels of mind, which make things appear differently from the way they exist, but on deep awareness, which does not fabricate discordant appearances.

This does not mean to rely on deep awareness of what is ultimately true to ascertain the accuracy of a statement concerning what is conventionally true. A mind that validly cognizes the deepest truth about something can only ascertain the validity of how a conventional phenomenon exists. One needs to use a mind that validly cognizes the conventional truth about something to ascertain the validity of what something conventionally is.

The ultimate deepest truth about something is how it exists in terms of either voidness or the clear light mind. All phenomena exist as appearances of the clear light mind within the context of voidness. Thus, if one explains from the resultant point of view of a Buddha, then not only a specific protector or a specific tulku candidate is an emanation of an enlightened clear light mind, but all beings exist in that way. Therefore arguing from an ultimate or deepest point of view does not decide the question concerning the conventional identity of a protector or a candidate.

Resolution of the Disciples' Dilemmas

Dharmakirti gave another criterion to consider, which may be more helpful for resolving the dilemmas that many disciples face over disputed issues and thus more effective for dispelling fears over possible breaches of guru-devotion. If Buddha repeatedly stated a point throughout his teachings, then all disciples need to take it seriously as Buddha's true intention. On the other hand, if a point appears only in obscure texts, it either needs interpretation or is just for special persons and not for the general public.

Throughout his teachings, Buddha advocated that spiritual seekers rely on safe direction from the Triple Gem and on the constructive karma they accumulate for protecting themselves from suffering. Almost no where did Buddha recommend that seekers entrust their lives to Dharma-protectors or even rely on them. Therefore, in situations in which one cannot decide an issue such as whether a specific protector is an enlightened being, the best solution is to maintain a distance and to have no opinion. The issue of Dharma-protectors is not crucial to anyone's practice for attaining enlightenment. Most important is to stick to the main teachings of Buddha on safe direction and karma.

The same advice pertains to accepting one or another candidate as the reincarnation of a great teacher. Buddha spoke repeatedly about the necessity that a spiritual mentor has learning, realization, and a kind heart. He hardly ever mentioned the need for a title or property. Controversy over tulku candidates has repeatedly occurred throughout Tibetan history, for example with the Sixth Dalai Lama and the incarnation of the Drugpa Kagyü master Pema-karpo. No way exists to decide the issue rationally. It is best to show great respect to both candidates, to maintain equanimity about their identities, and to let the lamas sort out questions concerning hierarchy and monastic property. A disciple's only appropriate concern is to receive teachings from these candidates, if the candidates become properly qualified. The title and property that each nominee holds do not affect the quality of his or her teachings.

Deciding Sensitive Issues Pertaining to Karma and Discipline

Buddha did not create the laws of karma, nor did he forbid anyone to act destructively. In teaching about karma and ethical discipline, he merely stated which actions bring about detrimental results to oneself and, either directly or indirectly, bring harm to others. Each individual needs to use his or her discriminating awareness to decide how to act. Within this context, Buddha differentiated between actions that are naturally destructive, such as killing, and those recommended for certain groups to avoid, for a specific purpose. An example of the latter is monastics eating after noon, because it affects the clarity of their minds for meditating in the evenings and mornings.

Let us examine two additional examples of actions that are not naturally destructive, but which Buddha recommended for certain groups to avoid, for specific purposes. The actions are: (1) treating nuns and monks as equals, in the case of the Buddhist monastic community, and (2) engaging in homosexual acts, in the case of Buddhist practitioners with vows to refrain from inappropriate sexual behavior. When traditional mentors uphold Buddha's teachings that engaging in these actions causes problems for members of these groups, Western disciples often find it difficult to accept. Yet, they are perplexed about what to do. They fear that disagreeing with their teachers and insisting on the equality of women or of homosexuals constitute a breach of guru-devotion. To resolve the conflict, they need to understand the purpose behind Buddha's advice.

When Buddha established his monastic community, he hesitated at first to admit nuns. Because he felt strong compassion for all beings, he was concerned that society not disparage and reject the methods he taught for eliminating suffering. Indian society at his time would suspect improper sexual behavior if his monastic community consisted of monks and nuns mixing freely together and receiving equal treatment. Moreover, many of the monks lacked the maturity to deal with women in a nonsexist manner. Therefore, to avoid disrespect and trouble to his community and subsequent discredit of his teachings, he established the community of nuns as a separate entity, with a position inferior to that of the monks. In addition, he formulated additional vows for the nuns, to ensure that monastic conduct would be beyond suspicion. The community has followed these procedures ever since.

Similarly, under Kushan rule in third century Kashmir, Indian society encountered Iranian culture. The customs of the Iranians at that time differed greatly from those of India, especially concerning widely accepted sexual behavior. Following Buddha's guideline that respect for his community led to respect for his teachings, Vasubandhu expanded the traditional list of inappropriate forms of sexual behavior. He included for Buddhist laypeople sexual practices that Indian society at the time associated with foreign, "uncivilized" customs, such as incest and homosexuality.

The extent to which general Indian society and specifically Indian Buddhists engaged in these sexual practices prior to contact with Iranian culture is not the point. The point is that, in recommending against them, Vasubandhu was concerned with enhancing the respectability of the Buddhist community and teachings. Maintaining Buddhist ethics, after all, meant avoiding actions that caused problems; and condoning or following sexual customs associated with people whom society considered uncultured would surely lead to controversy and trouble. Since both Chinese and Tibetan Buddhism base their practice of ethical self-discipline on Vasubandhu's texts, their lineages still include homosexuality in their lists of inappropriate sexual behavior.

Buddha specified that, in the future, his community could change minor rules of discipline concerning actions recommended for certain groups to avoid for specific reasons. To change them, however, a council of monastic elders needs to convene, thoroughly research the issue, and reach a consensus. Modern Western society looks down upon discrimination against women and homosexuals. If Buddhist customs condone such prejudice, society may disparage the Buddhist community and

discredit Buddha's teachings. Therefore, to maintain Buddha's guideline for avoiding controversy and trouble, a council of elders may need
to reconsider these issues. His Holiness the Fourteenth Dalai Lama,
for example, has supported convening such a council, although he has
admitted that gaining a consensus would not be easy.

Before resolution of these issues, most Buddhist masters who are
responsible for maintaining the purity of their lineage have felt that
they need to uphold the traditional teachings. They would be irrespon-
sible to their position and duties if they were to do any less. Disagreeing with such a master when he or she is one of our spiritual mentors,
however, does not constitute a breach of guru-devotion. A breach
occurs only when disagreement boils over into distorted, antagonistic
thoughts that the mentor is an intolerant reactionary.

Western followers and disciples who are confused or impatient about
such issues need to understand that Buddhism is not an authoritarian
religion. No single person has the authority to modify the teachings—
not a head of a lineage or any other spiritual mentor. Therefore, it is
inappropriate to seek the approval of a traditional Tibetan lama for
one's actions as a woman or for one's sexual preferences. Each person
needs to try to understand the principles underlying Buddhist ethics and use his or her discriminating awareness to decide how best to
avoid problems and trouble.

~16

Blocks in Opening Oneself to a Spiritual Mentor

Paranoia and Vulnerability

ONE OF THE MOST important aspects of healthy disciple- mentor relationships is that of disciples receiving inspiration from their mentors. This can only occur if they are open to their mentors' uplifting positive influence. Some disciples, however, are paranoid that if they open themselves to a spiritual mentor they will come under the control of the person or be manipulated. Alternatively, they may feel that by opening up they become vulnerable. They fear being hurt, betrayed, or abused. If a mentor is not properly qualified, and particularly if the teacher has unscrupulous motives, their reticence is well founded. However, if the teacher is a properly qualified mentor, then to make the most efficient progress, they need to overcome their blocks.

We can open our hearts to receive inspiration in a healthy manner only if we have a basic understanding of voidness—particularly an understanding of how we exist. This is one of the reasons why, as explained earlier, becoming a disciple requires knowledge of the basic Buddhist teachings. Specifically, we need at least an intellectual understanding of the differentiation that Buddhism makes between a conventionally existent "me" and a totally fictitious or false "me." Western psychology speaks of a healthy ego and an inflated ego. A healthy ego is a sense of a conventionally existent "me." An inflated ego is a conception and belief that one's conventional "me" exists in the manner of a false "me."

A conventionally existent "me" is the person to whom the word *me* refers, based on the unbroken continuity of an individual's unique experience. With a healthy ego, one is able to organize one's life and take care of personal needs. A false "me" is a solidly existent "me," assumed to be findable somewhere inside oneself, acting as an independent boss trying to control one's experience. The notion that a conventional "me" could exist in such a concrete way does not refer to anything real. Modern science agrees: the brain functions as a complex network, without any control center. With an inflated ego, however, one identifies with a false "me" and mistakenly believes that one can completely control what happens.

With a correct understanding of voidness, one stops falling to either of two extremes. On the one hand, one stops projecting and believing that the conventional "me" exists as a false "me." On the other hand, one does not reject the idea that the conventional "me" exists at all. Thus, qualified mature disciples maintain a balance between being open to a mentor's enlightening influence, without projecting a false "me" onto themselves, and being able to preserve their individuality and integrity on the basis of a conventional "me." Let us explore the issue more fully.

Assorted personal and cultural factors may support one's fear of opening to a spiritual mentor; nevertheless, from a deep point of view, the fear arises from falling to one of the two extremes. A disciple may fear manipulation from having an inflated sense of a false "me" that must resist or become totally out of his or her control. This often occurs with people who are obsessed with trying to control everything in their lives and all situations with others around them. Their obsession makes them particularly leery of manipulation through suggestion, as in guided meditation. Alternatively, paranoia and fear may arise from a dysfunctional sense of a conventional "me," unable to maintain its valid identity in the face of a seemingly independently existent external onslaught.

If, instead of closing, one opens to a mentor while unconsciously maintaining either of the two extreme views, one may develop yet other forms of unhealthy relationships. With a strong sense of a false "me," one may inflate one's ego even further by joining it with the inflated "me" of an inflated mentor. This frequently occurs in disciples who join fascist spiritual cults and gain existential empowerment through the strength of the leaders and the groups. The syndrome also occurs in "spiritual groupies" who follow qualified mentors.

On the other hand, with a dysfunctional sense of a conventional "me," one may become submissive and excessively devotional. One may try to gain a sense of a solid, false "me" by inflating and identifying with the conventional "me" of the mentor, as opposed to doing the same with one's own conventional "me." The result is usually emotional overdependence, with the danger of either transference and degenerative regression, or exploitation and possible abuse.

Thus, opening to inspiration from a spiritual teacher needs great care. To avoid possible pitfalls, the opening needs to be a gradual process, coupled with an ever deeper understanding of the voidness or impossibility of the conventional "me" existing as a false "me." Sutra-level guru-meditation may be helpful here, since it standardly includes focusing on the mentor's conventionally existent weaknesses and faults as devoid of existing as inherent flaws and therefore as features that dependently arise. We may supplement the meditation by also focusing on the conventional "me"s of both the mentor and us. Both are devoid of existing in the manner of a false "me," and yet conventionally existent and functional as a "me" that arises dependently on the aggregate factors of experience.

Systems Analysis

To understand the nonlinear fashion in which such voidness meditation benefits the disciple-mentor relationship, let us borrow some analytical tools from Maturana and Varela's application of systems analysis to deep ecology in *The Tree of Knowledge* and *The Embodied Mind*. Understanding voidness, opening to a mentor, and receiving inspiration form a feedback loop. The more we understand, the more we open. The more open we are, the more inspiration we receive. The more inspiration we receive, the more we understand voidness.

As with all feedback loops within living systems, the dynamic is self-regulatory. In other words, at each stage of the development, the disciple-mentor relationship stabilizes into a different pattern. When viewed over long periods, the patterns become progressively more healthy, although in any short period the relationship may go up and down.

The living system here is an open one: in other words, the energy of inspiration continually flows through it. Consequently, at certain points, the living system of the relationship reaches a critical stage. At these points, the system releases and sheds tied-up energy, such as the energy bound in paranoia, inflation, submission, or fanatic devotion. Consequently, the system transforms into a new structure of increased efficiency. The relationship reaches a new quantum level of energy as we begin to relate to and to receive inspiration from our inner guru—our clear light mind.

Openness from the Side of the Mentor

Serkong Rinpochey once imparted a profound guideline instruction to me. He said that when, in the future, your disciples see you as a Buddha and you know full well that you are not yet enlightened, do not let this sway you from seeing that your own mentor is a Buddha. The implication is that a spiritual teacher, in understanding the nonliteral meaning of seeing that the mentor is a Buddha, tries to provide the circumstances conducive for disciples to access their clear light minds.

Because qualified spiritual mentors understand voidness, their ways of relating to disciples are free of ego-games. Moreover, the mentors' honesty and sincerity provide open gateways for us, as disciples, to access safely levels of relationship deep beneath ego-trips. As our growing understanding of voidness and increasing inspiration carry us across the threshold, we feel sufficiently safe to begin shedding previous neurotic patterns. Our disciple-mentor relationships slowly become deeply authentic and honest from our sides as well. As we drop increasingly more preconceptions and concepts concerning the relationships, the directness of mind that we reach provides a circumstance conducive for opening to clear light mind.

First, we begin to realize the clear light nature of our mentors' minds—the inseparability of our mentors and Buddhas. With sufficient understanding of voidness, the release of neurotic energy that the insight brings allows us to calm down and shed even deeper levels of concepts, and thus to approach the clear light level within us.

Sometimes, however, unqualified spiritual teachers may play ego-games with us. For example, the teachers may try to convince us to adopt their avidly sectarian attitudes. To avoid the hellish consequences that may follow if teachers attempt to exploit us while we are trying to be sincere, we again need to focus on voidness in guru-meditation. The mentors' faults are devoid of existing as inherent flaws and the seemingly independently existing "me"s that the mentors are trying to assert are devoid of existing in the ways in which they appear.

Moreover, our conventional "me"s are devoid of existing as seemingly independent "me"s that must struggle to resist in order to survive. A correct understanding of voidness allows us the emotional transparency to allow a domineering mentor's ego-trip to pass through us, without causing upset. We may then either say no to the mentor's pressure or keep a respectful distance if a working relationship has become untenable.

Dealing with the Death of a Mentor

The death of one's spiritual mentor may be a devastating occurrence. We may feel abandoned or betrayed, especially if we have inflated the mentor into an actual Buddha, able to decide when to die. We may feel like someone who has lost a beloved spouse and, feeling that no one can ever replace the person, decides never to remarry. Thus, we may feel that no one can ever replace the mentor and so we close to the possibility of relating deeply to another spiritual master again.

One source of the block may be an inflation of the mentor into "the one and only mentor for me." The concept hints at an unconscious influence from the Biblical belief in Jehovah as the one and only God. Belief in another God is not only disloyal, but also heretical, strictly forbidden by divine commandment.

A mentor, however, is not a jealous, vengeful God. To consider someone "the only one"—whether it be the only mentor or the only partner to whom we can relate—is to inflate the person into an independently existent individual with the concrete identity of being the only one. Conventionally, each mentor, like each partner, is a unique individual. No one can exactly replicate someone else or provide the circumstances for the exact same relationship. Nevertheless, if the disciple-mentor relationship has been relatively free of ego-trips, we may be able to see more easily that opening to other mentors is not a betrayal of our relationships with the deceased.

Moreover, a healthy relationship with a spiritual mentor does not end with the teacher's death. Even after the mentor has died, we may still receive inspiration from the person in our memories and dreams. In fact, sometimes there may be even fewer blocks to being open. While a teacher is alive and geographically distant, we may feel that the teacher could still be with us but is not. This may seem like a glaring fault and may cause annoyance and complaint. If, on the other hand, we have accepted the mentor's death and sufficiently grieved, ironically we no longer feel distant from the person. The deceased seems present at all times, deep within our hearts.

Inflation, Projection, and Idealization

Unconscious inflation and projection often describe the psychological mechanism of unhealthy relationships with spiritual teachers. For example, we may be working to develop selfless compassion. In the process, however, while still influenced by disturbing patterns, we may deny or repress the narcissistic sides of our personalities. Unconscious inflation may then manifest in an attitude of "holier than thou." The inflation may further manifest in narcissistic preoccupation with and overemphasis on feelings of devotion. We may also project the inflation onto a mentor and, subsequently, aggrandize and identify emotionally with the teacher or his or her lineage.

In projecting and becoming overemotional about a mentor and a lineage, a complementary deflation may emerge. In contrast to them, we may feel that we are inadequate. The more perfect the teacher and lineage appear, the worse we may seem in our own eyes. If we then inflate the negative self-image, we may morbidly fixate on feelings of self-mortification. We may feel that we must sacrifice ourselves. Subsequently, our practice of selfless compassion may unconsciously transform into an exercise of martyrization to glorify the mentor and the lineage.

We may then further inflate and project negativity onto teachers and lineages that are supposedly our mentors' rivals. Consequently, we may aggrandize them into the Devil and become fanatically sectarian. Moreover, if a glorified mentor somehow disappoints or neglects us, we may inflate our low self-esteem and one or more of our so-called inadequacies and feel that we are bad disciples and deserve the punishment. Alternatively, or in addition, we may inflate the neglect and feel that the mentor is as cruel as Satan.

To try to avoid inflating and projecting negativity, we may supplement sutra-level guru-meditation with bringing to consciousness not only our mentors' faults and shortcomings, but also our own. In acknowledging our own shortcomings, we need to see that they do not exist as inherent flaws. The insight may allow us to develop healthy attitudes regarding the disturbing emotions and attitudes still left at the current stages of our development. The balance gained helps to prevent the relationships with our mentors from becoming unhealthy.

Care is also required not to idealize the teacher. Idealization imputes good qualities onto others that they in fact do not have. For example, we may project and see good qualities in our mentors that we feel that we ourselves lack or that we ourselves need. Often, we projected these qualities onto our parents in childhood, but did not receive the treatment from them that corresponded to our expectations. Even when our mentors have the qualities that we feel we lack, or need, or wish that our parents had possessed, we may inflate these to impossible proportions and thereby thrust our teachers beyond our reach.

Because self-disparagement usually accompanies either idealization or inflation, we need to realize that the good qualities we see reflect the hidden potentials of our own Buddha-natures. This realization is valid whether or not our mentors actually possess the qualities corresponding to our projections. In healthy relationships with spiritual mentors, however, we accent only the good qualities that teachers actually have, without exaggerating or embellishing them with further qualities that we wished they had.

Devotion

As discussed earlier, a healthy relationship with a spiritual mentor does not contain the neurotic devotion that combines emotional fervor with mindless obedience. Nevertheless, even when some of the potentially positive aspects of devotion are present, difficulties may arise. Consider, for example, the uplifting feeling derived from a loss of self in awe of something greater. Devoted persons may lose themselves in the splendor of rituals, or in the face of God, country, just causes, or great figures. When the loss of self entails a loss of the sense of a false "me," devotion is a healthy, constructive emotion.

In some theistic religious contexts, however, pious persons totally devoted to God or to a saint lose themselves in awe of an unknowable mystery. In its classical form, devotion occurs with a leap of faith. This form of devotion sometimes brings problems, because devotees may project the entire unconscious sides of their personalities. Consequently, so long as they regard the object of devotion as a mystery, beyond what they may know, they may block integration of their unconscious potentials into their conscious states. From a Buddhist point of view, they may block realization of their Buddha-natures. Moreover, in losing themselves in awe of the unconscious, they may surrender rational functionality. With feet no longer on the ground, they may be subject to manipulation or possible abuse in moments of religious fervor.

If Western disciples project an unknowable mystery onto a mentor and lose themselves in adoration and awe, the result may be a serious block to healthy relationships. If we suffer from this problem, we may lose all sense of not only a false "me," but also of a conventional "me," and become overdependent on an idolized mentor whom we can only worship and adore. Moreover, viewing the mentor's qualities and actions as an unknowable mystery—beyond all thought, conception, words, and sense of good or bad—may court disaster.

A Mentor's Actions as Inconceivable

Many Nyingma and Kagyü texts describe a Buddha's actions, and thus a mentor's actions, as beyond all thought and conception. One may fathom these actions only when one comprehends the deepest truth and, since the deepest truth is beyond thought and conception, so are the actions that are its "play." Some disciples misunderstand the point. They think that even a teacher's abusive behavior is inconceivable and therefore they had best keep quiet because they are insufficiently spiritually advanced to comprehend its mystery. Resolution of their confusion requires a correct understanding of inconceivability and of the relation between conventional and deepest truths.

We may understand the inconceivability of deepest truth and thus of a mentor's actions in two ways. If we take the deepest truth to be "self-voidness"—the absence of impossible ways of existing—straightforward, nonconceptual understanding of voidness is beyond conceptual thought, words, and so forth. If the deepest truth refers to "other-voidness"—an understanding of reality with a clear light mind—its direct realization is beyond all grosser levels of mind at which conceptual or verbal thinking occur. *Inconceivable*, then, does not mean *unknowable*. It merely means that the fullest understanding is beyond the level of conceptual thought.

Whether we take the deepest truth as self- or other- voidness, the appearances of a mentor's actions as the play of voidness are conventionally true phenomena. Appearances' being the play of self-voidness means that conventionally true appearances arise as knowable, comprehensible phenomena only because they are dependently existent. If they were independently existent, they could neither arise nor be known or comprehended. Appearances' being the play of other-voidness means that giving rise to conventionally true appearances is the natural activity of the clear light mind, just as giving rise to rays of sunlight is the natural activity of the sun.

In Buddhism, then, the deepest truth and the conventional truth are two valid facts about an item, seen by two valid ways of knowing something about it. The deepest truth about the appearances of a mentor's actions is how they exist; the conventional truth about them is what they are. The two truths are thus inseparable facts—if one is true, so is the other. Thus, the deepest truth is not a transcendental absolute totally beyond conventional phenomena. Consequently, the nonconceptual realization of the deepest truth does not require transcending and discarding conventional truth with a mystical leap of faith. The realization follows rationally from sufficient strengthening of our networks of good qualities, positive potentials, and deep awareness. If we conceive of the deepest truth as existing independently of conventional truth and if, in addition, we conceive of the valid cognition of the deepest truth as existing independently of the valid cognition of conventional truth, we have not understood the deepest truth or valid cognition.

As explained earlier, the Nyingma and Kagyü literatures typically speak from the resultant viewpoint of a Buddha. A Buddha apprehends the conventional and deepest truths about phenomena simultaneously and inseparably. Thus, since a Buddha's apprehension of self- and other-voidness is beyond the level of conceptual thought, similarly beyond conceptual thought is a Buddha's simultaneous and inseparable apprehension of a mentor's actions as the play of voidness.

From the basis and pathway points of view of disciples, however, a mentor's actions are knowable and comprehensible only with a mind that apprehends conventionally true phenomena nonsimultaneously with and separably from self-voidness and the clear light mind. Such a mind normally can understand things only conceptually. Nevertheless, viewing a mentor's actions and trying to understand them with a conceptual mind does not spell inevitable failure and does not render those actions unknowable mysteries. A mind that can validly cognize conventional truths—in this case, the appearances of a mentor's actions—can correctly discriminate between actions that accord with the Dharma and those that contradict it. Thus, the statement that the actions of a mentor are inconceivable does not render disciples incapable of ascertaining correctly what the actions are. Nor does it render the mentor unaccountable for the consequences of them.

The Difference between Seeing That a Mentor Is a Buddha and Projection

Projecting one's "unknowable" unconscious onto a mentor differs significantly from seeing that one's mentor is a Buddha. Similarly different are regarding his or her actions as a mystery and regarding them as a play of clear light mind and self-voidness. If we make our mentors and their qualities and actions into unknowable mysteries, we must accept them as enlightened through a mystical leap of faith. In so doing, we may close our eyes to reality. We may no longer look at or see our mentors' actual good qualities, let alone their actual conventional faults. This starry-eyed blindness creates a block to relating realistically to mentors.

In a healthy relationships with spiritual mentors, and specifically with tantric masters, disciples see that the mentor is a Buddha, but understand clearly what this means. The understanding allows for a strong positive feeling of devotion in which they may lose themselves in awe of something greater than themselves. Here, however, that something greater is knowable, rather than unknowable and a mystery. Consequently, the devotion felt toward it is grounded to earth and does not entail religious ecstasy or the projection of unconscious contents.

Grounded devotion, then, is another connotation of the word *awe*—sometimes inadequately translated as *dread* or *fear*—that, as explained earlier, Vasubandhu used to describe a positive emotion that accompanies appreciating the kindness of a spiritual mentor. The loss of self that characterizes this type of awe and devotion, then, is a loss of an inflated ego-sense of a false "me," rather than a loss of a healthy ego-sense of a conventional "me." Thus, grounded devotion to a spiritual mentor leads to a mature and stable opening of oneself to inspiration and balanced joy.

~17

Generational and Life Cycle Issues

Stages in the Contemporary Life Cycle

IN *New Passages*, Sheehy explained that the stages of the human life cycle vary according to socioeconomic class and the conditions of the times. Using this thesis, she discovered a new paradigm for the adult life cycle of contemporary, middle-class or semi-affluent, socially mobile, educated Caucasian-Americans. The paradigm contains three stages: provisional, first, and second adulthood.

Sheehy then analyzed the manner in which each of the current generations within this group has been passing through the three stages. Her proposition is that understanding the behavior of people from this socioeconomic class requires placing them within the context of their generations and their stages in life. Moreover, she contended that Canadian, Latin American, Western European, and Australasian members of this mobile class are fast approaching a similar pattern of threefold adulthood. In each country, however, cultural factors will modify the pattern as it emerges.

Most spiritual seekers who go to Western middle-class Dharma centers in the United States fall into the class of people that Sheehy analyzed. Sheehy's scheme provides a useful analytical tool for understanding some of the problems that these people have encountered in building relationships with spiritual teachers. It may also be relevant for understanding problems that may arise in the future in other subcultures, both in the United States and elsewhere.

Provisional adulthood is a prolonged adolescence characterized by experimentation and noncommitment to either a career or a marriage. It lasts through one's twenties. The times in which it occurs tend to set the general tone for the rest of one's life. First adulthood follows from around thirty to the mid-forties, during which one tries to prove oneself through a career and/or raising a family. Second adulthood then begins in the mid-forties, starting with "middlescence," a period of experimentation akin to a second adolescence, from the mid-forties to around fifty. During this period, one may be laid off or forced into early retirement and one's children may be away at college. An age of mastery follows until the mid-sixties, often with a new career or a new life partner. One may find a new synthesis of one's life that brings more fulfillment. After sixty-five comes an age of integrity during which one no longer feels the need to prove oneself and can enjoy the synthesis that one has found.

The generation that has consistently comprised the majority of spiritual seekers attracted to Tibetan Buddhism in the United States has been the Baby Boomer or Vietnam Generation, born from the mid-forties to the mid-fifties. A far smaller proportion has come from the Me Generation, born from the mid-fifties to the mid-sixties, and even less from Generation X or the Endangered Generation, born from the mid-sixties to around 1980. Let us examine how factors of generation, life stage, and the times have affected the approach of these groups to spiritual practice and their relationships with their spiritual teachers.

Stages in the Spiritual Life History of Baby Boomers

A belief that things can be perfect has set the emotional tone characteristic of the Baby Boomer Generation. Thus, during a prolonged adolescence of noncommitment in the late 1960s and through much of the seventies, many of them experimented with new alternatives. Often, they did so as a rebellion against restriction by their parents or because of the pressures of the Vietnam War. Typically, they rebelled against the traditional religion, culture, or values into which they were born, or against a combination of the three. In many cases, the rebellion led to an attraction to Tibetan Buddhism.

A lack of serious economic pressure allowed the idealism characteristic of being in their twenties to bubble over into romantic idealization of the Tibetans, their culture, and Buddhism. This led to a romanticization of Tibetan masters, fostered by relatively easy access to the lineage heads and the greatest lamas of the time. Inadequate translation and sparse reading materials further allowed for idealization and fantasy.

Consequently, the relationships that most seekers built with mentors were unrealistic. A number of Baby Boomers, in fact, went to teachings in the seventies while under the influence of psychedelics or recreational drugs.

During first adulthood in the 1980s, Baby Boomers became achievers. Wishing to gain approval from their Buddhist teachers and peers, many tried to prove themselves by making a hundred thousand prostrations, doing long retreats, performing ornate rituals (Skt. *pujas*), studying in geshey training programs, or serving their mentors devotedly by building and working in Dharma centers. The spirit of unbridled, self-centered achievement that characterized the eighties in the United States fanned the "spiritual materialism" of the day.

Because the Baby Boomers, often subject to low self- esteem, were trying to justify their worthiness, they tended to project that their teachers were judging them. Many unconsciously felt that they needed to perform in order to establish their self-worth and to win acceptance and love. Some also felt an element of competition with fellow seekers. They felt that they had to outshine the others in devotion or in the number of prostrations they made. Cliques of "inner-circle" disciples formed around the major Tibetan teachers in the West. The disciple-mentor relationship became increasingly unhealthy.

Middlescence came to the Baby Boomers in the 1990s, coinciding with the emergence of scandals and controversies involving spiritual teachers. Learning of several famous mentors' abusive behavior or involvement in heated disputes with each other, many Baby Boomers either experienced disillusion or went into denial. Seeing the flaws of the Tibetan Buddhist system and the discredit of several of its leading stars was extremely traumatic. It resembled the shock of seeing themselves or their peers contracting cancer or their parents coming down with Alzheimer's disease.

Many Baby Boomers shed the rigid false self of a spiritual achiever and became lax in meditation and practice commitments. They emotionally distanced themselves from their relationships with their spiritual mentors, both those still living and those already passed away. As with a second adolescence, many became experimental and looked toward psychology and other disciplines for methods to handle their midlife crises. The breakdown of rigid categories that characterized the nineties fanned their searches for new models of spiritual practice.

As Baby Boomers progressed into second adulthood in the late nineties, many rediscovered the dormant values that they had suppressed with the spiritual-achievement dynamic of their first adulthood. They found the sensibility and practicality of their Western cultures and gained a sense of self-worth from these positive aspects. Having entered the age of mastery, some gained the spiritual self-confidence to integrate their experiences into new syntheses. They reached levels of maturity that enabled them to relate in healthier ways to their spiritual mentors and to approach their meditation practices more realistically. Success in this endeavor depends on openness to inspiration from their spiritual mentors.

The Spiritual Life History of the Me Generation

Members of the Me Generation came to Tibetan Buddhism as provisional adults during the 1980s. The emotional tone of their generation has been set by the wish to have everything. Because opportunities abounded to make money quickly, fewer of them were drawn to Buddhism than were members of the preceding generation. The spirit of the eighties in the United States fostered greed and professionalism. Young people with capital, talent, and favorable socioeconomic backgrounds felt that any effort to get ahead would guarantee easy success. As part of their prolonged adolescence during this decade, members of the Me Generation rebelled against the impractical, hippie romantic mentality and applied themselves to acquiring money, goods, and experiences. Idealizing materialism, many regarded happiness as a commodity and felt they could buy it.

People from this generation who followed spiritual paths often applied themselves with equal narcissistic focus on the practices. They set about "collecting merit" with the same attitudes they held in accumulating collections of music tapes and designer clothing. Many expected to gain and have everything, without emotional commitment and, as symbolized by the answering machine, without intimacy. Carrying these attitudes into their relationships with spiritual mentors, many idealized their teachers as means for getting spiritually ahead and used them to collect more merit, but without actually opening their hearts to them.

In the nineties, the Me Generation faced the scandals and controversies as achievers in first adulthood. Many felt robbed of what they had wanted to achieve in the spiritual sphere and, sorely disillusioned, turned to winning success in business and in raising families. Others became incensed and applied themselves ardently to achieving the downfall of abusive mentors. Those who kept up their spiritual practices followed the spirit of the nineties and dropped rigid models. Many emotionally distanced themselves further from their mentors and went only infrequently to Dharma centers.

The Spiritual Path of Generation X

Very few members of Generation X sought spiritual paths during their prolonged adolescence and provisional adulthood in the nineties. Several factors contributed to this happening. AIDS, unemployment, and environmental disaster endangered prospects for a secure future. Leaders on all levels of society were involved in lies and scandals. Consequently, most members of this generation felt it impossible to trust anything or anyone, especially the integrity of people in positions supposedly of respect. Many resigned themselves to expecting that everything and everyone would let them down, as perhaps they felt that their parents had done when divorcing or leaving them in day care, especially when they were babies, without spending quality time with them. When they learned of scandal and controversy among Buddhist spiritual leaders, they thought, "What do you expect?" Naturally, most felt little draw or need to build a relationship with a spiritual mentor.

In keeping with the spirit of the nineties and the ethos of prolonged adolescence, members of Generation X rebelled against rigid models. Most adopted a "whatever" attitude, which set the tone for the generation. Anything was OK; nothing really mattered. Many felt their idealism quashed. They experimented with whatever, without committing themselves, since commitment surely would lead to disappointment. Many felt comfortable to communicate only at safe distances, through email or under fantasized identities in chat rooms. They could simply turn off the computer or not reply if someone disappointed them.

Members of Generation X who went to Dharma centers often carried these attitudes with them. Many found familiar atmospheres in large Buddhist organizations in which the head lamas either visited rarely or had already passed away. Being in centers away from the head lamas and under the substitute care of less qualified junior teachers may have unconsciously reminded them of being in day care centers away from their parents who were too busy with other priorities to give them the quality time that they needed. If they had felt that they could do whatever in day care, away from parents whom they felt would leave them there regardless of how they behaved, then, with large distances between themselves and the head lamas, they could do whatever at the centers. Since the head lamas would ignore them anyway and the local spiritual teachers were not their real lamas, there was no need to open to deep relationships with either of them.

Those who did open their hearts and minds often projected images from their unconscious of someone totally structured and reliable onto the head lamas. They idealized them, but from safe emotional distances, and sometimes became fanatic and rigid in structured practice. Unable to integrate their own unconscious good qualities, many maintained a "whatever" attitude in other aspects of their lives.

Avoiding Problems Typified by Provisional Adulthood

Although each generation experiences each stage of adulthood slightly differently depending on culture and the times, the basic structure of each stage suggests a particular form of unhealthy relationship with a spiritual teacher. Various elements of sutra-level guru-meditation indicate methods for possibly avoiding or overcoming those dangers.

Provisional adulthood suggests the problem of idealizing and romanticizing a spiritual mentor, while keeping an uncommitted emotional distance. When idealization and characteristically Western confusion join forces, disciples typically experience low self-esteem as part of their conscious personalities and project ideal perfection. Thus, romantic idealization of a mentor—especially when coupled with seeing the person as a Buddha—often entails inflating the actual good qualities the mentor has or interpolating positive features that he or she lacks. It may also entail denying the teacher's actual shortcomings and faults.

Placing the mentor on an unreachable pedestal enables adulation from a safe emotional distance. In other words, because the emotion of adulation—similar to romantic love—focuses on a superhuman object, it may be intense and exciting. However, it lacks the deeper, relaxed intimacy that comes from accepting someone despite his or her faults. Thus, although personal factors play a role, emotional distance often derives from relating to a fantasy rather than to an actual person. After all, relating to a fantasy of perfection is safer than risking disappointment, betrayal, or abandonment when relating to an actual teacher with both strong and weak points. The unconscious emotional distancing can occur whether the teacher is resident at a Dharma center or visits only rarely.

Focusing on the good qualities of a teacher in sutra-level guru-meditation, however, is not romantic idealization. It focuses on the actual qualities of the person, without aggrandizing or adding anything. Moreover, it acknowledges the person's faults, also without inflating or fabricating any aspects. A lack of interpolation or denial also applies to seeing that the mentor functions as a Buddha or that he or she is a Buddha. In either case, the pure vision recognizes and labels a mentor's positive features as Buddha-qualities and sees their foundation in Buddha-nature. It does this, however, without invalidating an accurate accounting of the person's conventional assets and shortcomings. In short, conviction in a mentor's factual qualities and appreciation for his or her actual kindness help to prevent the distance created by romanticization. Thus, they allow for a deeper-reaching emotional relationship.

To avoid the problems of idealization, it may be helpful to adapt the deconstruction methods used in sutra-level guru-meditation regarding a mentor's shortcomings. After gaining a realistic view of a mentor's weak points, we would bring to mind the impression we have of his or her good qualities and kindness and try to discriminate between our projections and fact. Peeling off projections is always a difficult task because our minds make them appear to be factual and we believe them to be so. The process requires considerable firsthand experience with the mentor and deep introspection. Nevertheless, once we have cleared away conventionally inaccurate projections, we would then focus on the conventionally accurate features as devoid of existing as inherent wonders. Then, we would be ready to focus on them with conviction and appreciation.

By dispelling naivety, such a procedure may facilitate becoming clearheaded about the mentor. It may also enhance a conviction in the qualities, based on understanding their dependently arising nature, and confidence that we may attain them ourselves. Further, when free of confusion, a tendency toward idealization may then be an asset. Because the tendency leads to looking up to something, it may help us to gain inspiration from our mentors' actual qualities and kindness.

The unconscious mechanism to defend ourselves from certain emotions may then help us to maintain a conscious distance from immature feelings toward our mentors. It may also help us to avoid committing ourselves to unhealthy relationships. Such harnessing of idealization and emotional distancing accords with the Kadam lojong advice to turn potentially negative circumstances into positive ones.

Avoiding Problems Typified by First Adulthood

The characteristic psychological feature of first adulthood is the drive to establish oneself. When coupled with the confusion of low self-esteem, transference, and inflation of a teacher, the drive may become an obsession with proving one's worth. One feels unconsciously compelled to perform in order to please a judgmental parent figure and to gain acceptance and approval.

As with neurotic forms of provisional adulthood, this syndrome also interpolates fantasized qualities onto the teacher. Here, the primary delusion is considering the teacher to be a judge of our worth. This confusion often comes from unconsciously interpolating the characteristics of the supreme judge, God, when trying to see that the mentor is a Buddha. Dispelling inaccurate conventional truths about our mentors in guru-meditation may help to alleviate the problem. Also helpful would be clearing away inaccuracies concerning ourselves, such as the idea that we are unworthy. When free of the confusion that causes obsession with achievement, the drive to establish ourselves may help us to channel the mentor's inspiration toward making true progress on the path.

Avoiding Problems Typified by Second Adulthood

The middlescent phase that begins second adulthood typically involves reevaluation of one's previous patterns of behavior, discarding outdated factors that no longer work, and experimenting with new models. If we have previously related to our spiritual mentors in unhealthy manners or have discovered serious faults in them, we may forsake not only the mentors, but also the entire spiritual path. If, however, we correctly identify the sources of unhealthiness in the relationships, we may correct improprieties and go beyond the unsatisfying plateaus we may have reached in our practices.

During the age of mastery within second adulthood, people typically reintegrate the legacies of their past into new syntheses. If we have been dwelling on the faults and shortcomings of our mentors, we run the danger of unconsciously being loyal to their negative aspects and passing that on to the next generation. This may occur whether or not we discard the relationships with our teachers. For example, we may be emotionally dishonest with younger disciples. We may pretend to have qualities that we lack.

Further, disciples in second adulthood may regress and degenerate to earlier stages of behavior, such as intensely competing to out-achieve junior practitioners and emotionally distancing themselves from any commitment to offer them help. If, however, we have focused properly on our mentors' good qualities, the new syntheses may incorporate the positive legacies we have gained. We may take full advantage of this phase of life by encouraging and nurturing the next generation.

Those in Second Adulthood Can Help Inspire Provisional Adults

In renouncing past patterns and finding new syntheses, disciples in second adulthood may turn primarily inward or outward. Moreover, they may do so either with or without the confusion of inflated egos. For example, turning inward, they may focus on meditation as a source of happiness, either narcissistically or in a balanced manner. Turning outward, they may seek satisfaction in tending to the needs of others, either in a stifling oppressive fashion or in a nurturing supportive way. For example, they may dominate a Dharma center or they may serve as resources of experience and advice, available for the next generation to draw upon for developing a center further.

In the present age of scandal, controversy, school violence, and AIDS, people tend to distrust everything. Thus, people who involve themselves with a spiritual path are naturally wary of trusting spiritual teachers. On the one hand, critical evaluation of a teacher before establishing a relationship is a healthy precaution and may help to avoid disappointment, harassment, or abuse. On the other hand, morbid skepticism and paranoia prevent gaining the inspiration from a qualified teacher needed to energize and sustain serious practice.

The hesitancy to commit oneself, which characterizes provisional adulthood, may create an additional emotional block for opening to a spiritual teacher during the current critical times. Second adulthood spiritual elders, however, may help younger seekers to overcome their blocks and to establish trust by becoming sources of inspiration themselves.

To inspire the younger generation, disciples in second adulthood do not need to become gurus. Instead, they may serve as second magnifying glasses to focus inspiration from the great masters they have met. Many of these masters are now inaccessible to newcomers because of either being too internationally active or having already passed away. Thus, through sutra-level guru-meditation, second adulthood disciples may focus on the good qualities of these figures to gain inspiration and then pass on positive legacies through their own examples. Doing so enables them to avoid unconsciously passing on negative legacies of neglect or abuse through spiritual narcissism or the stifling domination of a Dharma center.

~Epilogue
Relating to a Western Spiritual Teacher

Authorization of a Western Spiritual Teacher

As BUDDHISM takes root in the West, more Westerners are becoming spiritual teachers in its traditions. Some Tibetan mentors have formally given permission for their accomplished Western disciples to teach. A few have even named Westerners as their spiritual successors. In most cases, the authorization has brought qualified Western disciples to the fore. Occasionally, however, letters of endorsement from Tibetan lamas have derived from insufficient experience with the Western character to allow a correct evaluation of the disciples' intentions. In addition, several Westerners have declared themselves spiritual teachers without any reference to their spiritual mentors. Some of them have been properly qualified; others have been deficient in training or character.

His Holiness the Fourteenth Dalai Lama has explained that appointment by a mentor or self-proclamation does not make someone a spiritual teacher. Authorization comes from the person's qualifications and effectiveness in teaching, as well as from a student's acceptance of him or her as a teacher. Seeking permission from a mentor comes after a student requests a person to teach, not before.

Following a Middle Path in Intercultural
Student-Teacher Relationships

Some people feel that only if spiritual teachers are from traditional Asian societies can they be authentic. However, whether teachers come from traditional Asian or modern Western backgrounds, each cultural package carries with it advantages and drawbacks. One of the qualifications of a disciple, according to Aryadeva, is being free of prejudice.

Thus, although for some people spiritual teachers from one cultural background may be more fitting than are those from another, seekers need to be open to both. Westerners who find spiritual teachers inspiring only if they are Tibetans need to check if their biases may be due to rejecting their own cultures, having only minimal knowledge of Tibetan ways, projecting fantasies about exotic, mystical Tibet, or some combination of these factors.

In relationships between Western students and Tibetan teachers, each side may avoid problems by understanding the other's culture and finding a comfortable middle path. A compromise structure might entail, for example, following traditional protocol while giving teachings, yet discarding the custom of public scolding. Tibetan mentors commonly scold Tibetan disciples not only in private, but also frequently in front of others. This helps to correct proud disciples who are preoccupied with not losing face. For most Western disciples, however, public scolding is inappropriate. It is tantamount to humiliation and may reinforce negative feelings about themselves. Even private scolding needs to be approached with sensitivity.

A middle path is also necessary when people of Asian descent with Buddhist backgrounds study with Western spiritual teachers. This group of seekers includes young Tibetans in the West who are out of touch with their culture, Tibetans in India or Nepal with modern educations, and people from Tibetan cultural areas in Russia or Mongolia who have received Soviet schooling. It also includes East, South, and Southeast Asians, both in their homelands and overseas as first- or later-generation immigrants. A middle path might include, for example, allowing traditional forms of showing respect, yet honoring the Western need for explanations reconcilable with the findings of science.

A Student-Teacher Relationship between Two Westerners

When Western spiritual seekers study with Western teachers, problems frequently arise if one or both sides try to follow a traditional Tibetan model in the relationship. This is especially true when the relationship becomes one of disciple and mentor. Because traditional Tibetan protocol often feels artificial and insincere, the interaction may become stilted. Western culture, however, does not provide a suitable alternative model. A Buddhist disciple-mentor relationship is hardly the same as that between a student and teacher in a secular school or that between a church or synagogue member and his or her pastor, priest, or rabbi.

If the setting of the disciple-mentor relationship is a Dharma center that is part of the organization of a Tibetan master, the Western seekers often feel the dilemma more sharply. This is because maintaining a double standard of behavior toward their Tibetan and Western mentors may introduce a subtle element of racial prejudice that makes everyone uncomfortable. A strictly Western form of student-teacher relationship may evolve more naturally in centers that are not directly associated with specific Tibetan masters or which are totally Western.

Further, the Western cultures from which the Western students and teachers derive will also affect the forms that the relationships between the two will take; modern cultures differ greatly. Some societies are more formal than others. Even within one country such as the United States, the disciple-mentor relationship between two Southerners and between two Californians will undoubtedly be different. Moreover, when the two parties come from different Western countries or cultures, a comfortable middle path between the customs of each is also required.

One general guideline, however, may be helpful. Most Westerners prefer verbal acknowledgment in establishing a relationship, rather than merely unspoken understanding of its formation. Therefore, in establishing a Mahayana disciple-mentor relationship between two Westerners when the disciple does not take bodhisattva vows in the presence of the mentor, both sides may avoid confusion if the seeker requests to become a disciple and the mentor explicitly accepts.

Showing Respect to a Western Spiritual Teacher

The procedures of guru-meditation apply equally to Tibetan and Western spiritual teachers. However, the manner of showing respect to the teacher may need to differ with culture. General customs of politeness, such as being quiet and attentive when a teacher enters the classroom, suit any society. However, certain ritual Asian forms of showing respect, such as prostrating, may be uncomfortable when both parties are Western.

A foreign custom of showing respect is often an inadequate vehicle for generating and communicating a heartfelt emotion. Although some

Westerners may feel comfortable in following a traditional Asian custom, for others it may seem like play-acting. Offering prostration may simply serve to aggravate their emotional distance. Yet, if no formal means are available for expressing respect—especially in a disciple-mentor relationship—a disciple's conviction and appreciation of the mentor may remain too amorphous to stimulate growth. A mutually recognized and comfortable form of expression may help to nurture inspiration.

A sincere expression of respect needs to arise naturally. Moreover, if Western mentors expect or demand shows of respect from Western disciples and dictate the forms, the disciples often respond as they would to demanding parents. They either obey begrudgingly, while feeling demeaned, or simply refuse. Mentors need to let Western disciples express their respect in their own ways and need to learn to read the gestures that the disciples use.

Most Westerners value freedom of choice. Restriction merely reinforces their feelings of low self-esteem or rebellion. Thus, to express their respect in emotionally comfortable manners, they need a choice of acknowledged conventions that do not make them feel like fools or like shallow imitators of foreign ways. Examples of respectful gestures before a class or meditation session would be to stand or sit silently as the mentor enters, or to bow the head. After a lecture, a round of applause may comfortably express appreciation and respect.

Generational Differences in Ways of Showing Respect

Each stage of the adult life cycle may be conducive to different forms of expressing respect. Moreover, each generation in each culture and in each period of time may do things differently in each life-cycle stage. When Baby Boomers were provisional adults, for example, they were willing to experiment. During first adulthood, many mimicked foreign customs in an attempt to compete with other students to be the most devoted disciple. In middlescence, Baby Boomers often found these forms empty. Second adulthood then afforded them the opportunity to rediscover older ways of showing respect, which they had either rejected or repressed in their youth.

Members of Generation X, on the other hand, who are presently in provisional adulthood, may be more cautious to show respect than previous generations, because of fear of betrayal. With little tolerance for anything phony, they are extremely critical of a teacher's qualities and find most formalities hypocritical and meaningless. Only someone who consistently lives up to what he or she teaches and who nonjudgmentally lets them be themselves commands their respect. Moreover, they prefer to show respect straightforwardly, without pretense, simply by coming to class regularly, paying attention, and taking the instructions seriously.

When members of Generation X feel inspired by spiritual teachers, they still reject as artificial and superfluous the emotional displays characteristic of Baby Boomers and the Me Generation. They typically express their inspiration nonverbally, with more dedication to their practice. Western teachers from the Baby Boomer generation need to check any tendencies they may have to feel insecure if others do not acknowledge them in ways to which they are accustomed.

The Disciple-Mentor Relationship in the Context of the Practical Realities of a Dharma Center

Western Dharma centers may hire teachers as resident Buddhism professors, Dharma instructors, or meditation or ritual trainers. In such cases, the centers usually follow normal business procedures, with contracts, conditions, and options to terminate the contracts if either side fails to meet the terms. Dharma centers, however, cannot hire teachers as resident mentors, since establishing a disciple-mentor relationship is an individual matter, and not an institutional decision. One cannot impose a spiritual teacher as the required mentor for everyone at a center, especially for newcomers.

Traditional Tibetans often have difficulties when becoming the resident teachers at Dharma centers since they assume that if centers invite them to teach, the students wish to establish disciple-mentor relationships with them. Moreover, they are accustomed to being given offerings for free instruction, not salaries based on a charge for courses. Western teachers, however, can more easily understand and accept these arrangements. Therefore, to avoid confusion, Western teachers need to keep the financial arrangements between Dharma centers and themselves strictly on the bases of business terms, even if the administrators of the centers are their disciples. The traditional protocols of the disciple-mentor relationship do not pertain to the financial sphere, although politeness and respect need always to be present.

Both Western and Tibetan spiritual teachers may establish and run their own Dharma centers. In such cases as well, the teachers cannot expect that everyone who comes to the centers will be their disciples. They need to accept that many will be only their Buddhism students, Dharma pupils, or meditation or ritual trainees. As with other teaching institutions, they need to run their centers along sound financial guidelines.

A Student Working Personally with or Indirectly for a Western Teacher

As explained previously, in Tibetan society certain disciples, known as *getrug*, live with their mentors, normally from childhood, and receive full financial support from the household. This occurs whether they live with their mentors in the teachers' own homes or in the homes of the teachers' patron/disciples, and whether the mentors are monastics or married or single laypeople. They may serve as attendants, cooks, secretaries, interpreters, ritual assistants, or some combination of roles, and may or may not receive spiritual teachings from the mentor.

Like members of an Asian extended family, household- member disciples receive neither salaries nor pocket money for their work. In the case of monastics, the only private funds that they normally have they receive at large monastic ceremonies, empowerments, or discourses, when the lay patrons of the proceedings make small financial offerings to all the monks and nuns who attend. In the case of lay teachers, the disciples included in the finances of the household are usually younger relatives and may occasionally receive pocket money from other family members. Household-member disciples may choose to leave their mentors' homes; but no matter how poorly they serve or behave, Tibetan mentors rarely ask them to leave. They merely assign their duties to other members of the household.

Westerners, on the other hand, who serve as personal secretaries, assistants, or interpreters for Western teachers do not necessarily have disciple-mentor relationships with the teachers, although they are usually at least their students. They normally live in separate housing or in separate quarters within Dharma centers. Like going to jobs, they go to work each day with the teachers and have the usual expenses of modern Western lives. The Dharma centers, private patrons, or the teachers themselves may provide their funding. Alternatively, they may have other sources of income and either serve as volunteers or work only for token remuneration. Some students may also work indirectly for Western teachers, either at the teachers' Dharma centers or in affiliated businesses, with financial arrangements similar to those for the teachers' personal staff. In all these cases, several practical guidelines may be helpful to follow.

When working for the teacher is the students' sole source of income, the salary needs to be appropriate to the work done and sufficient to cover health insurance and other normal Western expenses. To pay inadequate wages or, as in indentured labor, to provide simply room and board at a center and perhaps a tiny monthly allowance so that student staff and workers can never accumulate enough savings to move out on their own is exploitation. The exploitation is even more pronounced if the students are lured into accepting the positions because they are made to feel that they are the "chosen ones" given the honor to serve the teacher.

Some Dharma organizations follow a socialist model. The organization runs a business and the profits pay for the living expenses of the spiritual teachers, their student staff, and the student workers. The staff members and workers frequently live together in communal houses. Each person, upon approval from a financial committee, may draw a reasonable amount from a common fund for pocket money and personal matters, based on need. Participation in such arrangements, however, requires selfless dedication and honesty on everyone's part; otherwise, the situation may likewise result in authoritarian exploitation and may similarly leave the students without the financial resources to leave communal life. To avoid the latter from happening, the organization might contribute monthly to individual accounts for each student, somewhat like contributing to an employee's pension plan, and the funds made available to anyone who decides to leave.

Further, the main criterion for hiring students needs to be their professional skills and commitment to the Dharma, not their spiritual levels or devotion to the teacher. It must be made clear to everyone that efficiency and effectiveness at work does not reflect spiritual competency or the sincerity of the student-teacher relationship. Moreover, as an explicit part of the contract, both sides need the option to terminate the arrangement for any reason, without this indicating a breach of guru-devotion or disapproval of the workers or staff members as spiritual seekers.

The relationships between spiritual teachers and their private secretaries, assistants, and interpreters tend to work most effectively when the people chosen are personal disciples. Because protection of the disciple-mentor bond must take top priority, only extremely mature and emotionally stable disciples are suited to work in close personal contact with their mentors.

A Disciple/Assistant Living with a Western Mentor as an Apprentice

When Western teachers are old or infirm, they may require assistants to live with them. Normally, however, Western teachers who are in good health do not require live-in attendants, although they may find assistants helpful on extended lecture tours. The other major situation in which living with an assistant may be beneficial is when Western mentors train especially receptive disciples as apprentices.

Spiritual apprenticeship is more than the typical Western training program for spiritual teachers. It does not encompass merely learning the subject matter and pedagogic skills, participating in workshops to explore personal attitudes about authority, sex, and money, and receiving supervision. It entails living closely with a mentor, normally as part of the household, and learning from observation of the teacher's interpersonal relations and handling of daily activities, from participation in them as an assistant, when appropriate, and from intense interaction with the mentor. The relationship may be extremely demanding, as was the case in my own nine-year apprenticeship with Serkong Rinpochey to become an interpreter and spiritual teacher. For example, to train my mindfulness and memory, he would stop our conversation at any time and ask me to repeat word for word what either he or I had just said. The emotional challenge of such training requires strict adherence to the guideline of not becoming annoyed with the mentor and viewing every action as a teaching.

The spiritual apprentice-mentor relationship between two contemporary Westerners living together is still a largely unexplored area. Although certain modern Western cultural features may make it more difficult than in Tibetan or other Asian societies, the possible benefits of such a relationship between two qualified, mature people with a healthy, strong bond as disciple and mentor make it worthwhile to explore. Let us look at some tentative guidelines. Most of them would also pertain to disciples living with elderly or infirm Western mentors, even when they are not training as apprentices.

The live-in arrangement would probably work best either when both parties are single—whether they are monastic or lay—or, in cases of one or both parties having life-partners, when the mentor and partner form a teaching couple or when the disciple and partner are to be trained as a team. If the partner of either side is not personally involved with the teaching or training process and, particularly, if either side has children, too many problems of jealousy, resentment, division of loyalties, possible exploitation of the apprentice or partner as a servant, and so on, may arise. If such problems occur even in cultures that have the custom of people living in extended families, how much more so will they happen in Western cultures that lack the custom? In such cases, a nonresident apprenticeship may be best. Moreover, regardless of the genders and sexual orientations of an unmarried apprentice and mentor, it must be clear from the start that the relationship of living together is not a "spiritual marriage" with Prince or Princess Charming.

In traditional Indian and Tibetan societies, spiritual apprentices maintain celibacy (Skt. *brahmacharya* conduct) while undergoing intensive training. In a modern Western context, it is perhaps unrealistic to expect total celibacy from lay apprentices living and training with mentors. However, it would be inappropriate for single lay apprentices to bring their partners to sleep in the mentor's house or, if lacking established sexual relationships, to look for partners while residing with the mentor. The apprentice-mentor relationship needs to be the main intense relationship, especially within the shared home. Moreover, if single lay mentors have lovers, it probably would be too difficult for most apprentices if the mentors slept with them overnight at home.

For the resident apprentice-mentor relationship to remain healthy, however, it must not be the only close, nonfamilial relationship that each side has. Both the apprentice and the mentor need to have personal friends. Further, as in any relationship between two people sharing an apartment or a house, each side needs to be able to invite friends home, without feeling awkward, but also without disturbing the other. Although they may share mutual friends, neither side needs to feel obligated to include or exclude the other when friends come to visit. In addition, the apprentices need to feel free to receive instruction from other spiritual teachers—although in consultation with the mentors they live with—and the mentors naturally will have other disciples and perhaps even apprentices.

Regardless of the age differences between live-in apprentices and their mentors, it is important to try to prevent the apprentices from feeling as if they are children. To avoid undue transference, the relationship must be between two adults who can communicate openly to each other. Particularly delicate is the issue of money. If the apprentices receive partial or full financial support from the mentors or the mentors' patrons, it might be best if they receive it each week or month like a normal salary, not like a child's allowance. Moreover, to help maintain self-respect, they need to earn their salaries, for instance by doing household or secretarial work for the mentors. Payment by the hour may help to minimize feelings of guilt or resentment when the apprentices take necessary time to relax, to visit family or friends, or to take care of personal matters. As a precaution in case the mentors or patrons can no longer afford to pay them salaries, it is helpful if the apprentices have savings or professional skills to turn to as alternative sources of income. In some cases, holding outside part-time jobs may not only alleviate financial pressures, but also help the apprentices to maintain balance and to prevent the intensity of the relationships with their mentors from overwhelming them.

It is best if the apprentices contribute their fair shares to the household expenses from their salaries or other sources of income. To receive room, board, and unlimited use of the telephone and car as part of the arrangements may easily cause them to regress to the stage of indulged teenage dependents. Further, the apprentices need to have their own rooms, except perhaps when travelling with their mentors, so that they can relax, listen to music, and entertain friends, without feeling self-conscious.

Before starting to live together, it might be best if both sides agree on a specified period of time for the apprenticeship, which can be extended or shortened depending on the usefulness of the arrangement. As in the case of disciples working for mentors, it must be clear that either side may terminate the arrangement at any time, without implying a break or weakening of the disciple-mentor bond. Both sides need to acknowledge, however, that even when the apprenticeship reaches its natural conclusion at the completion of the training, they will naturally feel sad.

In a Tibetan context, disciples who are members of a mentor's household often remain in this role for the rest of their lives. If the mentor is a tulku or starts a line of tulkus, they may even remain after the mentor's death to find and raise the next incarnation. In the case of two Westerners, a lifelong relationship of a disciple/apprentice/assistant and a mentor living together may evolve, if both sides find it beneficial, even without the issue of a possible future tulku's being involved. However, just as Tibetan mentors often have several disciples who live with them as part of the household, similarly Western mentors need to make clear to live-in apprentices, even lifelong ones, that they do not hold the exclusive rights to these types of relationship with them. Emotional space must always be available for additional apprentices to join the household.

Western-Style Friendship between a Disciple and a Mentor

In Western countries with the predominantly Protestant values of egalitarianism, most people feel uncomfortable in hierarchical relationships. They tend to view such relationships in patriarchal or matriarchal terms, which carry for them negative connotations of manipulation, control, and suffocation of individuality. Therefore, disciples and mentors from such societies often prefer relationships with each other that more resemble friendship between equals.

On one level, the disciple-mentor relationship contains an equal exchange. Both parties gain inspiration from the other. However, as in the dynamic between a single parent and an only child, if a Western mentor tries to make the relationship into a friendship between equals, the disciple suffers. Both sides need to be clear, for example, that it is not the student's job to give emotional support to the teacher. Although most Western disciples are averse to authoritarian mentors who remain emotionally aloof, nevertheless they need stable examples of attainment to look up to and respect.

Western spiritual seekers with low self-esteem often need reassurance that they are not unique in having shortcomings. Thus, they may gain inspiration from spiritual teachers who, in the manner of Dharma instructors, share their doubts and weaknesses and indicate how they are using the Dharma to overcome them. Yet, sometimes the emotional struggles the teachers are working through are struggles with the students, such as being sexually attracted to some or being frustrated and disappointed that certain students do not come regularly to teachings. In such cases, it is inappropriate for teachers to share those feelings with students, as friends might share them with each other. Spiritual teachers, and especially mentors, need always to refrain from saying or doing anything that might undermine the students' respect and trust.

Westerners tend to need and to like personal interaction with spiritual teachers more than Tibetans do. They also are more accustomed to expressing their own and listening to others' emotional difficulties. Thus, sharing personal problems with Western teachers may be more appropriate and easier than sharing them with Tibetan ones. In this sense, Western mentors may resemble close friends. Yet, care is required to avoid confusing this type of intimacy with romantic intimacy. Some disciples may feel that the mentor is the only one who understands them and thus fall in love. At the other extreme, unconscious fear of homosexuality or of male or female domination may cause some disciples suddenly to distance themselves from the mentor when they start to feel love and affection. Western teachers need sensitivity and strict attention to avoid unconscious countertransference.

Occasionally, a spontaneous friendly handshake or hug between disciple and mentor may be appropriate upon meeting or departing if shaking hands or hugging is a cultural custom shared between them and both sides feel natural and relaxed about it. If shaking hands or hugging becomes a forced ritual, however, or misinterpretation of its intent begins to arise, it is best to avoid these types of physical contact.

Nevertheless, each encounter outside the classroom or meditation hall need not be deep and meaningful. Forced intensity quickly becomes artificial and stifling. Sharing relaxed informal time may sometimes be more beneficial. Yet, teachers need to avoid encouraging being so relaxed that students become sloppy with them or take undue advantage of their time.

Geshey Ngawang Dhargyey once said that spiritual teachers are like wild animals. It is best not to stay too close. If spiritual seekers spend all day with them, they are more apt to find or see faults than if they keep a certain distance. The implicit meaning is that seekers' moods go up and down, and a teacher's actions may not always be enlightening. If disciples lack a strong foundation in sutra-level guru-meditation, they may derive more confusion than inspiration. Even in a Tibetan context in which attendants or child disciples live with their mentors, the two parties nearly always stay in separate rooms and do not spend all their unstructured time with each other. Thus, in spiritual friendships between Western disciples and Western mentors, a middle path between closeness and distance may be beneficial. The boundaries of propriety need to be clearly defined and strictly maintained, even in the case of apprentices living with mentors.

Western-Style Life-Partnership between a Disciple and a Mentor

His Holiness the Fourteenth Dalai Lama has said that if unmarried lay mentors develop sexual love for students or disciples, one cannot say that partnerships between them are totally taboo. However, the mentors' intentions need to be the establishment of long-term committed partnerships and not just one-night stands. It is completely inappropriate and abusive for mentors to use the lure of long-term relationships, or to play on the fantasies of disciples, just to get them into bed. In committed relationships, the two may relate to each other as equals in bed. Afterwards, however, they may relate as mentor and disciple. There is no inherent contradiction, as is shown in the relationships between married Tibetan lamas and their Tibetan wives.

Such arrangements may be more difficult to maintain with Westerners who feel uncomfortable in hierarchical partnerships or marriages. For most people, having several roles in a relationship is difficult to juggle. When one person is in the mode of one role, the other may be in the mode of another. The dynamic may be very delicate, especially during the courtship period.

In the West, the family of a doctor normally relies on an outside physician for medical treatment. Similarly, Western disciples and mentors who become life-partners may perhaps avoid many problems by suspending active pursuance of their disciple-mentor relationships. The disciples may make better spiritual progress if they rely primarily on other teachers as their mentors, while still deriving inspiration and encouragement from their spouses. In the case of an unmarried lay mentor and an apprentice developing sexual love for each other, the long-term relationship would probably need eventually to shift to one of a teaching team.

Conclusion

The tantras unanimously agree that the inspiration gained from a healthy disciple-mentor relationship is a source of true joy and spiritual attainment. On the other hand, when misunderstood and mixed with confusion, the relationship becomes unhealthy and may give rise to spiritual devastation and emotional pain. Misunderstanding may occur on the side of the disciple, the mentor, or both; and cultural factors often add to the confusion.

Shantideva explained that without seeing the target, an archer cannot hit a bull's-eye. Thus, to build healthy relationships and to heal the wounds that may have occurred from unhealthy ones, disciples need to identify correctly the principal source of the problems—lack of awareness. Lack of awareness derives from confusion about the Dharma teachings and about the cultural factors unconsciously affecting the thought and behavior of each party in the relationship. When Westerners are involved, imprecise or misleading translation terms frequently worsen the confusion. A rectification of terms, together with cultural sensitivity, may help to bring emotional clarity.

Many people, disillusioned or outraged at failures in the disciple-mentor relationship in the West, have called for a serious revision of the relation. Revision, however, does not require overturning tradition and inventing something entirely new. Revision may come from clearing away confusion about Buddha's teachings and by following the time-proven method of transmission of Buddhism from one culture to another.

Throughout the history of Buddhism, the teachings have successfully passed to different cultures by emphasizing and expanding Dharma points that resonate with the thought and customs of the recipient society. For success in the ongoing historical process of transmitting the Tibetan Buddhist lineages to the West, Kadam sutra-level guru-meditation may provide points of resonance and serve as an appropriate framework for building healthy disciple-mentor relationships. Time-tested Dharma methods adapted and applied to new situations have provided the solutions to the culturally based problems that inevitably arise. Thus, with Asian-style creativity, harmonious fits have grown within the framework of Buddhist tradition.

~Appendix

Summary of the Stages of Expanded Sutra-Level Guru-Meditation

Our analysis of some of the problems that have caused unhealthy relationships with spiritual teachers in the West has suggested Kadam sutra-level guru-meditation as a framework for the healing process. In several cases, additional steps in the meditation have seemed appropriate, but within the context of the traditional method. Let us summarize our findings in terms of a Mahayana disciple-mentor relationship.

The meditation begins with imagining our mentors or looking at photos of our them and offering the seven-part invocation: prostrating, making offerings, admitting mistakes, rejoicing in the virtues of others, requesting teaching, beseeching the gurus not to pass away, and dedicating the positive potential of the practice. As part of admitting mistakes, we may also acknowledge the wrongs we might have experienced from less-than-perfect teachers.

Following the invocation, we remind ourselves of the advantages of focusing on our mentors' good qualities and the disadvantages of dwelling on their faults. Then, we bring to mind the teachers' shortcomings, clear away conventional inaccuracies, and meditate on the conventionally accurate faults as devoid of existing as inherent flaws. We may repeat the procedure with our own shortcomings. Then, we may follow a similar procedure regarding first our own good qualities and then those of our mentors. The process entails bringing the qualities to mind, clearing away any inflation or interpolation, and then focusing on the conventionally accurate ones as devoid of existing as inherent wonders.

Free of naivety, we then focus on the actual good qualities of our mentors with the clearheaded belief that they have these qualities. When the actual qualities are perfectly clear, we reinforce our belief in their presence by thinking of the process whereby our mentors have gained them and by the positive effects that they have on others and on us. We then focus with belief on the fact that these qualities are attainable and on the conclusion that we can and shall attain them ourselves, to benefit others. This section of the practice concludes with focusing intently on our mentors with firm conviction and trust, and then absorbing our concentration totally on these feelings so that we integrate them fully.

Next, we turn to our mentors' kindness. We may supplement this step by bringing to mind our feelings of their lack of kindness, examine any degenerative regression that may be affecting our feelings, and clear away conventional inaccuracies and exaggeration of our mentors' behavior. Then we focus on the accurate facts as devoid of indicating that our mentors are inherently inconsiderate or cruel. Reminding ourselves that people sometimes show kindness in ways other than what we might normally recognize or want, we bring to mind our mentors' kindness. Clearing away again any exaggeration or interpolation, we then focus on the conventionally accurate kindness as devoid of existing as an inherent favor or boon. If we find it relevant, we may also focus on ourselves as devoid of congenital flaws that would render us, by their own powers, inherently unworthy of kindness or love. As when focusing on our mentors with firm conviction, we then focus intently on them with clearheaded, heartfelt appreciation and loving respect, and then absorb ourselves into these feelings.

With firm conviction, trust, appreciation, and loving respect for our mentors, we now request inspiration. The inspiration enters our hearts in the form of white or yellow light emanated from our mentors' hearts—white to diminish shortcomings such as low energy or yellow to stimulate good qualities. We then imagine tiny images of our mentors coming to the crown of our heads. They sit there for the remainder of the day to act as witnesses of our behavior and thought and to serve as continuing sources of inspiration. Before going to sleep at night, we may imagine that these tiny images of our mentors come to our hearts and dissolve, or we may imagine that we fall asleep with our heads in our mentors' laps.

The meditation ends with dedicating the positive potential of the practice. We think, "May the positive legacy of my mentor's good qualities and kindness integrate with my networks of good qualities, positive potentials, and deep awareness. May it ripen and affect my behavior so that I may pass on this legacy to others and help them to achieve emotional well-being, more fortunate rebirth, liberation, and eventually enlightenment for the benefit of all."

～Bibliography

Sanskrit and Tibetan Sources

Aku Sherab-gyatso (A-khu Shes-rab rgya-mtsho) (1803–1875). *'Dus-pa lam rim-pa dang-po'i khrid-dmigs-kyi brjed-byang* (A Reminder for Not Forgetting the Visualizations Described for the First Stage of the Path of Guhyasamaja).

Anangavajra (Anaṅgavajra, Yan-lag med-pa'i rdo-rje) (9th century). *Prajñopāyaviniścayasiddhi* (Thabs-dang shes-rab gtan-la dbab-pa grub-pa; Establishing Method and Discriminating Awareness).

Aryadeva (Āryadeva, 'Phags-pa lha) (3rd century). *Catuḥśataka-śāstra-kārikā* (bsTan-bcos bzhi-brgya-pa zhes-bya-ba'i tshig-le'ur byas-pa; Four Hundred Stanzas).

Aryashura (Āryaśūra, sLob-dpon dPa'-bo) (2nd century). *Jātakamālā* (sKyes-rabs 'phreng-ba; A Garland of Past-Life Accounts [of the Buddha]).

Asanga (Asaṅga, Thogs-med) (3rd century). *Abhidharmasamuccaya* (Chos mngon-pa kun-las btus-pa; An Anthology of Special Topics of Knowledge).

_____. *Mahāyānasūtrālaṃkāra* (Theg-pa chen-po'i mdo-sde rgyan; Filigree of Mahayana Sutras).

Ashvaghosha II (Aśvaghoṣa; rTa-dbyangs) (10th century). *Gurupañcāśatikā* (Bla-ma lnga-bcu-pa; Fifty Stanzas on the Guru).

Atisha (Atiśa, Dipaṃkaraśrijñāna; A-ti-sha, dPal Mar-me mdzad ye-shes) (982–1054). *Bodhipathapradīpa* (Byang-chub lam-gyi sgron-me; A Lamp for the Path to Enlightenment).

_____. *Bodhipathapradīpavṛtti* (Byang-chub lam-gyi sgron-me'i dka'-'grel; An [Auto-]Commentary on the Difficult Points of *A Lamp for the Path to Enlightenment*).

_____. *Gurukriyākrama* (Bla-ma'i bya-ba'i rim-pa; The Stages of Practice with a Guru).

Bla-ma sgrub-pa thun-mong-ba'i khrid-dang 'brel-ba'i nyams-len ngag-'don-gyi rim-pa khrigs-su bkod-pa mun-sel nyin-byed snang-ba (The Properly Arranged Stages of Recitation for Practice in Conjunction with a Discourse on the Common

Level of Actualizing through the Guru: Eliminating Darkness and Bringing Daylight).

Chaykawa ('Chad-kha-ba) (1101–1175). *Blo-sbyong don-bdun-ma* (Seven Points for Cleansing Attitudes; Seven-Point Mind Training).

Chandrakirti (Candrakirti; Zla-ba grags-pa) (6th century). *Bodhisattva-yogacaryā-catuḥśataka-ṭikā* (Zhi-brgya-pa'i 'grel-ba byang-chub sems-dpa'i rnal-'byor spyod-pa; Yogic Deeds of Bodhisattvas: A Commentary on [Āryadeva's] *Four Hundred Stanzas*).

_____. *Madhyamakāvatāra* (dBu-ma-la 'jug-pa; A Supplement to [Nagarjuna's *Root Stanzas on*] *the Middle Way*).

_____. *Mūlamadhyamaka-vṛtti-prasannapadā* (dBu-ma rtsa-ba 'grel-ba tshig-gsal; Clear Verses: A Commentary on [Nāgārjuna's] *Root Stanzas on the Middle Way*).

Chandrakirti II (Candrakirti; Zla-ba grags-pa) (9th century). *Pradipoddotana-nāma-ṭikā* ('Grel-ba sgron-gsal; An Illuminating Lamp: A Commentary [on *The Guhyasamāja Tantra*].

Dagpo Jampel-lhündrub (Dvags-po 'Jam-dpal lhun-grub) (19th century). *Lam-rim myur-lam-gyi sngnon-'gro'i ngag-'don-gyi rim-pa sbyor-chos bskal-bzang mgrin-rgyan* (Supplementary Practices: An Ornament for the Throats of Fortunate Ones, Stages for Recitation as a Preliminary for [the Second Panchen Lama's] *Graded Stages of the Path: A Speedy Path*; The Lam-rim Puja).

The First Dalai Lama (rGyal-ba dGe-'dun grub) (1391–1474). *mDzod-tik thar-lam gsal-byed* (Clarifying the Path to Liberation: A Commentary to [Vasuban-dhu's] *Treasure-House [of Special Topics of Knowledge]*).

The Third Dalai Lama (rGyal-dbang bSod-nams rgya-mtsho) (1543–1588). *Lam-rim gser-zhun-ma* (The Graded Stages of the Path: Refined Gold).

The Fifth Dalai Lama (rGyal-mchog lnga-pa chen-po Ngag-dbang blo-bzang rg-ya-mtsho) (1617–1682). *Lam-rim 'jam-dpal zhal-lung* (The Graded Stages of the Path: Personal Instructions from Manjushri).

The Seventh Dalai Lama (rGyal-dbang bsKal-bzang rgya-mtsho) (1708–1757). *dPal gsang-ba 'dus-pa mi-bskyod rdo-rje'i dkyil-'khor-gyi cho-ga'i rnam-par bshad-pa dbang-don de-nyid yang-gsal snang-ba rdo-rje sems-dpa'i zhal-lung* (An Expla-nation of the Mandala Ritual of Glorious Vajra Akshobhya Guhyasamaja, Illumination Clarifying the Actual Meaning of Empowerment: Personal In-structions from Vajrasattva).

Dharmakirti (Dharmakirti; Chos-kyi grags-pa) (7th century), *Pramāṇavārttika* (Tshad-ma rnam-'grel; A Commentary on [Dignaga's *Compendium of*] *Validly Cognizing Minds*).

mDo mtshams-sbyor (The Connections Sutra).

Dragpa-gyeltsen (Grags-pa rgyal-mtshan) (1147–1216). *Bla-ma bsten-pa'i thabs shlo-ka lnga-bcu-pa'i gsal-byed* (Clarifying [Ashvaghosha's] *Fifty Stanzas*, The Method for Relating to a Guru).

————. *Byin-rlabs tshar-gsum khug-pa* (Three Rounds of Inspiration).

Drigungpa ('Bri-gung 'Jig-rten mgon-po Rin-chen dpal) (1143–1217). *Dam-chos dgong-pa gcig-pa* (The Single Intention of the Sacred Dharma).

————. *Theg-chen bstan-pa'i snying-po* (The Essence of the Mahayana Teachings).

Gampopa (sGam-po-pa Zla-'od gzhon-nu) (1079–1153). *Lam-mchog rin-po-che'i phreng-ba* (A Precious Garland for the Supreme Path).

————. *Thar-pa rin-po-che'i rgyan* (A Precious Ornament for Liberation; The Jewel Ornament of Liberation).

Gaṇḍavyūhasūtra (sDong-po bskod-pa'i mdo; A Sutra Spread Out Like a Tree-Trunk).

Ghanavyūhasūtra (sTug-po bkod-pa'i mdo; A Sutra [on Pure Realms] Spread Out in a Dense Array).

Gorampa (Go-bo rab-'byams-pa bSod-nams seng-ge) (1429–1489). *Blo-sbyong zhen-pa bzhi-bral-gyi khrid-yig zab-mo gnad-kyi lde'u-mig* (A Key to the Essential Profound Points: Discourse Notes on the Cleansing of Attitudes, [Manjushri's] *Parting from the Four [Stages of] Clinging*).

Gyelrong Tsültrim-nyima (rGyal-rong Tshul-khrims nyi-ma) (19th century). *Kha-chems rlung-la bskur-ba'i 'phrin-yig* (A Last Testament Letter Cast to the Wind).

Jñānavajrasamuccaya (Ye-shes rdo-rje kun-las btus-pa; An Anthology of Vajra Deep Awareness).

The Eighth Karmapa (rGyal-ba Kar-ma-pa Mi-bskyod rdo-rje) (1507–1554). *dBu-ma gzhan-stong smra-ba'i srol legs-par phye-ba'i sgron-me* (A Lamp for Clearly Revealing the Other-Voidness Madhyamaka Tradition).

The Ninth Karmapa (rGyal-ba Kar-ma-pa dBang-phyug rdo-rje) (1554–1603). *Phyag-chen ma-rig mun-sel* (Mahamudra Eliminating the Darkness of Ignorance).

Kaydrub Norzang-gyatso (mKhas-grub Nor-bzang rgya-mtsho) (1423–1513). *Dam-tshig gsal-ba'i sgron-me* (A Lamp to Illuminate the Closely Bonding Practices).

————. *Bka'-dge dgongs-pa gcig-bsgrub-kyi phyag-rgya chen-po gsal-ba'i sgron-ma* (A Lamp for Clarifying Mahamudra to Establish the Single Intention of the Kagyü and Gelug Traditions).

————. *Phyi-nang-gzhan-gsum gsal-bar byed-pa dri-med 'od-kyi rgyan* (An Ornament for [Pundarika's] *Stainless Light*, Clarifying the External, Internal, and Alternative [Kalachakras]).

Kongtrül ('Jam-mgon Kong-sprul Blo-gros mtha'-yas Yon-tan rgya-mtsho) (1813–1899). *rGyud bla-ma'i 'grel-ba phyir mi-ldog-pa'i seng-ge'i nga-ro* (The Irrevocable Lion's Roar: A Commentary on [Maitreya's] *Sublime Continuum*).

————. *Nges-don sgron-me* (A Lamp for the Definitive Meaning; Torch of Certainty).

_____. *Shes-bya mtha'-yas-pa'i rgya-mtsho* (Ocean of Infinite Knowledge).

Langri-tangpa (Glang-ri thang-pa) (11th century). *Blo-sbyong tshig brgyad-ma* (Eight Stanzas on Cleansing Attitudes; Eight-Verse Mind Training).

Longchenpa (Klong-chen Rab-'byams-pa Dri-med 'od-zer) (1308–1363). *Chos-bzhi rin-po-che'i 'phreng-ba* (A Precious Garland for the Four Themes [of Gampopa]).

_____. *Rin-po-che'i man-ngag mdzod* (A Treasure-House of Precious Guideline Instructions)

_____. *Sems-nyid ngal-gso* (Rest and Restoration in the Nature of the Mind, Kindly Bent to Ease Us).

Mahāvyutpatti (Bye-brag-tu rtogs-par byed-pa chen-po; The Great [Sanskrit-Tibetan] Etymological Dictionary).

Maitreya (Maitreya, Byams-pa). *Mahāyānottaratantraśāstra* (Theg-pa chen-po rgyud bla-ma bstan-bcos; The Sublime Continuum: A Mahayana Treatise; The Changeless Nature).

Manjushri (Mañjuśrī, 'Jam-pa'i dbyangs). *Zhen-pa bzhi-bral* (Parting from the Four [Stages of] Clinging).

Naropa (Nāropa; Nā-ro-pa) (1016–1100). *Gurusiddhi* (Bla-ma sgrubs-pa; Actualizing through a Guru).

Ngari Panchen (mNga'-ris Paṇ-chen Pad-ma dbang-gi rgyal-po) (1487–1542). *sDom-gsum rnam-nges* (Ascertaining the Three Vows).

Ngawang-pelzang (Ngag-dbang dpal-bzang) (19th century). *Kun-bzang bla-ma'i zhal-lung-gi zin-bris* (Lecture Notes on [Peltrül's] *Personal Instructions from My Totally Excellent Guru*).

Ngojey-raypa (Ngo-rjes ras-pa Zhe-sdang rdo-rje) (12th century). *Theg chen bstan-pa'i snying-po legs-bshad lung-gyi rgya-mtsho* (Ocean of Quotations Explaining Well [Drigungpa's] *Essence of the Mahayana Teachings*).

Ngorchen Könchog-lhündrub (Ngor-chen dKon-mchog lhun-grub) (1497–1557). *rGyud-gsum mdzes-rgyan* (A Beautiful Ornament for the Three Continua).

_____. *sNang-gsum mdzes-rgyan* (A Beautiful Ornament for the Three Appearances).

Niguma (Niguma, Ni-gu-ma) (11th century). *sGyu-ma lam-gyi rim-pa* (The Graded Stages of the Path of Illusion).

_____. *sGyu-ma lam-gyi rim-pa'i don-'grel* (A Commentary on the Meaning of *The Graded Stages of the Path of Illusion*).

Pabongka (Pha-bong-kha Byams-pa bstan-'dzin 'phrin-las rgya-mtsho) (1878–1943). *rNam-grol lag-bcangs* (Liberation in the Palm of Your Hand).

_____. *Thun-drug bla-ma'i rnal-'byor-dang sDom-pa nyi-shu-pa Bla-ma lnga-bcu-pa sNgags-kyi rtsa-ltung sbom-po bcas-kyi bshad-khri gnang-ba'i zin-tho mdor-bsdus* (Abbreviated Notes from Explanatory Discourses Given on [the First Panchen Lama's] *Six-Session Guru-Yoga*, [Chandragomin's] *Twenty [Stanzas* on the Bodhisattva] Vows, [Ashvaghosha's] *Fifty Stanzas on the Guru*, and the Root and Secondary Tantric Vows).

Padmasambhava (Padmasaṃbhāva; Pad-ma 'byung-gnas) (8th century). *Bar-do thos-grol* (Liberation through Hearing in the Bardo; The Tibetan Book of the Dead).

The First Panchen Lama (Paṇ-chen Blo-bzang chos-kyi rgyal-mtshan) (1570–1662). *Bla-ma mchod-pa* (A Ceremony for Honoring the Gurus; Lama Chöpa; The Guru Puja).

_____. *dGe-ldan bka'-brgyud srol phyag-chen rtsa-ba rgyas-par bshad-pa yang-gsal sgron-me* (An Extensive [Auto-]Explanation of *A Root Text for the Gelug/Kagyü Lineage of Mahamudra*: A Lamp for Further Illumination).

_____. *rGyud thams-cad-kyi rgyal-po dpal gsang-ba 'dus-pa'i bskyed- rim-gyi rnam-bshad dngos-grub-kyi rgya-mtsho'i snying po* (The Essence of [Kaydrubchey's] *Ocean of Actual Attainments: An Explanation of the Generation Stage of Glorious Guhyasamaja, the King of All Tantras*).

_____. *Lam-rim bde-lam* (The Graded Stages of the Path: A Blissful Path).

The Second Panchen Lama (Paṇ-chen Blo-bzang ye-shes) (1663–1737). *Lam-rim myur-lam* (The Graded Stages of the Path: A Speedy Path).

Peltrül (rDza dPal-sprul O-rgyan 'jigs-med chos-kyi dbang-po) (1808–1887). *Kun-bzang bla-ma'i zhal-lung* (Personal Instructions from My Totally Excellent Guru; The Words of My Perfect Teacher).

Pema-karpo ('Brug-chen Pad-ma dkar-po) (1527–1592). *Bla-ma mos-gus-kyi khrid-kyi dmigs-rim byin-rlabs-kyi snye-ma* (Graded Visualizations as a Thrust for Conviction and Appreciation of a Guru: A Cluster of Fruit of Inspiration).

_____. *Dvags-po chos-bzhi'i rnam-bshad skyes-bu gsum-gyi lam nyin-mor byed-pa* (An Explanation of the Four Themes of Gampopa: Bringing Daylight to the Path of the Three Scopes of Spiritual Seekers).

Pundarika (Kalki Puṇḍarika, Rigs-ldan Pad-ma dkar-po). *Paramasevā* (Don-dam bsnyen-pa; Approximating the Deepest Level).

_____. *Vimālaprabhā-nāma-laghu-kālachakra-tantra-rāja-ṭīkā* (bsDus-pa'i rgyud-kyi rgyal-po dus-kyi 'khor-lo'i 'grel-bshad dri-ma med-pa'i 'od; Stainless Light: A Commentary Explaining *The Regal Abbreviated Kalachakra Tantra*).

Ratnameghasūtra (dKon-mchog sprin-gyi mdo; A Cloud of Jewels Sutra).

Rigdzin Chökyi-dragpa (Rig-'dzin Chos-kyi grags-pa) (b. 1595) *rGyud-sde'i snying-po lnga-ldan-gyi nyams-len* (The Heart of the Tantras: The Fivefold Practice [of Mahamudra]).

Sakya Pandita (Sa-paṇ Kun-dga' rgyal-mtshan) (1182–1251). *sDom-gsum rab-dbye* (The Divisions of the Three Sets of Vows).

_____. *Lam zab-mo bla-ma'i rnal-'byor* (The Profound Path of Guru-Yoga).

_____. *Legs-bshad rin-po-che'i gter* (A Precious Treasury of Elegant Sayings).

Sangwayjin (gSang-ba'i byin). *sKyes-bu gsum-gyi lam-rim rgyas-pa khrid-su sbyar-*

ba (An Extensive Presentation of the Graded Stages of the Path for the Three Scopes of Spiritual Seekers, Arranged in a Discourse).

Shantideva (Śāntideva, Zhi-ba lha) (8th century). *Bodhisattvacaryāvatāra* (Byang-chub sems-pa'i spyod-pa-la 'jug-pa; Engaging in a Bodhisattva's Deeds).

Sherab-senggey (rGyud Shes-rab seng-ge) (1383–1445). *sGron-gsal rgya-cher bshad-pa le'u dang-po rgya-cher bshad-pa* (An Extensive Explanation of [Chandrakirti's] *Illuminating Lamp*: An Extensive Explanation of Chapter One).

Sönam-tsemo (bSod-nams rtse-mo) (1142–1182). *Chos-la 'jug-pa'i sgo* (The Gateway for Entering the Dharma).

Taranata (Tā-ra nā-tha) (1575–1634). *rGyal-ba'i bstan-pa-la 'jug-pa'i rim-pa skyes-bu gsum-gyi man-ngag-gi khrid-yig bdud-rtsi'i nying-khu* (The Stages for Engaging in the Triumphant One's Teachings: Discourse Notes on the Guideline Instructions Concerning the Three Scopes of Spiritual Seekers: The Essence of Nectar).

Terdag Lingpa (gTer-bdag gLing-pa sMin-gling gter-chen 'Gyur-med rdo-rje) (1646–1714). *Rin-chen them-skas* (A Precious Ladder; The Jewel Ladder).

Tsangpa-gyaray (Tsang-pa rgya-ras Ye-shes rdo-rje) (1161–1211). *Bla-ma'i ngo-sprod rmus-long mig-'byed* (Introduction by the Guru to Open Blind Eyes).

_____. *Bla-ma'i sgrub-thabs thugs-rje nyi-rgyas* (Actualizing through One's Guru: The Expansive Sun of Compassion).

Tsarchen (Tshar-chen Blo-gsal rgya-mtsho) (1502–1566). *bShes-gnyen dam-pa bsten-par byed-pa'i thabs shlo-ka lnga-bcu-pa'i 'grel-ba* (Methods for Building a Relationship with a Proper Spiritual Mentor: A Commentary on [Ashvaghosha's] *Fifty Stanzas [on the Guru]*).

Tsongkapa (Tsong-kha-pa Blo-bzang grags-pa) (1357–1419). *Bla-ma lnga-bcu-pa'i rnam-bshad slob-ma'i re-ba kun-skong* (An Explanation of [Ashvaghosha's] *Fifty Stanzas on the Guru*: The Complete Fulfillment of Disciples' Hopes; The Fulfillment of All Hopes).

_____. *dBu-ma-la 'jug-pa'i rgya-cher bshad-pa dgongs-pa rab-gsal* (Totally Clarifying the Intention: An Extensive Explanation of [Chandrakirti's] *Supplement to [Nagarjuna's "Root Stanzas on] the Middle Way"*).

_____. *Drang-nges legs-bshad snying-po* (The Essence of Excellent Explanation of Interpretable and Definitive Phenomena; The Essence of True Eloquence).

_____. *Lam-gyi rim-pa mdo-tsam-du bstan-pa* (A Brief Indication of the Graded Stages of the Path).

_____. *Lam-rim bsdus-don* (The Abbreviated Points of the Graded Stages of the Path).

_____. *Lam-rim chen-mo* (A Grand Presentation of the Graded Stages of the Path).

_____. *Lam-rim chung-ngu* (A Short Presentation of the Graded Stages of the Path; The Middle-Length Presentation of the Graded Stages of the Path).

_____. *Lam-gtso rnam-gsum* (The Three Principal Aspects of the Path).

_____. *Legs-bshad gser-phreng* (A Golden Garland of Excellent Explanation).

_____. *gSang-sngags-kyi rim-pa chen-mo* (A Grand Presentation of the Graded Stages of the Secret Mantra Path).

Udānavarga (Ched-du brjod-pa'i tshoms; Special Verses Grouped by Topic; The Tibetan *Dhammapada*).

Vajramālā (rDo-rje phreng-ba; A Vajra Garland).

Vanaratna (Vanaratna, Nags-kyi rin-chen) (b. 1384) and Gö Lotsawa ('Gos Lo-tsā-ba gZhon-nu dpal) (1392–1481) (transl.) *Gurvāradhanapañjika* (Bla-ma'i bsnyen-bkur-gyi dka'-'grel; A Commentary on Difficult Points [in Ashvaghosha's *Fifty Stanzas on the Guru*] concerning Helping and Showing Respect to a Guru).

Vasubandhu (Vasubandhu, dByig-gnyen) (3rd century). *Abhidharmakośa* (Chos mngon-pa'i mdzod; A Treasure-House of Special Topics of Knowledge).

_____. *Abhidharmakośabhāṣya* (Chos-mngon-pa'i mdzod-kyi rang-'grel; An Auto-Commentary on *A Treasure-House of Special Topics of Knowledge*).

Wönpo Sherab-jungnay (dBon-po Shes-rab 'byung-gnas) (1187–1241). *Dam-chos dgong-pa gcig-pa'i 'grel-chen* (A Grand Commentary to [Drigungpa's] *Single Intention of the Sacred Dharma*).

Yeshey-gyeltsen (Yongs-'dzin dKa'-chen Ye-shes rgyal-mtshan) (1713–1793). *Bla-ma mchod-pa'i khrid-yig gsang-ba'i gnad rnam-par phye-ba snyan-rgyud man-ngag-gi gter-mdzod* (Discourse Notes on [the First Panchen Lama's] *Ceremony to Honor the Gurus*: A Treasure-House of Guideline Instructions from the Oral Tradition Revealing the Hidden Important Points).

_____. *Sems-dang sems-byung-gi gsal-bar ston-pa blo-gsal mgul-rgyan zhes sdom-'grel* (An [Auto-]Commentary on *Mnemonic Verses*, Indicating Clearly the Primary Minds and Mental Factors: A Necklace for a Clear Mind; The Necklace of Clear Understanding).

Translations and Secondary Literature

Āryadeva and Gyel-tsap. *Yogic Deeds of Bodhisattvas: Gyel-tsap on Āryadeva's "Four Hundred," with commentary by Geshe Sonam Rinchen*. Trans. and ed. Ruth Sonam. Ithaca: Snow Lion, 1994.

Aryasura. *The Marvelous Companion: Life Stories of the Buddha*. Berkeley: Dharma Publishing, 1983.

Atiśa. *A Lamp for the Path and Commentary*. Trans. Richard Sherburne, S. J. London: George Allen & Unwin, 1983.

Berzin, Alexander. *Developing Balanced Sensitivity*. Ithaca: Snow Lion, 1998.

_____. *Taking the Kalachakra Initiation*. Ithaca: Snow Lion, 1997.

Berzin, Alexander, Jampa Gendun, et al., trans. *The Guru Puja*. Dharamsala: Library of Tibetan Works and Archives, 1979.

Berzin, Alexander and Sharpa Tulku, trans. "A Letter of Practical Advice on Sutra and Tantra: A Brief Indication of the Graded Stages of the Path, Lam-gyi rim-pa mdo-tzam-du bstan-pa." In Robert A. F. Thurman, ed. *Life and Teachings of Tsong Khapa*. Dharamsala: Library of Tibetan Works and Archives, 1982, pp. 67–89.

_____. "Lines of Experience: The Abbreviated Points of the Graded Path, Lam-rim bsdus-don." In Robert A. F. Thurman, ed. *Life and Teachings of Tsong Khapa*. Dharamsala: Library of Tibetan Works and Archives, 1982, pp. 59–66.

Boszormenyi-Nagy, Ivan and G. H. Spark. *Invisible Loyalties*. New York: Brunner/Mazel, 1984.

Capra, Fritjof. *The Web of Life: A New Scientific Understanding of Living Systems*. New York: Anchor Books, 1996.

The Dalai Lama, H. H., Tenzin Gyatso. *Path to Bliss: A Practical Guide to Stages of Meditation*. Trans. Geshe Thubten Jinpa. Ithaca: Snow Lion, 1991.

_____. *The Path to Enlightenment*. See Gyatso, Sonam, The Third Dalai Lama, *Essence of Refined Gold*.

_____. *The Union of Bliss & Emptiness: A Commentary on the Lama Choepa Guru Yoga Practice*. Trans. Thupten Jinpa. Ithaca: Snow Lion, 1988.

_____. *The World of Tibetan Buddhism: An Overview of Its Philosophy and Practice*. Trans. Geshe Thupten Jinpa. Boston: Wisdom, 1995.

The Dalai Lama, H. H. and Alexander Berzin. *The Gelug/Kagyü Tradition of Mahamudra*. Trans. and ed. Alexander Berzin. Ithaca: Snow Lion, 1997.

Dhargyey, Geshe Ngawang. *An Anthology of Well-Spoken Advice*, vol. 1. Trans. and ed. Alexander Berzin, with Sharpa Tulku. Dharamsala: Library of Tibetan Works and Archives, 1984.

Gampopa, Je. *The Jewel Ornament of Liberation*. Trans. Khenpo Konchog Gyaltshen Rinpoche. Ithaca: Snow Lion, 1998.

Gtsan-smyon He-ru-ka. *The Life of Milarepa*. Trans. Lobsang P. Lhalungpa. New York: Dutton, 1977.

Guenther, Herbert V., trans. *The Life and Teachings of Naropa*. Boston: Shambhala, 1986.

Guenther, Herbert V. and Leslie S. Kawamura. *Mind in Buddhist Psychology: A Translation of Ye-shes rgyal-mtshan's "The Necklace of Clear Understanding."* Emeryville, CA: Dharma Publishing, 1975.

Gyatso, Sonam, The Third Dalai Lama. *Essence of Refined Gold, with commentary by Tenzin Gyatso, The Fourteenth Dalai Lama*. Trans. Glenn H. Mullin. Ithaca: Gabriel/Snow Lion, 1982. Reprint, The Dalai Lama. *The Path to Enlightenment*. Trans. Glenn H. Mullin. Ithaca: Snow Lion, 1995.

Holmes, Katia and Ken, trans. *The Changeless Nature (The Mahayana Uttara Tantra Shastra)*. Eskdalemuir, Scotland: Karma Drubgyud Darjay Ling, 1979.

Hopkins, Jeffrey. *Meditation on Emptiness*. London: Wisdom, 1983.

Karmapa IX. *Mahamudra Eliminating the Darkness of Ignorance, with commentary by Beru Khyentse Rinpoche and "Fifty Stanzas of Guru-Devotion" by Asvaghosa*.

Trans. and ed. Alexander Berzin. Dharamsala: Library of Tibetan Works and Archives, 1978.

Khenpo Karthar Rinpoche. *The Instructions of Gampopa: A Precious Garland of the Supreme Path.* Trans. Lama Yeshe Gyatso. Ithaca: Snow Lion, 1996.

Kongtrul, Jamgon. *Buddhist Ethics.* Trans. International Translation Committee founded by V. V. Kalu Rinpoche. Ithaca: Snow Lion, 1998.

_____. *The Teacher-Student Relationship.* Trans. and comm. Ron Garry. Ithaca: Snow Lion, 1998.

_____. *The Torch of Certainty.* Trans. Judith Hanson. Boston: Shambhala, 1986.

La Vallée Poussin, Louis de, trans. *L'Abhidharmakośa de Vasubandhu*, 6 vols. Brussels: Institut Belge des Hautes Études Chinoises, 1971.

Long-ch'en Rab-jam-pa. *The Four-Themed Precious Garland: An Introduction to Dzog-ch'en, the Great Completeness, with commentary by His Holiness Dudjom Rinpoche and Beru Khyentze Rinpoche.* Trans. Alexander Berzin, with Sherpa Tulku and Matthew Kapstein. Dharamsala: Library of Tibetan Works and Archives, 1979.

Longchenpa and Herbert V. Guenther. *Kindly Bent to Ease Us, Part One: Mind, from "The Trilogy of Finding Comfort and Ease."* Trans. Herbert V. Guether. Emeryville, CA: Dharma Publishing, 1975.

Maturana, Humberto and Francisco J. Varela. *The Tree of Knowledge: The Biological Roots of Human Understanding.* Boston: Shambhala, 1992.

Menninger, Karl. *Theory of Psychoanalytic Technique.* New York: Basic Books, 1958.

Minling Terchen Gyurme Dorjee. *The Jewel Ladder: A Preliminary Nyingma Lamrim, with commentary by Garje Khamtrul Rinpoche.* Trans. Tsepak Rigzin. Dharamsala: Library of Tibetan Works and Archives, 1990.

Ngari Panchen, Pema Wangyi Gyalpo. *Perfect Conduct: Ascertaining the Three Vows.* Trans. Khenpo Gyurme Samdrub and Sangye Khandro. Boston: Wisdom, 1996.

Pabongka Rinpoche. *Liberation in the Palm of Your Hand.* Trans. Michael Richards. Boston: Wisdom, 1991.

Paltrul Rinpoche. *The Words of My Perfect Teacher (Kunzang lama'i shelung): A Complete Translation of a Classic Introduction to Tibetan Buddhism.* Trans. Padmakara Translation Group. San Francisco: Harper, 1994.

Rabten, Geshe and Geshe Ngawang Dhargyey. *Advice from a Spiritual Friend.* Trans. Brian Beresford. Boston: Wisdom, 1996.

Rahula, Walpola, trans. *Le Compendium de la super-doctrine (philosophie) (Abhidharma-samuccaya) d'Asanga.* Paris: École francaise d'extrême-orient, 1971.

Rinchen, Geshe Sonam. *Atisha's Lamp for the Path to Enlightenment.* Trans. Ruth Sonam. Ithaca: Snow Lion, 1997.

_____. *The Three Principal Aspects of the Path: An Oral Teaching by Geshe Sonam Rinchen.* Trans. Ruth Sonam. Ithaca: Snow Lion, 1999.

Sakya Pandit. "A Precious Treasury of Elegant Sayings: Legs-bshad rin-po-che'i gter." In Nagarjuna and Sakya Pandit. *Elegant Sayings*. Berkeley: Dharma Publishing, 1977, pp. 61–114.

Śāntideva. *A Guide to the Bodhisattva Way of Life*. Trans. Vesna A. Wallace and B. Alan Wallace. Ithaca: Snow Lion, 1997.

Sheehy, Gail. *New Passages: Mapping Your Life across Time*. New York: Ballantine Books, 1995.

Sparham, Gareth, trans. *The Tibetan Dhammapada: Sayings of the Buddha: A Translation of the Tibetan Version of the Udanavarga*. London: Wisdom, 1986.

Thurman, Robert A. F., trans. *Tsong Khapa's Speech of Gold in the "Essence of True Eloquence."* Princeton: Princeton University Press, 1984. Reprint, *The Central Philosophy of Tibet: A Study and Translation of Jey Tsong Khapa's "Essence of True Eloquence."* Princeton: Princeton University Press, 1991.

Tsongkhapa, Je. *The Fulfillment of All Hopes: Guru Devotion in Tibetan Buddhism*. Trans., Gareth Sparham. Boston: Wisdom, 1999.

Varela, Francisco J., Evan Thompson and Eleanor Rosch. *The Embodied Mind: Cognitive Science and Human Experience*. Cambridge Mass.: MIT Press, 1991.

Waley, Arthur, trans. *The Analects of Confucius*. London: Allen & Unwin, 1938.

~ Also by Alexander Berzin

Developing Balanced Sensitivity
A Glimpse of Reality (with Thubten Chodron)
Taking the Kalachakra Initiation

Translator and Coauthor:

An Anthology of Well-Spoken Advice (Geshe Ngawang Dhargyey)
The Gelug/Kagyü Tradition of Mahamudra (His Holiness the
    Dalai Lama)

Translator:

A Compendium of Ways of Knowing (A-kya Yong-dzin)
The Four-Themed Precious Garland: An Introduction to Dzog-ch'en
    (Long-ch'en Rab-jam-pa)
The Guru Puja (The First Panchen Lama)
Kalachakra and Other Six-Session Yoga Texts
The Mahamudra Eliminating the Darkness of Ignorance (The Ninth
    Karmapa, Wang-ch'ug Dor-je)
The Wheel of Sharp Weapons (Dharmarakshita)

Contributing Translator:

Four Essential Buddhist Commentaries (His Holiness the Dalai Lama)
Four Essential Buddhist Texts
Life and Teachings of Tsong Khapa (Robert Thurman, ed.)

Translator of the Original English:

Il Diamente che Taglia le Illusioni (Serkong Rinpoche; Italian)

Een Lamp voor het Pad naar Verlichting (Atisha and Serkong Rinpoche; Dutch)

Meditation sur l'esprit (His Holiness the Dalai Lama; French)

Published Lectures Delivered Originally in English:

Alapvetö tanitások (Hungarian)

Coração e Mente: O Caminho do Budismo Tibetano (Portuguese)

Fünf Weisheiten (German)

Karma, Renacimiento y Mente (Spanish)

Obshii Obzor Buddiskih Praktik (Russian)

Podslawy Praktyki Buddyjskiej (Polish)

Tibetskii Buddizm: Istoriya i Perspektivy Razvitiya (Russian)

Trzy wyklady (Polish)

Vorträge von Dr. A. Berzin (German)